Design Vienna
1890s to 1930s

Joann Skrypzak

With essay by Barbara Copeland Buenger

Elvehjem Museum of Art
University of Wisconsin–Madison
2003

ISBN 0-932900-96-8

Catalogue published on the occasion of the exhibition
Design, Vienna 1890s to 1930s
Organized by the Elvehjem Museum of Art with curator Joann Skrypzak
Elvehjem Museum of Art
April 26–June 29, 2003

Library of Congress Cataloging-in-Publication Data

Skrypzak, Joann, 1964-
Design, Vienna, 1890s to 1930s / Joann Skrypzak ; with essay by
Barbara Copeland Buenger.
p. cm.
Catalog of an exhibition to be held at the Elvehjem Museum of Art,
Madison, Wisc., April 26-June 18, 2003.
Includes bibliographical references and index.
ISBN 0-932900-96-8
1. Art, Austrian—Austria—Vienna—20th century—Exhibitions. 2.
Modernism (Art)—Austria—Vienna—Exhibitions. 3.
Design—Austria—Vienna—History—20th century—Exhibitions. 4.
Kaerwer, Barbara Mackey—Art collections—United States—Exhibitions.
5. Art—Private collections—United States—Exhibitions. I. Buenger,
Barbara Copeland. II. Elvehjem Museum of Art. III. Title.
N6810.V5S57 2003
745.4'4943613'07477583—dc21
2002156754

Cover: Iridescent Glass Vase, ca. 1900, see cat. 27.
Back cover: Silver-gilt Buckle designed by Koloman Moser, ca. 1904, see cat. 34;
Gilt Brass Ball Program Cover designed by Josef Hoffmann, 1909, see cat. 84;
Woodcut by Erwin Lang, 1921, see cat. 100.
Page 4, Emil Orlik's *Self-Portrait at the Easel with Fools*, 1920, see cat. 14;
page 6 Karl Krenek's untitled woodcut, 1906, see cat. 6;
page 8 Wilhelm List's untitled page from *Ver Sacrum*, 1902, see cat.18.
Details of artists' fabric designs: inside covers,
Felice Rix-Ueno's block-print of blue and black on white silk, 1924, see cat. 63;
page 31, Mathilde Flögl's block-print of red and yellow on crêpe de chine, 1928, see cat. 64;
page 49, Clara Posnansky's brown, beige, and red on white crêpe de chine, 1930, see cat. 65.

With tremendous gratitude and deep sadness
we dedicate this exhibition and catalogue
to the late William C. Bunce

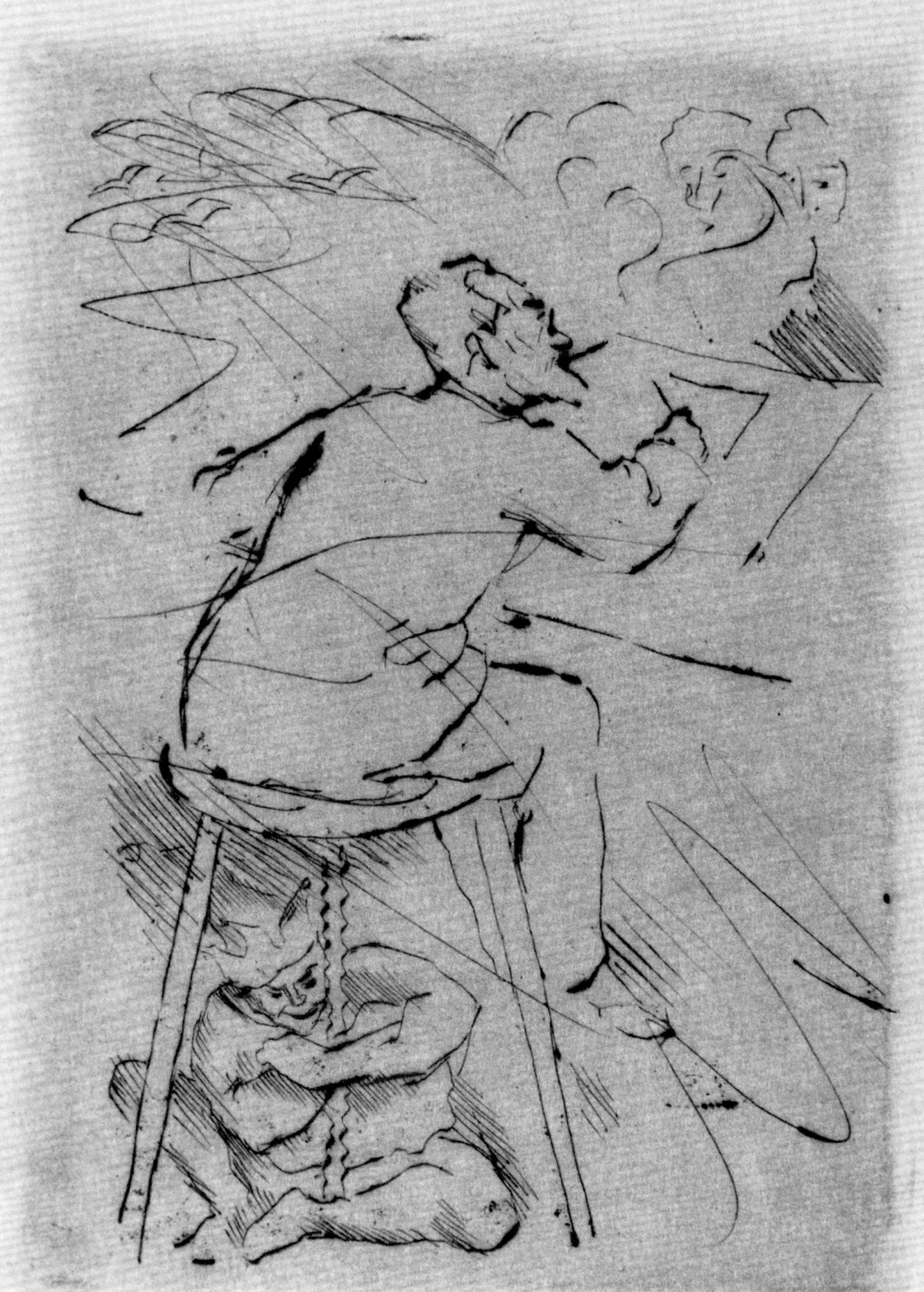

f. Fredr. Schöne g.f.E. 1920

Orlik 1920

Table of Contents

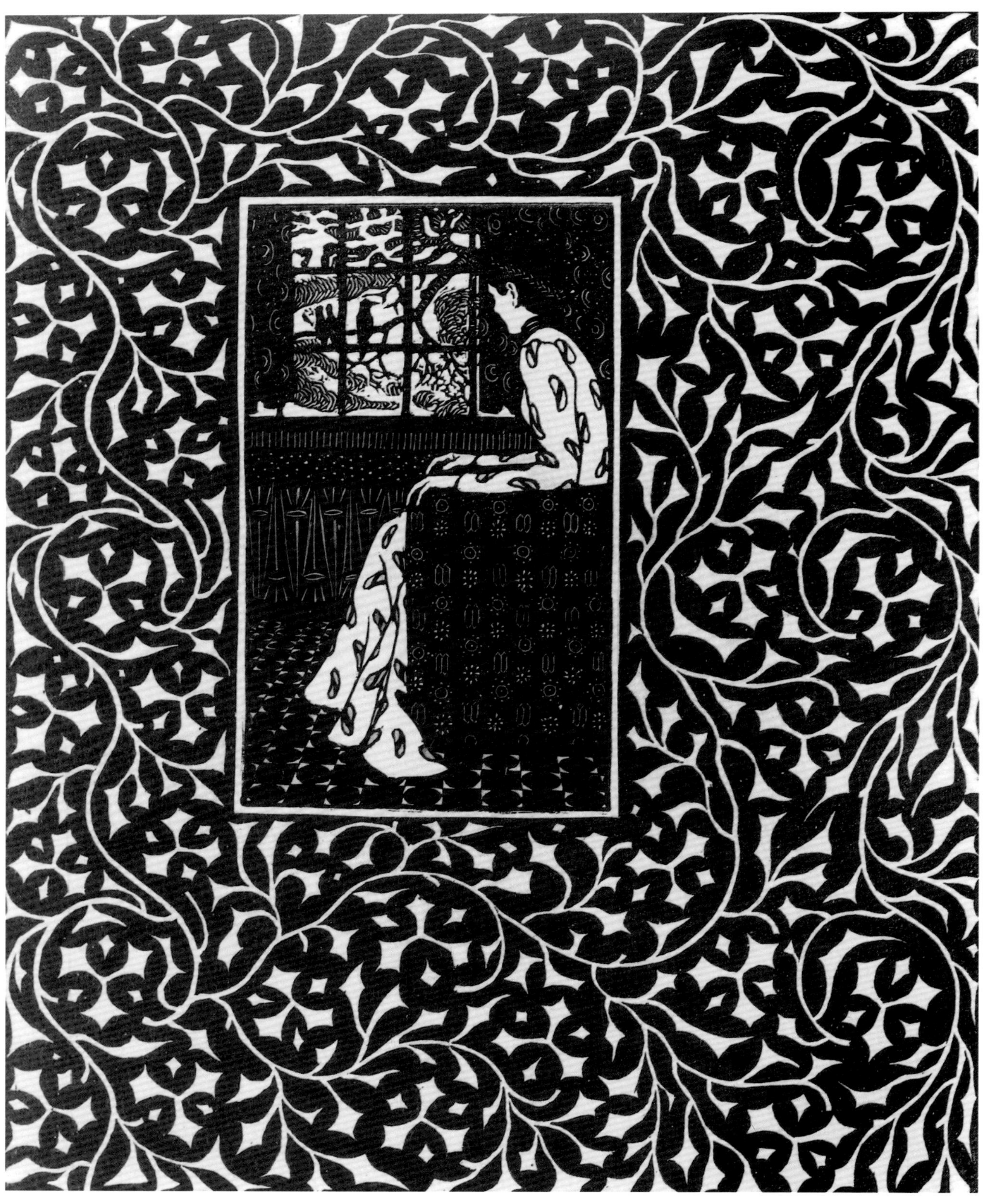

Foreword

Barbara Mackey Kaerwer, whose collection we are proud to present to our visitors, is well versed in art history and has a long history of personal dedication to teaching about art history and art appreciation. The exhibition of a collection assembled by such an individual is particularly appropriate to a university museum such as the Elvehjem whose mission closely parallels her passion. At the outset, I wish to express the gratitude of all of us here at the UW–Madison to Barbara for so selflessly sharing this extraordinary collection with us.

The presentation of this collection of fine and decorative arts, produced in Austria by the Vienna Secession and Wiener Werkstätte movements between the 1890s and 1930s, is particularly resonant at the UW–Madison at this time. In recent years, the university has developed a broad-based interdisciplinary program in material culture, which has a need for material displays. The Kaerwer collection, itself a study in Viennese material culture around the turn of the twentieth century, will be used for teaching and research by students and faculty from various academic departments while it is on view. These Viennese movements are particularly interesting for students in this field because of their basic concept of *Gesamtkunstwerk* (a unified work of art). Their designs synthesized the aesthetic and practical and blurred the distinction between the fine and applied arts; single objects and entire living environments were carefully orchestrated ensembles that coordinated a variety of sumptuous materials.

The Kaerwer Collection has been, moreover, a superb training ground for its curator, doctoral candidate Joann Skrypzak. Ms. Skrypzak who has been working simultaneously on her dissertation, Sporting Modernity: German Artists and the Athletic Body, 1918–1945, visited with Barabara Kaerwer on several occasions and prepared the current exhibition and its accompanying catalogue. She spent 2001–02 academic year in Germany on Fulbright grant and received the first Dana-Allen Dissertation Fellowship at the Institute for Research in the Humanities for 2002–03. We are grateful to her for the devotion to this subject and her analysis of this wonderful collection.

This catalogue and exhibition would not have been possible without the expertise and assistance of many people. I especially want to acknowledge Professor Barbara Buenger who played a pivotal role. She joined Joann in several visits to the Kaerwer home and provided valuable guidance in the selection of objects for the exhibition. She also has contributed an important essay for this catalogue. Professor Buenger and Barabara Kaerwer have been friends for many years sharing a deep pleasure in modern German art.

I also wish to acknowledge the work done by the Elvehejem staff in implementing every stage of this project from fundraising by development specialist Kathy Paul to management by assistant director for administration Carol Fisher. Exhibition designer Jerl Richmond and preparator Steve Johanowicz have done their usual immaculate exhibition installation; curator for education Anne Lambert had been diligent in educational program planning. Assistant registrar Jennifer Stofflet worked with the photographer and made travel arrangements for the collection. Editor Patricia Powell has given editorial direction and managed the catalogue production process. In addition to our immediate staff I want to thank Jim Wildeman for his excellent photography and David Alcorn for his sensitive design for the catalogue.

As usual generous public and private benefactors made this exhibition and catalogue possible. I want to thank the Anonymous Fund, Brittingham Fund, Dane County Cultural Affairs Commission with additional funds from the Madison Community Foundation and the Overture Foundation, the Wisconsin Humanities Council and the National Endowment for the Humanities, and Hilldale Fund.

Finally, I once again wish to recognize the lifelong dedication to arts and teaching of Barbara Mackey Kaerwer. Barbara's relationship to this university and the Elvehjem Museum of Art is long-standing and profound. She graduated from the University of Wisconsin in Madison in 1942 with a B.A. in political science, and, despite graduate experience at other universities, she always retained a fondness for this institution. Barbara was good friend of art historian Jim Watrous, who was instrumental in getting this university art museum established, and she has been a good friend not only to me but to each director of the museum since its opening. She has been especially interested in the educational mission of our museum, particularly in its support of the art history curriculum. She is excited by and supportive of the new program in material culture. In September 1984, Barbara was invited to join the Elvehjem Council and has faithfully attended meetings and given advice through nearly twenty years. She has been a generous benefactor to the university through the years. She has also been and is a wonderful friend of the Elvehjem.

Russell Panczenko
Director, Elvehjem Museum of Art

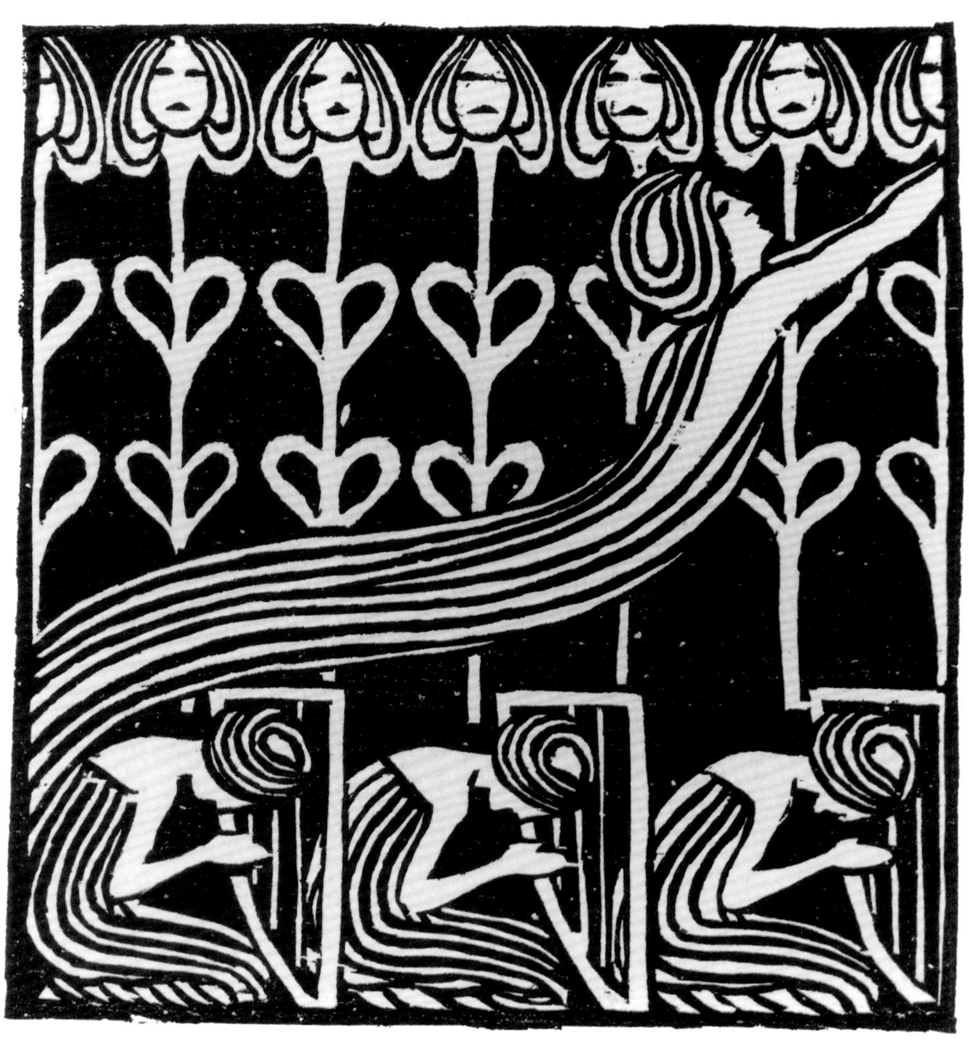

Curator's Acknowledgements

Most curatorial and academic projects are the result of work that extends over years and, in some cases, continents. My involvement with this exhibition began as a summer project in 2000, when Elvehjem Director Russell Panczenko invited me to undertake preliminary research for a show of Viennese Modern art and design from the Kaerwer Collection. I owe this good fortune to my academic advisor, Professor Barbara Buenger, who, familiar with both my studies in German art history and curatorial experience as well as my growing interest in material culture studies, recommended me for the task. At the end of spring semester, Professor Buenger and I made an initial trip to examine the collection and gather information. Barbara Mackey Kaerwer, an alumna, Elvehjem supporter, and champion of the University of Wisconsin's material culture studies program, enthusiastically assisted us in every way possible. She gave us full access to objects and documentation and supplemented these with her knowledge and experience as a collector devoted to education. After several days working among the richness and good organization of the collection, we returned to Madison fired with ideas and plans. We drafted an initial list of selections, and I began the process of organization and research.

We wanted this exhibition to be an introduction to the modern applied arts of Austria that not only demonstrated the dominant roles played by the Vienna Secession and Wiener Werkstätte but also presented the sense of taste that defined the period from the 1890s to 1930s. As I grew further acquainted with Barbara Kaerwer and her aims as a collector, it also became clear that relating aspects of her efforts could provide valuable insight into the issues of collecting art. With these ideas in place, I assumed the role of curator and resumed exhibition preparations the following summer.

I am especially grateful for the trust, support, and flexibility of the many people who helped bring this exhibition to fruition. Barbara Mackey Kaerwer represents the keystone of the project. Her openness and inimitable vibrancy ensured that my trips to the collection were a stimulating retreat. With unflagging confidence in my efforts, she joined me in inspiring museum visits and fruitful exchanges, responded to numerous inquiries, engaged in several hours of interviewing, and suggested additions to the exhibition list. Her assistant, Lori Harney, who set up the original collection database, provided me with a well-organized framework for research and eased the difficult task of dealing with a large number of artists working in various media.

My existing relationships with the Elvejhem Museum staff proved invaluable in ways that I expected and did not. I owe special thanks to Drew Stevens, Maria Saffiotti Dale, and Jerl Richmond for wise recommendations at early stages of the project; to Pat Powell, Anne Lambert, and Kathy Paul, who patiently followed me during my dissertation year in Germany and kept deadlines on track; and to Jennifer Stofflet and Jim Wildeman, who deftly handled the demands of photographing a variety of two- and three-dimensional works.

In the University of Wisconsin-Madison art history department, Professors Gene Phillips and Ann Smart Martin contributed expertise in the areas of Japanese art and decorative arts. Kohler Art Library Director Lyn Korenic assisted the project in several ways; Memorial Library reference librarian Christine Lee helped track down critical sources and details. We have Onno Brouwer and Caitlin Doran of the university's cartography lab to thank for maps in the catalogue. For additional information on artists and objects I am also indebted to Denis Gallion and Daniel Morris of Historical Design in New York; Dr. Dedo von Kerssenbrock-Krosigk of the Bröhan-Museum in Berlin; and Elisabeth Schmuttermeier and Angela Völker of the Museum der angewandte Kunst in Vienna.

Closer to home, friends and colleagues Robert Cozzolino, Professor Susan Funkenstein, Ryan Grover, and Laura Mueller and my parents Maria and Anthony Skrypzak have participated in countless discussions about the ideas, joys, and challenges involved in the project. Olaf Davidsmeyer provided expert technical assistance and served as a sensitive listener and insightful critic.

My final appreciation is due to Professor Buenger, who has contributed to this project in innumerable ways. She has unstintingly supported my endeavors, provoked new avenues of research, and supplied the type of rigorous critique that has strengthened my ideas and their means of expression. As both mentor and friend, her compassion, humor, and commitment to work and life have surpassed any reasonable expectations for her role as advisor and continue to be a source of inspiration and delight.

Joann Skrypzak
November 2002
Madison

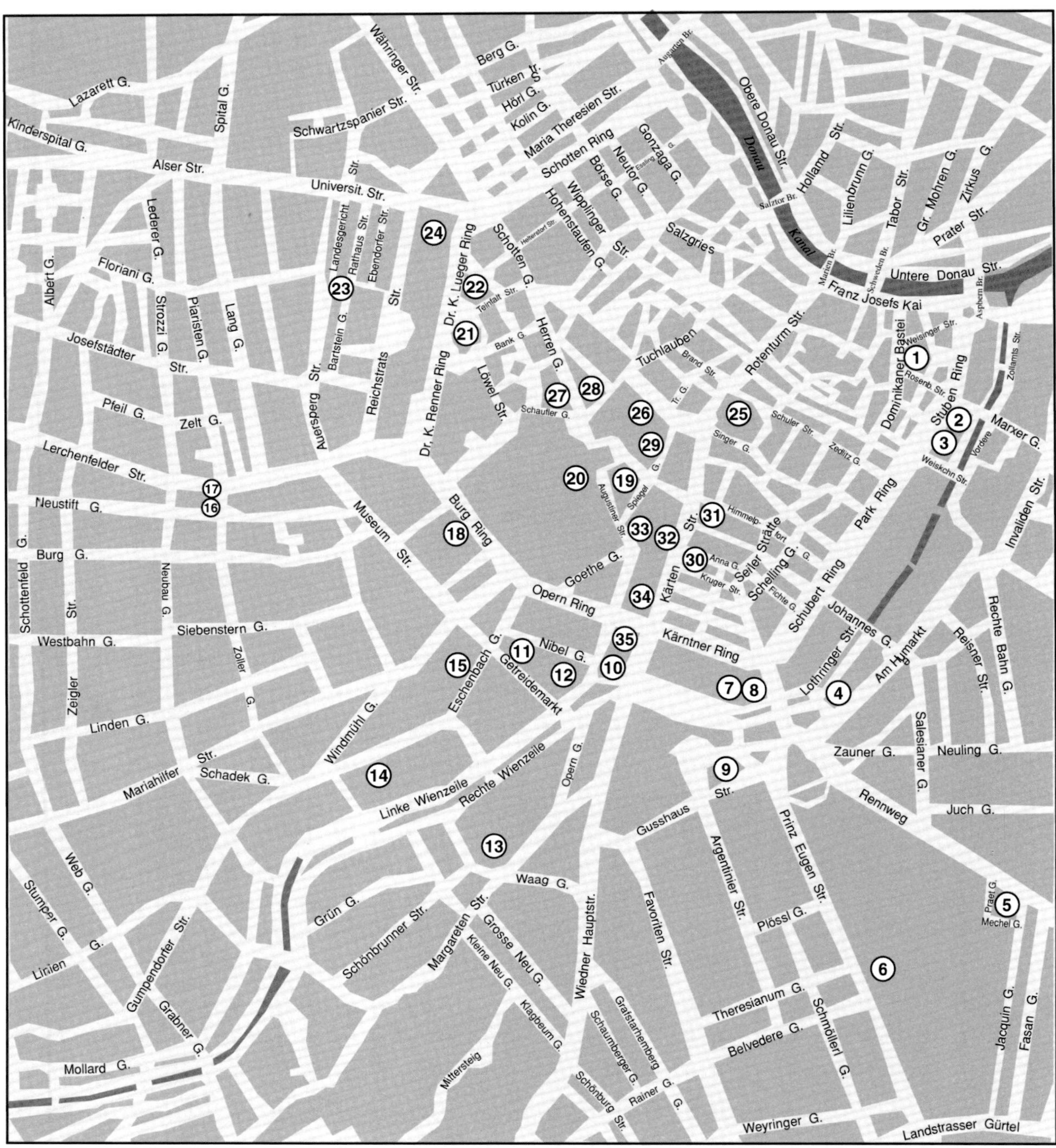

1 Post Office Savings Bank
2 Kunstgewerbeschule (School of Applied Arts)
3 Museum für angewandte Kunst (Museum of Applied Arts)
4 Konzerthaus [Kunstschau]
5 Rennweg 16 [Hof- und Staatsdruckerei (Court and State Printing Press)]
6 Belvedere
7 Karlsplatz 5, Künstlerhaus
8 Musikverein
9 Karlskirche (St. Charles Borromeo)
10 Café Museum
11 Akademie der bildenden Künste (Academy of Fine Arts)
12 Secession
13 Heumühlgasse 6 [first quarters of Wiener Werkstätte (WW)]
14 Linke Wienzeile 38, 40 (Otto Wagner)
15 [Casa Piccola; Salon Flöge]
16 Neustiftgasse 32-34 [main office/workshops of WW]
17 Döblergasse 4 [additional WW workshops]
18 Kunsthistorisches Museum (Museum of the History of Art)
19 Albertina
20 Österreichische Nationalbibliothek (Austrian National Library)
21 Burgtheater
22 Café Landtmann
23 Rathaus (City Hall)
24 Universität (University)
25 Stephansdom (St. Stephan's Cathedral)
26 Graben 15 [WW salesroom]
27 Loos Haus, Michaelerplatz 1
28 Michaelerplatz 2 [Café Griensteidl]
29 Dorotheergasse 11 [Galerie Miethke]
30 Kärtnerstraße 41/Palais Esterhazy [WW show and salesrooms]
31 Kärtnerstraße 33 [Cabaret Fledermaus]
32 Kärtnerstraße 32 [WW showroom]
33 Maysedergasse 4 [first WW fabric showroom]
34 Opera
35 Opernring 3 [Heinrichhof Café]

[no longer extant]

Unwieldy Wien[1]

Barbara Copeland Buenger

Barbara Kaerwer's superb collection presents welcome challenges to appreciate, study, and teach Vienna's art and history through its rich material culture.[2] The exhibition joins a large, wonderfully unwieldy range of items, a Koloman Moser chair and whole length of Lotte Hahn fabric, for instance, with a painting, numerous prints and drawings, fabric samples and needlework, ceramics, metalwork, glass, small objects of great variety, and books from the miniature to the monumental. These help us recognize the enormous contribution and versatility of the many modern Viennese and non-Viennese artists in and outside of the major groups of the Secession and Wiener Werkstätte. They also help us assess the immense achievement of modernist Vienna as it moved beyond the city to find, welcome, join, and stimulate the finest international art and design at home and abroad.

Of the three most frequently represented artists in this exhibition, for instance, Koloman Moser (1868–1918) produced works for Kaiser Franz Josef from the 1890s on, before and after he became a founding member of the Secession and the Wiener Werkstätte, and always worked concurrently in painting, design (he designed both the Wiener Werkstätte's Neustiftgasse premises and its logo), exhibitions, publishing, bookbinding, posters, fashion, and furniture (cats. 3, 31–36, 67, 76–78, 86, 87, 103).[3] The Prague-born Emil Orlik (1870–1932) studied art on lengthy visits to Japan and England before his short stay in Vienna. His long and prolific career in professional design (cats. 10, 11, 14, 15, 19) and teaching continued with his appointment to the Berlin Kunstgewerbeschule in 1905, where he decisively influenced students such as Hannah Höch, George Grosz, and Karl Hubbuch to join arts and crafts and design with life drawing and the "high" arts. Josef Hoffmann (1870–1956), the eminent architect and protégé of Otto Wagner (1841–1918), was the only founding member of the Secession and Wiener Werkstätte to stay with the groups throughout their long and frequently threatened existence. The designer (alone and with the Secession, Wiener Werkstätte, Austrian Werkbund, and city of Vienna) of such great undertakings as the artists' colony at Hohe Warte, 1902 Beethoven exhibition, Purkersdorf Sanitarium, Palais Stoclet, several exhibition pavilions, and much private and public housing, Hoffmann is chiefly represented here by his work in metal and design and by his contributions to Austria's showing at the 1925 Paris International Exposition of Modern Decorative and Industrial Arts and to the 1928 commemoration of the Wiener Werkstätte's twenty-fifth anniversary (cats. 39–43, 45, 46, 49, 52, 73, 74, 75, 79, 84, 88–90).

The Kaerwer works help us map out the world of the tinderbox, multinational Habsburg empire in which these artists worked before and after its dissolution in 1919 (maps 2, 3),[4] and thus recall a still passport-free world before World War I, when Europeans routinely saw more of the east and regularly visited cities such as Trieste, for instance, as they traveled south to Istria or eastward from Venice to Istanbul. The still young Rudolf Kalvach (cats. 8, 9) and Egon Schiele, for instance, joined Rainer Maria Rilke, James Joyce, and many other tourists who stopped at the great cosmopolitan port (the home of Italian writer Italo Svevo) that Habsburgs had dominated for centuries. Before, during, and after the war, the Wiener Werkstätte became widely known through its participation in international exhibitions in Rome, Paris, and several German cities and opening of salesrooms in the spa cities of Marienbad and Karlsbad (cat. 90) and Zurich, New York, and Berlin.

In Vienna these artists were well known not only for their many completed projects, public works, and exhibitions, but also for their continued collaboration with much older institutions, such as the Imperial and Royal Court and State Printing Office (cat. 77) as they established their own premises. As strongly as these modernists repudiated the provincialism of the Viennese institutions that restrained them, we should remember that most received vital support and training in many of those same institutions founded during the much-maligned building of the Ringstrasse in the 1860s. Gottfried Semper's majestic Museum of Art History, the Museum and School of the Applied Arts, and the Künstlerhaus exhibition hall, for instance, all played formative roles in the careers of most of the early members of the Secession and Wiener Werkstätte.

Three monumental works at the city's outskirts help us gain an idea of the Wiener Werkstätte's participation in the city's building. Carl Moll's woodcut (cat. 7) shows figures walking in a snowy Hohe Warte near the Vienna Woods at the north end of the city, not far from Beethoven's summer wandering grounds. The reversed image depicts the park to the east of the Geweygasse; and, in the rear, the neighboring homes of Moll and Moser, two of an ensemble of four Moser commissioned from Hoffmann in1900 to create an artists' colony for Secession friends.[5] Seven years later, to the south and far west,

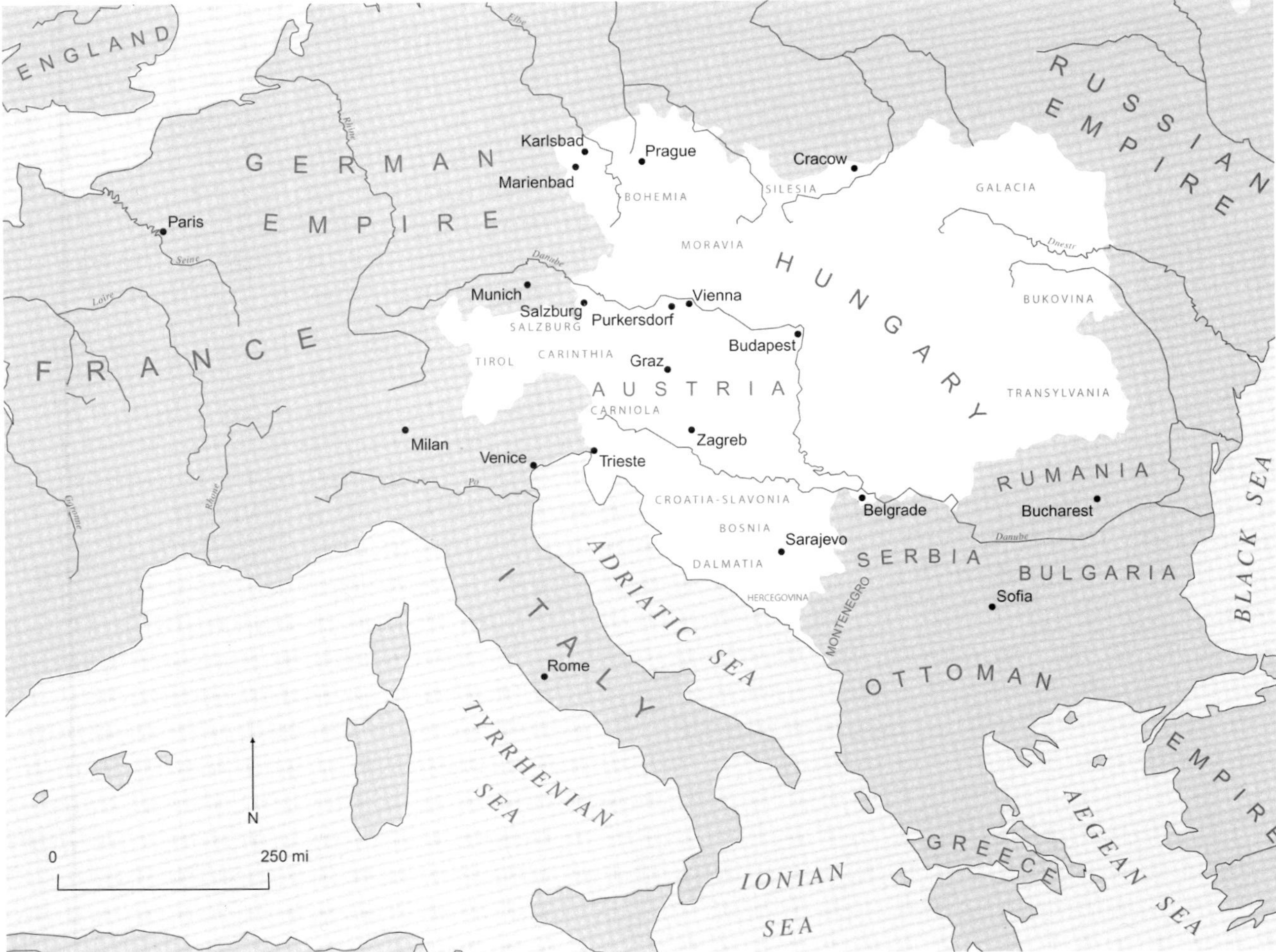

Map 2. Austrian-Hungarian Empire before World War I

Moser and Hoffmann joined other members of the Wiener Werkstätte to decorate Otto Wagner's last grand commission, the imposing Church am Steinhof built for the city mental asylum at Hütteldorf (1907).

Robert Philippi's 1921–1922 sketch (cat. 17) for his unsuccessful competition entry to decorate Clemens Holzmeister's crematorium at the Central Cemetery at the far southeast reminds us that although most new building was proscribed by dire economic straits in the immediate postwar period, the city did hire the best modern artists when it could undertake major projects. A friend of Schiele and one of the few Viennese artists who devoted himself chiefly to prints, Philippi drew from a broad range of international symbolism and expressionism as he developed his poignant, monumental rendering of the dead and ascending. Two of the artists finally chosen to decorate the crematorium, Anton Kolig (1886–1950) and Gudrun Baudisch (cat. 74) were members of the Neukunstgruppe and Wiener Werkstätte respectively; Holzmeister, renowned for the historical emphasis of his teachings, would give birth to a whole new era of Austrian architecture in the 1970s and 1980s.[6]

Study of these objects also leads us to consider how these artists exhibited their works in their own day and how they were received by contemporaries at home and abroad. Several illuminating examples come from the Wiener Werkstätte's final years. Josef Hoffmann coordinated Austria's contributions to the 1925 Paris International Exposition of Modern Decorative and Industrial Arts—the origin of the term art deco—to highlight several different contemporary directions (cat. 73, figure 1). Due to continued postwar acrimony, Germany was invited late and declined to participate, much to the consternation of its designers; Austria and Hoffmann, on the other hand, had been included in the planning of the Paris exhibition since it was first conceived as a response to the German Werkbund exhibitions in 1914. Eager to promote Austrian goods, the new republic and its president, Michael Hainisch, enthusiastically supported this Paris initiative. After the exposition's opening, French premier Paul Painlevé personally congratulated Hoffmann on his accomplishments, which also won Hoffmann the cross of the Legion of Honor.[7]

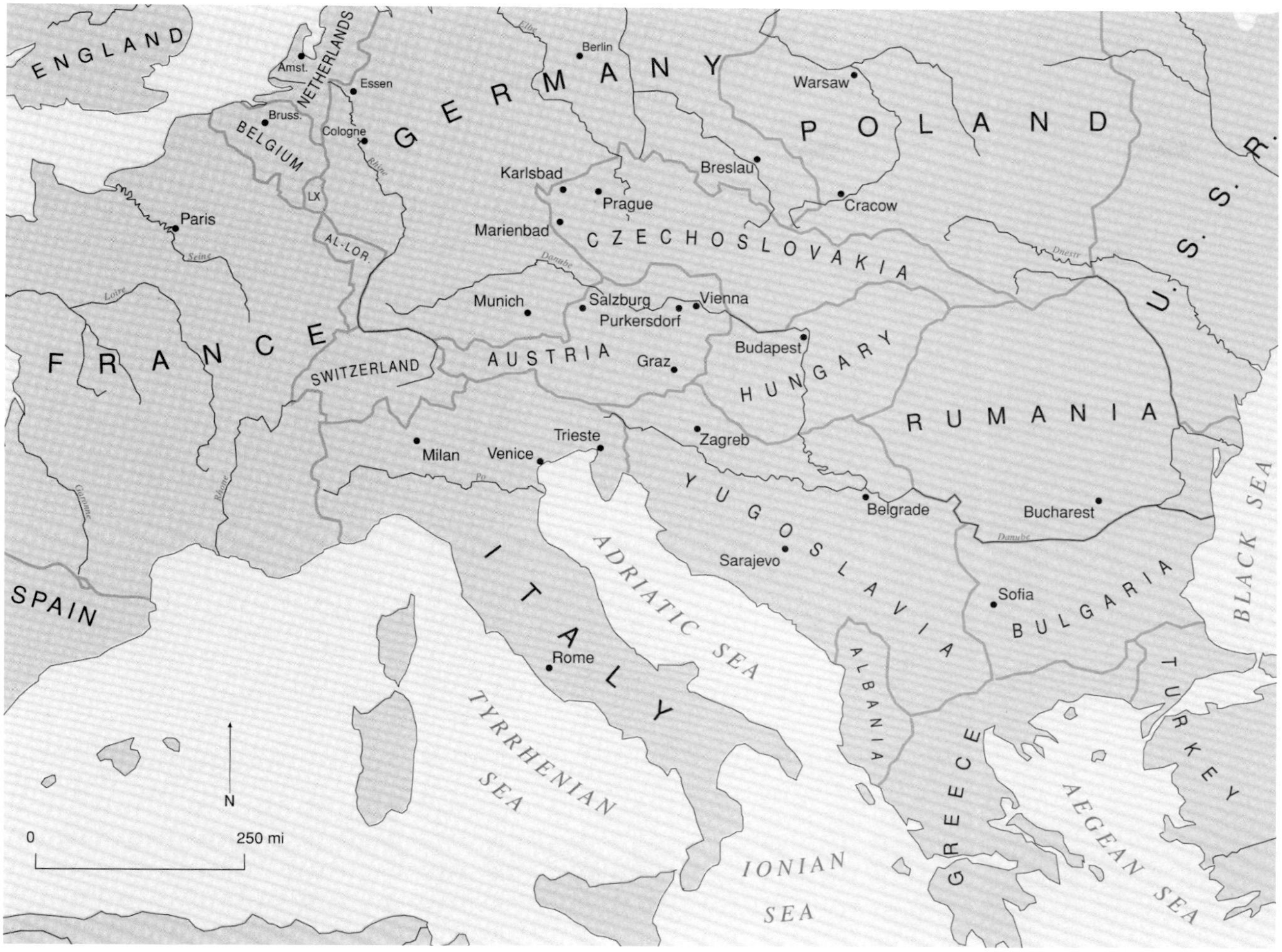

Map 3. Central and South-Eastern Europe after World War I

Aside from the bold and open, streamlined baroque of his own pavilion, Hoffmann chose the abstract, international style of architect Frederick Kiesler, for the Austrian theater exhibition (Kiesler's subsequent move to New York had great consequences for the American art scene).[8] Hoffmann also invited German architectural giant Peter Behrens to collaborate on the main pavilion, and thus enabled Behrens, who then lived and taught in Vienna, to represent the absent Germany. By decorating both the interiors and exteriors of the pavilion's display cabinets with the exuberant floral- and folk-derived calligraphy of the Wiener Werkstätte's recently deceased director, Dagobert Peche,[9] Hoffmann also highlighted the Wiener Werkstätte's latest directions.

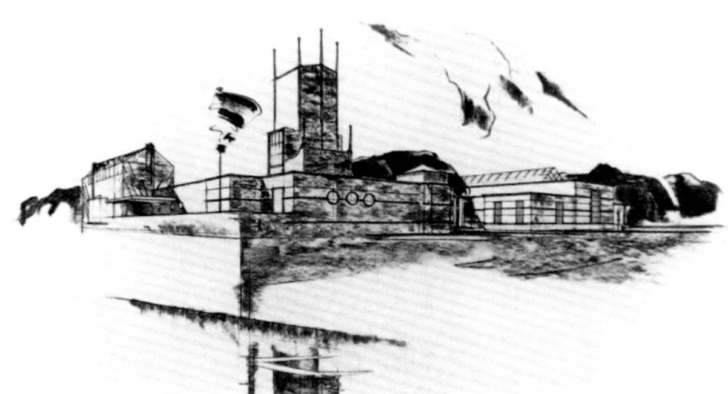

Figure 1. Josef Hoffmann's drawing of the Austrian pavilion at the International Exposition of Modern Decorative and Industrial Arts in Paris, from *L'Autriche à Paris* (1925)

Hoffmann continued to work and collaborate with the rank-and-file of Wiener Werkstätte artists, increasingly women, who remained productive until the business was finally liquidated in 1932. Like the lively patterns of Peche, many of the works that filled the Austrian cabinets at the Paris exhibition were colorful, decorative, and playful. This tendency directly reflected realistic concessions to attract a broader audience to less expensive and more accessible decorative products, but also demonstrated the more animated, jaunty tastes of a younger generation.[10]

The critical response to the Austrian pavilion and goods was mixed: highly positive, for the most part, in the French press, with the exception of those who favored the starker international style, and more negative in Vienna, which noted the pavilion's lack of commercial success, and continued long-standing criticisms of the Wiener Werkstätte's decorative tendencies led by that traditional enemy of decoration, Adolf Loos (1870–1933). Many considered these later works as no better than kitsch, and some attributed this decline to the predominantly female staff. A particularly Viennese penchant for punning word play led many to mock the group's name and logo: Loos spoke on "Das Wiener Weh" (The Viennese Woe); others attacked the group as "Wiener Weiberkunstgewerbe" (Viennese vixens' arts and crafts).[11]

Two women, Vally Wieselthier and Gudrun Baudisch, joined Hoffmann and others as producers of the 1928 volume that commemorated twenty-five years of the Wiener Werkstätte, although the majority of its illustrations showed the later works exhibited in the 1925 Paris show (cat. 74, figure 2). Although the group had already experienced several brushes with insolvency, a few sponsors spent large amounts for the celebration and publication, rather surprising in the year immediately following the

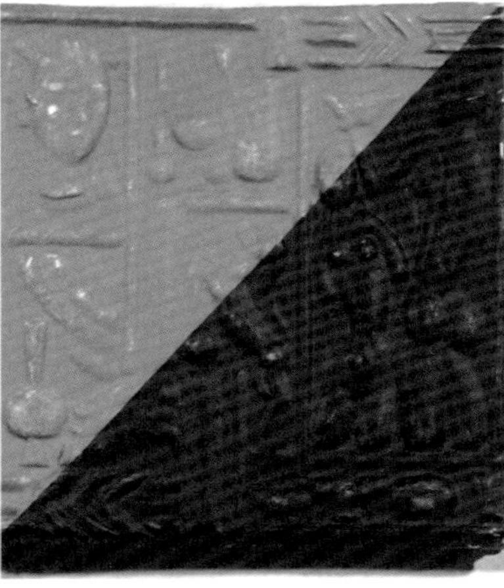

Figure 2. Front cover of *The Wiener Werkstätte 1903–1928* (1929), designed by Vally Wieselthier

severe Vienna riots. The commemorative volume was printed lavishly in several colors, but several corners were cut. The publication did not emulate the elegant standards of the group's earliest publications or the most advanced typography of its own day, but its appeal and contemporaneity are undeniable. Texts ran close to the page edges and colors fell unevenly against them, but the typeface was thoroughly contemporary, and the title page was probably designed by Walter Tiemann, the respected teacher of one of Germany's most progressive designers, Jan Tschichold.[12] The volume's outstanding features were its endpapers and molded papier maché art deco covers, the latter realized by a toy maker. Wieselthier and Baudisch's front and back covers recall both tiles and ancient scrolls, as they pair windblown deco women with vases and animals. The figures move between a simplifying antiquity and a modernity of freedom and sun, alternately orange- and black-figured as they are traversed by the covers' subdividing triangles.

A large piece of cloth by Lotte Hahn dated 1930 (cat. 66, figure 3) also represented the group's later years. Hahn's fabric augments several smaller fabric samples and pieces of lacework by showing a whole length; indeed, the Wiener Werkstätte often suspended such long pieces in store displays and exhibitions. This fabric shows that the

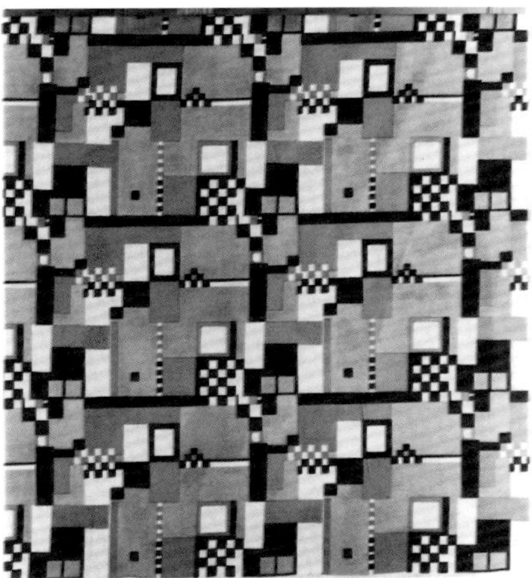

Figure 3. Lotte Hahn, geometric textile of woven cotton, ca. 1930

textile workshops fully joined the international, mid-1920s tendency towards abstract geometric decoration. Like much better-known artists such as Max Snischek, Maria Likarz-Strauss, Felice Rix-Ueno, and Mathilde Flögl (cats. 61–64), Hahn retained the Wiener Werkstätte taste for rich color combinations and complex patterns, but achieved more multidimensional, abstract effects by alternating circumscribed and unbounded forms against changing colored grounds. Internationally, her results are fully comparable with patterns of the Dessau Bauhaus and Sonia Delaunay, the latter first available at the 1925 Paris exposition.

Several of the works remind us how these modernists continued to face incomprehension and disapproval. Such is demonstrated, for instance, when we consider Emil Orlik's 1902 etched portrait of the distinguished composer and director Gustav Mahler (cat. 15, figure 4), and Egon Schiele's 1918 lithograph of friend and fellow Neukunstgruppe member, Paris von Gütersloh (cat. 16, figure 5). Orlik had arrived in Vienna by the high point of the Secession's great collective *Gesamtkunstwerk* of 1902, the exhibition coordinated to pay homage to Max Klinger's monumental statue of Beethoven and its celebration of a larger modern artistic ethos (Klinger, a German from Leipzig, was long closely associated with both the Vienna and Berlin Secessions).[13] Mahler, the director of Vienna's most important musical institution, the Hofoper (court opera) cemented his relationship with the Secession at this time[14] when he agreed to perform a concert of

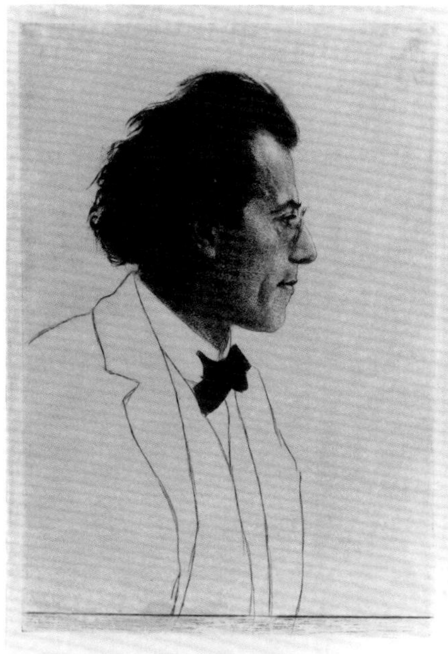

Figure 4. Emil Orlik, *Portrait of Gustav Mahler*, 1902

Schiele drew a lithograph of his close friend and fellow artist Paris von Gütersloh, as he painted the latter's great oil portrait (Minneapolis Institute of Arts), left unfinished when Schiele died from the influenza in December, 1918. From the start Schiele had planned his painting to portray Gütersloh with hands raised in inspiration, surrounded by a painterly astral glow that reflected the pair's mutual fascination with art's psychic and psychological communication.[17] Unlike Orlik's Mahler, Schiele's lithograph of Gütersloh's face and shoulders makes the latter's face (reversed in the print) look straight out (cat. 16, figure 5). The rumpled energies and intense absorption of Schiele's Gütersloh reverberate in the lively rendering of the bent nose, wide eyes, furrowed brow, shaded face, whorls of hair, and muscular line of shoulders, collar, and necktie. The fuller, three-dimensional realism of this and his other contemporary works is generally recognized to reflect Schiele's newly won sense of well-being. The lithograph was rejected,

Beethoven at the show's opening on April 15th; both he and the Secession hoped this might feature music from the Ninth Symphony that had inspired Gustav Klimt's *Beethoven Frieze*, the other major monument of that exhibition.[15] Friendly with several members of the Secession whom he would meet at Carl Moll's Hohe Warte home, Mahler was widely respected for his musicianship, but mercilessly chastised for his Jewishness, unusual interpretations of musical classics, and own new music; he was also repeatedly locked in power struggles with the Vienna Philharmonic, whose direction he had recently resigned. Although the opera chorus was willing to sing without pay for the Secession opening, the Philharmonic initially refused. Mahler ultimately employed only a small number of brass players to perform his arrangement of a short section from the Ninth's last movement.

Orlik, who would also produce contemporary portraits of Klinger and Ferdinand Hodler, probably developed the etching of Mahler from a photo and emulated photography's rich tonal qualities as he plied the varying graphic densities of drypoint, roulette, and mezzotint. Orlik charged the musician's bushy mane and curls, grainy facial texture, perpetually askew bow tie, and thin yet resilient jacket lines to emphasize Mahler's energy and concentration. He must have drawn the decisive bottom horizontal for a border or inscription at the beginning. After some errant jacket lines precluded an inscription or monogram such as he employed in other portraits,[16] Orlik burnished and covered that area with several groups of small horizontal stitches, producing an appropriately electric base for his alert subject.

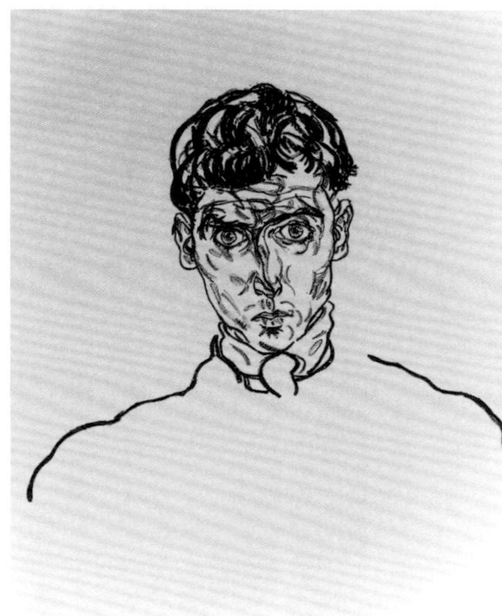

Figure 5. Egon Schiele, *Porträt Paris von Gütersloh*, 1918

however, by the graphics society that commissioned it, which lamented its departures from Schiele's "more original" early style.[18]

Two illustrated children's books based on different national legends illuminate some of the historical and political associations of style. The earliest, one of the finest small works associated with the early Wiener Werkstätte, was Franz Keim and Carl Otto Czeschka's tiny volume of *Die Nibelungen* published in the Gerlachs Jugendbücherei (cat. 96, figure 6). Keim, a former high school teacher who wrote several volumes in this series, sought to engage a young contemporary audience with the treasured Middle High German heroic epic, assumed to have been written by an Austrian in Passau around 1200. Keim's version drastically reduced the original 2400 strophes into thirty seemingly non-stop pages. He endowed

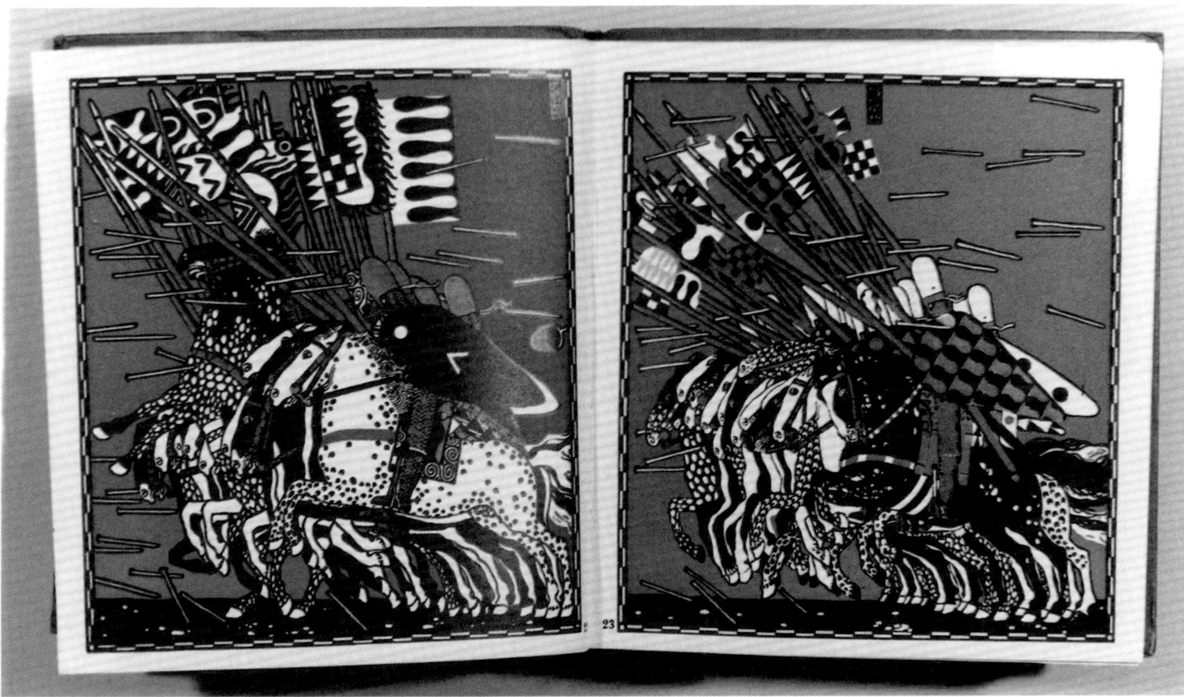

Figure 6. Carl Otto Czeschka's design for *Die Nibelungen dem Deutschen Volke wiedererzählt von Franz Keim* (1924)

Kriemhild and Brünnhilde with some modern, rather banal bourgeois ways but never compromised the violent dispatch of the medieval scenes of justice.

Czeschka framed each rectangular page with black-and-white checkerboard borders in the geometric style favored by the Wiener Werkstätte. He embellished the text in the Otto Eckmann Jugendstil typeface with elaborately turning scrolls and illuminated letters, small, square black-and-white vignettes of geometrically patterned figures, and eight lavishly decorated and colored full-page diptych illustrations of selected episodes.[19] Epitomizing the best Viennese Jugendstil of the day, these images told the story in abstractly modern, enlarged surface patterns. Beguiling combinations of geometric, biomorphic, and spiraling forms drawn from many different ages and cultures foreground the drama against fields of single colors, flattened medieval towers, and other decorated figures. Czeschka's elegant Middle Ages was enacted by chess players,[20] mostly anonymous, occasionally sentimental figures who abstractly and grandly evoke much of the *Nibelungenlied*'s courtly ritual that Keim had to suppress.

Czeschka began teaching in the Hamburg School of Arts and Crafts in 1909, but he maintained his connections with Vienna and continued to promote Wiener Werkstätte ideals in his north German work. As one of the group's greatest founders and practitioners, he has always received central notice in histories of modern Viennese art and design. Such is not true of Franz Wacik, widely admired as a political and social cartoonist for a popular Viennese humorous weekly, occasional theater designer, and illustrator of children's books (he designed three volumes in the Gerlach series). Wacik is all but forgotten in texts that present the Wiener Werkstätte as Vienna's only modern art movement and thus reminds us that a richer, more complicated history of modern art often falls outside a too-strictly-construed modernist canon. Wacik was a regular member and exhibitor with the Secession,[21] and illustrated Hugo von Hofmannsthal's famous wartime children's book, *Prinz Eugen der edle Ritter* (Prince Eugene the Noble Knight) in 1915 (cat. 98, figure 7). The content and layout of this work provide fascinating contrast with the Keim/Czeschka *Nibelungen*.

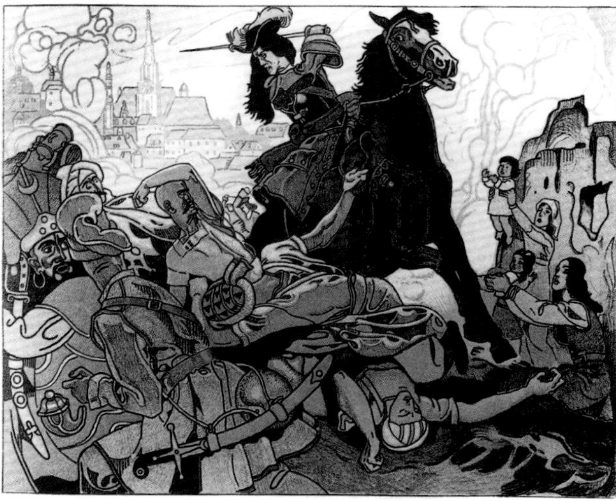

Figure 7. Franz Wacik's illustration of Prince Eugene battling the Turks for *Prinz Eugen der edle Ritter* (1915)

Hofmannsthal, one of Vienna's preeminent cosmopolitan writers, was the author of such magnificient libretti as *Der Rosenkavalier* and *Ariadne auf Naxos* and a vast literary and epistolary output. After a year in the reserves at the front, he returned to work in the war office, edit anthologies of Austrian and German literature, and become a leading figure in the conservative revolution that advocated a strong Middle Europe combining Germany and German-speaking Austria in direct violation of the Versailles Treaty.[22] During and after the war, Hofmannsthal joined the famed Austrian-born theater director Max Reinhardt to build the Salzburg Festival—perhaps the last great Viennese Gesamtkunstwerk—from the ashes of the lost Austro-Hungarian empire.[23]

Hofmannsthal nostalgically invoked the great ages of Austria's baroque and Holy Roman empire, as he joined others who championed similarly conservative views of a new Europe.[24] In talks, essays, and historical narratives since the start of the war, he repeatedly recalled the model of Prince Eugene of Savoy, one of the greatest modern military commanders, whom Austrian troops had always recalled in song as they marched into battle. Prince Eugene had joined the Holy Roman Emperor Otto I after he was refused a French commission, annihilated the always-dreaded Turkish army at Zenta (1697), joined forces with Marlborough against the French during the Wars of Spanish Succession, and became a grand patron of the arts in an effort to improve his image.[25]

Prince Eugene was long presented as Austria's counterpart to Frederick the Great, and the Hofmannsthal/Wacik renderings frequently echo Franz Kugler's and Adolf von Menzel's nineteenth-century renderings of Frederick as both a great war hero and a man of the people. Hofmannsthal and Wacik patriotically heralded the Austrian army's current exploits in World War I. Throughout the text Hofmannsthal emphasized a united, Holy Roman German Austria, hatred of France, and the need to arm the German people against foreign invaders.

The producers of *Prinz Eugen* also chose a modern, but not Jugendstil, typeface, Hans Koch's forthrightly Gothic boldface *Deutsche Schrift* type of 1906–1910.[26] The title page, originally hand-executed in calligraphy, reinforces the appropriateness of Koch's refined, explicitly calligraphic style to the baroque world evoked by Hofmannsthal. Wacik certainly knew the Keim/Czeschka *Nibelungen* (Czeschka had taught the artist Marianne Wacik, Franz Wacik's wife), and in many ways seems to respond to it. In this larger-format children's book, also ultimately published in an inexpensive edition, each black-and-white page was framed not by a geometric band, but by a border of stylized oak leaves and acorns that evoked Germanic strength. Each centered vignette incorporated black/white negative reversals, and many emulated the popular art of paper silhouettes. The vignettes were surrounded by circles and further elaborated by floral scrolls and winding details; they and the many spurting fountains found throughout are rendered in a thoroughly contemporary, rococo-deco style.

The twelve colored lithographs that commemorate Eugene's good works and vicious battles against the swarthy Turks are in a more realistic, if generalized, cartoonlike style that differs markedly from Czeschka's taut ornamentation. Figures and actions are dramatically differentiated by grand falls of light and are more alive with action, diagonals, and space. In comparison to Czeschka's *Nibelungen*, pattern is minimal, although Wacik used strong and unusually colored skies, waves of cloud lines, intricately silhouetted trees, and suggestively churning smoke and globular forms to dramatize his stories.[27]

Barbara Kaerwer's collection is valuable and unusual precisely because it includes both the Keim/Czeschka *Nibelungen* and the Hofmannsthal/Wacik *Prinz Eugen*, not just the finest gems of the best years of the Secession and Wiener Werkstätte, but also products of their much less-appreciated but equally noteworthy later periods. The collection includes works of both Viennese and non-Viennese artists, both in and outside of these groups, and thus a wide sampling of the many different kinds of art made and exhibited in Vienna. With this we gain a much rounder, richer, and more believable picture of the Viennese scene. Always founded on an unwieldy but fruitful coexistence of national and international, provincial and cosmopolitan, conservative and progressive, folk and modern, and inextricably entwined in the extremes of an extraordinary wealthy, decaying empire and of subsequent periods of war and postwar inflation, poverty, revolution, rising National Socialism, and final economic failure, Vienna's remarkable modern design is as forceful and unwieldy as the complicated period in which it was born.

Notes

1. I would like to express my warmest gratitude to Barbara Kaerwer, whose many years of bold and hard work in assembling and cataloguing her collection have facilitated its research and teaching. I would also like to thank many colleagues at the University of Wisconsin–Madison: the late William Bunce, Lynette Korenic, Linda Duychak, Beth Abrohams, and Linda Lunde of the Kohler Art Library; Tracy Honn, Robin Rider, Willa Schmidt, Ann Pollock, and the entire reference staff of Memorial Library; and Anne Lambert, Kathy Paul, Patricia Powell, Andrea Selbig, Andrew Stevens, and Jennifer Stofflet of the Elvehjem Museum of Art.

2. I enjoy the unusual pleasure and pride of drawing on the work of my doctoral student Joann Skrypzak, whose superb curatorial organization and unstinting hard work are responsible for this exhibition's excellence. Other indispensable sources are Colin B. Bailey, ed., *Gustav Klimt: Modernism in the Making* (exh. cat.) (New York: Abrams and Ottawa: National Gallery of Canada, 2001); Alessandra Comini, *Egon Schiele's Portraits* (Berkeley: University of California Press, 1974; Ernst Hanisch, *1890–1990. Der lange Schatten des Staates. Österreichische Gesellschaftsgeschichte* (Vienna: Ueberreuter, 1994); Jane Kallir, *Viennese Design and the Wiener Werkstätte* (New York: Galerie St. Etienne and Braziller, 1986); Waltraud Neuwirth, *Wiener Werkstätte. Avantgarde, Art Deco, Industrial Design* (Vienna: Neuwirth, 1984); Carl E. Schorske, *Fin-de-Siècle Vienna: Politics and Culture* (New York: Knopf, 1980); Werner J. Schweiger, *Wiener Werkstaette: Design in Vienna, 1903–1932*, tr. Alexander Lieven (New York: Abbeville Press, 1984); Eduard F. Sekler, *Josef Hoffmann: The Architectural Work. Monograph and Catalogue of Works* (Princeton: Princeton University Press, 1985); Debora L. Silverman, *Art Nouveau in Fin-de-Siècle France: Politics, Psychology, and Style* (Berkeley: University of California Press, 1989); Kirk Varnedoe, *Vienna 1900: Art, Architecture and Design* (exh. cat.) (New York: Museum of Modern Art, 1986); and Angela Völker with the collaboration of Ruperta Pichler, *Textiles of the Wiener Werkstätte, 1910–1932* (New York: Rizzoli, 1994).

3. On the full range of Moser's activities see Maria Rennhofer, *Koloman Moser* (Vienna: Brandstätter, 2002).

4. For the execution of the maps I am indebted to Onno Brouwer and Caitlin Doran of the University of Wisconsin–Madison Cartography Lab; Christian M. Nebehay, *Wien speziell. Architektur und Malerei um 1900* (Vienna: Brandstätter, 2000); and the Austrian Tourist Bureau in Vienna, <http://www.info.wien.at> and <http://www.wien.gv.at>

5. Sekler, *Josef Hoffmann*, 44–51, 266–70, 273–75 (cats. 52–54, 63).

6. Michael Spens, "Holzmeister, Clemens," *The Grove Dictionary of Art Online*, ed. L. Marcy (Accessed 22 October 2002), <http://www.groveart.com>

7. On the fair's history and the Austrian contributions see Joan Campbell, *The German Werkbund* (Princeton: Princeton University Press, 1978), 231–33; Sekler, *Josef Hoffmann*, 181–87, 403–4 (cats. 266–68); Kenneth Silver, *Esprit de Corps* (Princeton: Princeton University Press, 1989), 362–99; and Nancy J. Troy, *Modernism and the Decorative Arts in France: Art Nouveau to Le Corbusier* (New Haven: Yale University Press, 1991), 159–228.

8. Lisa Phillips, *Frederick Kiesler* (exh. cat.) (New York: Whitney Museum of Art and Norton, 1989), 13–15.

9. See Peter Noever, ed., *Dagobert Peche and the Wiener Werkstätte* (New Haven: Yale University Press, 2002).

10. To appreciate the contemporary spread of these tendencies throughout Austria, see L. W. Rochowanski, ed., *Ein Führer durch das Österreichische Kunstgewerbe* (Leipzig: Heinz, 1930).

11. Schweiger, *Wiener Werkstätte*, 98, 118, and Kallir, *Viennese Design*, 108.

12. I am tremendously indebted to Tracy Honn's superb and generous assistance in identifying several typefaces, which has illuminated both them and many other features of the books discussed here. On the typographers in context see Jeremy Aynsley, *Graphic Design in Germany: 1890–1945* (Berkeley: University of California Press, 2000).

13. Illustrated in Varnedoe, *Vienna 1900*, 42.

14. See Henry-Louis de La Grange, *Gustav Mahler. Vienna: The Years of Challenge* (Oxford: Oxford University Press, 1995), 502–15.

15. De La Grange, *Gustav Mahler*, 511–12, notes that many read the knight in Klimt's *Beethoven Frieze* as an idealized portrait of Mahler. See also Alessandra Comini, *Gustav Klimt* (New York: Braziller, 1975), 20 (figs. 34 & 35), 24.

16. Cf. Margret Schütte, *Emil Orlik* (Berlin: Mann, 1983), cats. 153, 157, 159, 161.

17. Illustrated in Comini, *Egon Schiele's Portraits*, pl. 190.

18. On the portraits see Comini, *Egon Schiele's Portraits*,180–83 and Jane Kallir, *Egon Schiele: The Complete Works*, 223, 342 (cat. no. P. 322), 634 (cat. nos. D. 2447 and D. 2448), and 650 (cat. no. G. 16b).

19. See *Die Nibelungen. In der Wiedergabe von Franz Keim*, with fore- and afterword by Helmut Brackert (Frankfurt am Main: Insel, 1972); Frances Carey and Antony Griffiths, *The Print in Germany, 1880–1933* (exh.cat.) (London: The British Museum, 1984; reprint New York: Dover,1993): 240–41; and Friedrich C. Heller, "Gerlachs Jugendbücherei," *Die Schiefertafel* 4, 3 (December 1981): 138–62.

20. Czeschka also designed Nibelungen chess figures and many toys; cf., for instance, Gabriele Fahr-Becker, *Wiener Werkstaette 1903–1932*, tr. Karen Williams and High Warden (Cologne: Taschen, 1995), 206.

21. Hans von Ankwicz, "Wacik, Franz," in *Allgemeines Lexikon der bildenden Künstler* 35, ed. Ulrich Thieme und Felix Becker (Zwickau: Ullmann, 1964–1966), 6–8.

22. Oswalt von Nostitz, "Hofmannsthal, Hugo von," in Caspar v. Schrenck-Notzing, *Lexikon des Konservativismus* (Graz: Stocker, 1996), 256–58.

23. See Michael P. Steinberg, *The Meaning of the Salzburg Festival* (Ithaca: Cornell University Press, 1990) and Walter Weiss, "Salzburger Mythos? Hofmannsthals und Reinhardts Welttheater," *Zeitgeschichte* 2, 5 (February 1975): 109–19.

24. On his involvement with one of these groups see Guido Müller, *Deutsch-französische Gesellschaftsbeziehungen und europäische Gespräche nach dem Ersten Weltkrieg. Das Deutsch-Französische Studienkomitee und der Europäische Kulturbund 1923/24–1932/33* (Munich: Oldenbourg, 2002).

25. See Nicholas Henderson, *Prince Eugen of Savoy* (London: Wiedenfeld and Nicolson, 1964).

26. See Aynsley, *Graphic Design in Germany*, 106, 185, and Sebastian Carter, *Twentieth Century Type Designers* (London: Trefoil, 1987), 59–61.

27. Wacik could be seen as a distanced, more eminent first cousin of the illustrators of the *Classics Illustrated* comic books.

Viennese Modern Design and the Taste for Living

Joann Skrypzak

Modernism in Austria is largely associated with its thriving capital city, Vienna. Home to the Habsburgs since the thirteenth century and center of the Austro-Hungarian Empire, Vienna also served as the birthplace for fin-de-siècle art movements the Vienna Secession and the Wiener Werkstätte (Vienna Workshop). These two movements, which span the period from 1897 to 1932, gave dominant shape to Viennese Modernism. The Secession developed out of a reaction to prevailing historicism and conservative exhibition practices. It saw itself as a vital, regenerative force that would produce art forms that were in keeping with modern life. Similarly motivated by reform concerns and stylistically unrestricted, the Werkstätte was formed out of a desire to save the decorative arts from their aesthetic devaluation through mass production. This group aimed to unite the fine and decorative arts and sought to bring the consumer into a closer relationship with the designer and craftsman.

Both movements were concerned with cultivating a new awareness of culture and the arts among the public and endeavored to eliminate the traditional distinction between the fine and decorative arts. Indeed, the new appreciation of the applied arts was an international fin-de-siècle phenomenon and found expression in the many national variants of art nouveau. In Vienna, however, the belief that all aspects of daily life could be enhanced by an aesthetic sensibility led the new art to be associated especially with the concept of the *Gesamtkunstwerk*, or unified work of art. Much more than it championed any one style of expression, Viennese modernism—through its ideals and designs—cultivated a taste for living aesthetically. For the Werkstätte the implications of this concept would be turn out to be as much a detriment to its existence as a creative impetus.

The era in which the Vienna Secession artists banned together in 1897 was that of the Ringstrasse. This large-scale civic development undertaken by Emperor Franz Josef in the late 1850s and 1860s was a response to the city's exploding population and the demands for better sanitation, public health, and recreation spaces. As a result in 1857 Franz Josef allocated land of the city's peripheral fortifications for urban improvement, and the Ringstrasse, a broad, two-mile long boulevard with numerous public buildings, was built. The architecture of the Ring was grand in scale and characterized by ornate historicist styles. On a symbolic level, this monumental display was meant to convey the Habsburgs's esteem and achievements and to raise the visibility of Vienna as a major European capital. On a functional level, the buildings provided for a variety of civic, legal, educational, religious, and cultural needs and represented the rational state-supported organization of institutions. Undertaken during an extended period of recession followed by a market crash in 1873, the project helped stimulate the economy. The Ringstrasse, however, had its more modernist-minded critics. Many disparaged the regressive appearance of the buildings and their huge scale that dwarfed humans and lacked a central communal square. Yet, the project ultimately had a great positive effect on culture and the arts. It drew many artists to Vienna and provided them with training and employment from which they expanded or departed.

In 1861 during the Ringstrasse development the emperor founded the city's one exhibition facility for contemporary art known as the Künstlerhaus. This institution was meant to present the work of living artists and promote cultural exchange with other European countries, an aim similar to that of its later rival, the Secession. Although predicated on democratic rule, the Künstlerhaus came to be dominated by a conservative majority that left little room for the younger generation of avant-garde artists. Its exhibition politics were increasingly perceived as corrupt as it favored older members' work that presumably was regarded as commercially more lucrative in light of the institution's ten percent sales commission. Moreover, the exhibition of foreign artists' works was similarly curbed in order to promote the domestic market. By 1897, fed up with this situation, nineteen members seceded from the Künstlerhaus and formed the Association of Austrian Artists—Vienna Secession (Vereinigung Bildender Künstler Österreichs—Wiener Seccession). Among this group of young artists were its elected president Gustav Klimt, Josef Hoffmann, Carl Moll, Koloman Moser, and Josef Maria Olbrich.

Hoffmann and Olbrich had studied under the progressive architect Otto Wagner, who was appointed professor of architecture at Vienna's Academy of Fine Arts. Wagner's conviction that artistic work should be based in modern life became a guiding principle for Hoffmann and Olbrich. Hoffmann drew on the classical and vernacular architecture he encountered when traveling in Italy as a Rome Prize scholar. Moser had trained at the Academy and, like Gustav Klimt, at Vienna's Applied Arts School (Kunstgewerbeschule). With Hoffmann he later would found the Wiener Werkstätte.

The Secession aspired to intensify Viennese artistic life by bringing it into more lively contact with art developed abroad. Works were to be exhibited based on artistic merit alone, apart from commercial considerations, although the Secession ultimately also had to contend with such matters. The group further aimed to stimulate the public's consciousness of an art that was modern and of its time and to raise the interest in art on official levels. Along with a concern for modernity, the Secessionists also integrated a new interest in the applied arts. In bridging the separation between fine and decorative arts, the Secessionists believed that the potential for artistic creativity was present in all forms of art. This attitude was to manifest itself in the design of the Secession's new exhibition hall, the publication of its periodical, *Ver Sacrum* (Sacred Spring), and in the range of exhibitions it organized.

After the success of the Secession's first show in March 1898, Olbrich was commissioned to design a permanent exhibition space for the group. By the autumn of that year the Secession building, which was located behind the Academy of Arts, was completed (figure 1). Conceived as a temple of art, the building announced the Secession's belief in the necessity of art's contemporaneity and liberation. Above the entrance its motto read: To the age its art, to art its freedom. The structure's classical design vocabulary freely combines elements of Apollonian rationality and Dionysian irrationality, an echo of Friedrich Nietzsche's idea of the eternal struggle between these two forces. The design is based, for instance, on simple, white, cubic forms and flat surfaces that enclose a central courtyard covered with a glass roof. As a dazzling counterpoint to this pared down symmetry, a spherical dome of gilt bronze laurel leaves rises above a four-pylon structure set over the center of the courtyard. This crowning dome signifies light in its gold color, and eternity, triumph, and Apollo, the god of music, poetry, and prophecy, in its laurel leaves. The discrete ornamentation applied to the building's surfaces—geometric elements and plant and animal forms—derives from the architectural structures and reinforces the interplay between the rational and irrational. The characteristic Secession styles that developed in the following years exhibited a similar synthesis of flat surfaces, geometric abstraction, and symbolic content.

The Secession's periodical, *Ver Sacrum*, published between 1898 and 1903 was intended as an exhibition in miniature. It reported on contemporary artists, Secession members, exhibitions, and reproduced artworks. Similar to many of its conceptual forerunners, such as *Pan*, *Revue Blanche*, and *Simplicissmus*, *Ver Sacrum*'s presentation was of essential importance. High quality papers, new type fonts, and texts accompanied by illustrations or decorative borders became means to produce a new type of periodical. *Ver Sacrum* brilliantly integrated all these elements so that each page was a synthesized artwork in itself. In accord with the Secession's idealistic aspirations, this harmonious fusion of form and content was intended to have a restorative effect on its readers.

Between 1898 and 1905 the Secession organized a series of exhibitions that displayed the latest in European artistic developments as well as its own achievements within that context. As part of their didactic efforts to make the public more aware and discerning of modern art, the Secession offered worker groups guided tours on Sundays at a reduced admission price.[1] The selection of European art included recent examples of symbolist, realist, and postimpressionist painting, as well as sculpture, graphic art, and photography. Exhibitions presented works by such leading artists as Munch, Signac, Toorop, Khnopff, Crane, Segantini, Böcklin, Gauguin, van Gogh, the Nabis, Toulouse-Lautrec, Hodler, and Stuck. The sixth show in 1900 was devoted to Japanese art; the eighth exhibition that same year presented the latest applied arts by some of the foremost European designers, including works from Meier-Graefe's *Maison Moderne*, Henry van de Velde, Charles Ashbee's Guild of Handicraft, and the Glasgow Four in addition to works by

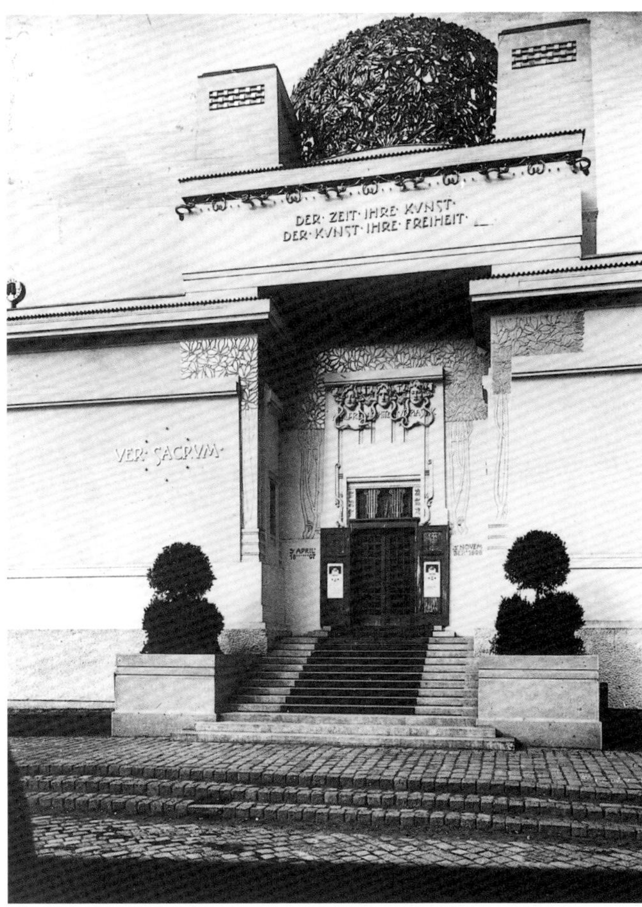

Figure 1. Josef Maria Olbrich designed the Secession Building, built in Vienna in1898, main façade. Photograph courtesy Österreichische Nationalbibliothek, Vienna

Hoffmann and Moser. The positive critical response to Hoffmann's and Moser's contributions gave further impetus to their desire to form a cooperative of designers and craftsmen skilled in all media.[2]

Subsequent exhibitions emphasized works by the Austrian members of the Secession. With this change of focus they presented the progress of Secession artists against the backdrop of international modernism. As explained in the catalogue of the tenth exhibition, "If we appear on this occasion without foreign guests, it is not because we mean to celebrate a goal already attained, but because we wish to demonstrate our own origins, the point of departure of our own creativity."[3] In fact, two factions developed within the Secession, the "naturalists" devoted to painting, and the "stylists," who more thoroughly integrated the fine and applied arts. This and other differences brought the latter group, led by Gustav Klimt, to break with the Secession in 1905.

The Secession's fourteenth exhibition dedicated to Beethoven and Klinger was the culmination of the stylists' efforts. Mounted in the Secession building from April 15 to June 27, 1902, the show's central goal was the presentation of Max Klinger's monumental polychrome sculpture of Beethoven. Secession artists organized and decorated the exhibition space around this work as a simple and uncluttered but thoroughly synthesized *Gesamtkunstwerk*. Orchestrated into a type of temple, the space celebrated Beethoven as a model artist-hero. Drawing on the ideas of Richard Wagner and Nietzsche, Klinger presented the artist as a hero who would lead humanity to redemption. The exhibition also expressed Wagner's vision of music as supreme among the arts, derived from his reading of Schopenhauer. All works were subordinated to the main utopian themes of mankind's longing for happiness and the triumph of the human spirit.

The Secessionist's interest in synthesizing the fine and decorative arts was certainly not a new concept, nor an idea confined to Vienna. Similar movements designed to bring about a renewal of the arts and to forge a link between art and industry developed throughout Europe and the United States. These movements were ultimately linked to developments in the natural sciences, psychology, philosophy, technology, the arts, design, and industry—developments underscored by Joseph Paxton's Crystal Palace in 1851 and subsequently by the alternative reform ideas of William Morris and the British Arts and Crafts movement in the 1870s and 1880s. These advancements stimulated the large, ranging international art nouveau phenomenon that came to be known as Jugendstil in German-speaking countries. Organic forms, curvilinearity, abstract patterning, and a sense of movement and rhythm dominated the movement's styles. At the same time, its national variants took on distinct characters often related to local and folk art traditions.

In Vienna, the early nineteenth-century Biedermeier style, associated with comfortable, middle-class interiors and based on simple neoclassical forms, was a crucial source of inspiration for Secession and Werkstätte artists. Viennese art nouveau often combined strict rectilinearity and geometry. Although the Viennese style appeared relatively late in comparison to those of other countries, its development was aided through its ties to the Museum of Art and Industry with its Applied Arts School in Vienna and network of technical and crafts schools throughout the empire.

In 1897, the same year that the Secession was founded, Arthur von Scala became the new director of the Museum of Art and Industry and Felician von Myrbach was made head of its school. Their appointments signaled a new vibrancy both for the institutions and for the crafts. The museum made its objects available to the technical schools, encouraged professionals to produce designs by the school's teachers and graduates, and organized annual exhibitions of the resulting works. In an effort to revitalize industry by exposing it to current art developments, Scala also arranged important applied art exhibitions from glass works by Tiffany and the Austrian firms Lobmeyer and Bakalowits to English furniture and Japanese prints. The Applied Arts School also was reorganized, giving it further autonomy, and in 1901 it gained a separate administration. Within the next few years Myrbach added Secession artists to his staff, including Hoffmann in 1898 and Moser in 1899. With some graduates from the school Hoffmann and Moser founded the group, Viennese Art in the Home (Wiener Kunst im Hause) in 1901.[4] This group designed modern interiors and household objects, but since they still lacked their own workshops, the artists sought production through the best firms in Vienna.

With their continuing desire to combine design, production, and distribution in one enterprise, in early 1903, Hoffmann, following his study trip to England and Scotland, and Moser finally realized plans for the Wiener Werkstätte. The firm was formally registered with Hoffmann and Moser as directors and the industrialist and collector Fritz Waerndorfer as financer, and in October they moved into permanent quarters in the Neustiftgasse designed by Koloman Moser with workshops for jewelry making and metalwork, bookbinding, leatherwork, carpentry, and lacquer work. Hoffmann brought his architectural practice to the firm and the organization later added divisions for textile (1909–1910) and fashion design (1911).

In the Werkstätte's belief that the aesthetic endeavor should be extended to all aspects of daily life and promote cultural progress, the group thought that every object could be improved through the beauty of its design and production. The vision was all-encompassing. Designs ranged from complex architectural projects to the smallest detail or seemingly mundane item such as a postcard or dinner bell. Drawing on the ideals of Ruskin and Morris, the group's working program also articulated the need for establishing a humane and artistic work environment. The ideals for their designs emphasized functionality, a respect for materials, and craftsmanship. Advocating a restrained use of ornamentation, they stated: "Where it is appropriate, we will seek to adorn, nevertheless without compulsion and not at all costs."[5] The first Werkstätte exhibitions and commissions provide a sense of how their mission unfolded.

The Werkstätte's public debut in October 1904 took place not in Austria, but in Berlin at the Hohenzollern Applied Arts House (Hohenzollern Kunstgewerbehaus), founded in 1879. The four-month exhibition celebrated the Applied Arts House's twenty-five year jubilee and led to the commission to design the Berlin apartment of Margarethe Stonborough, the daughter of Leopoldine and Karl Wittgenstein.[6] A month afterwards the Werkstätte opened a small exhibition in the Galerie Miethke that displayed the Werkstätte's early bookbinding efforts. Conceived of in the *Gesamtkunstwerk* tradition of the Secession's periodical *Ver Sacrum* and the artist's book, the works unified the best in design, materials, and execution. Included among the works was the luxury edition *In Celebration of One Hundred Years of the Imperial and Royal Court and State Printing Works* (*Zur Feier des einhundertjährigen Bestandes der k.k. Hof- und Staatsdruckerei*) (cat. 77). This publication exemplifies communal endeavor, with its typeface by Rudolf von Larisch and woodcut illustrations by Carl Otto Czeschka. Moser, trained not only as a painter but also skilled in graphic, textile, and glass design, served as director of the printing production. His contributions include designs for the volume's watermark, initials, text frames, title, endpapers, frontispiece, as well as its dust jacket and bindings. This work signaled the start of the group's public commissions and the collaboration between the Werkstätte and the state press.[7]

Early commissions for interiors and architectural projects came from within the Werkstätte's circle of friends and acquaintances. Among these was a design for the fashion salon of Gustav Klimt's companion, Emilie Flöge, and her sisters, and the Purkersdorf Sanatorium (1904–1906), built for Victor Zuckerhandl, the brother-in-law of art critic and Werkstätte enthusiast Berta Zuckerhandl. The sanatorium embodied the characteristic architectural style of the Werkstätte, based on a combination of clean, white surfaces set off by dark, square latticework, restrained ornamentation, functionality, and comfort. Despite the architecture's impression of simple austerity, it was also an essay in refined sophistication. Its use of expensive and luxurious materials matched its status as an institution for healing baths, treating nervous disorders, physical therapy, and convalescence intended for a wealthy clientele.[8] Two other early projects, the Palais Stoclet in Brussels (1905–1911) and the Cabaret Fleder-maus in Vienna's center (1908), further demonstrate the complex extent to which the *Gesamtkunstwerk* concept found articulation. The first of these was a prestigious residence for the Belgian industrialist and sophisticated art collector Adolphe Stoclet (figure 2). Unhampered by financial restrictions, Werkstätte artists conceived the exquisite modern designs down to the last detail. This coordinated theater for living spanned interior and exterior. The off-white exterior surfaces and openings are elegantly framed with gilt bronze moldings that emphasize the structure's tectonic quality. Franz Metzner's Atlas-type figures support the tower's floral cupola; Michael Powolny's *Pallas*

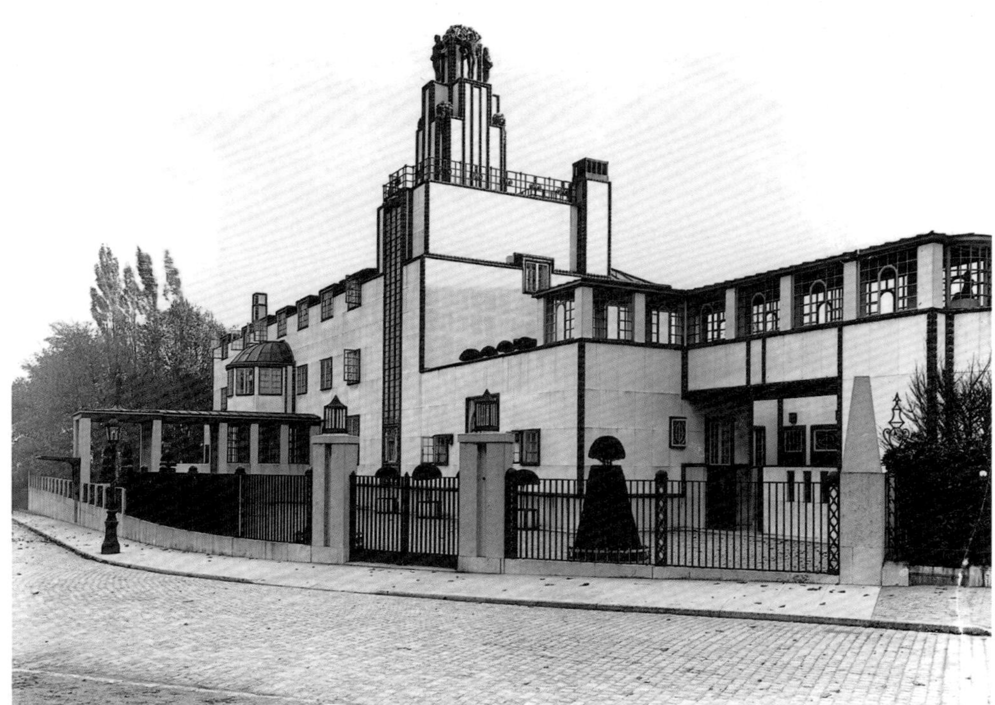

Figure 2. Josef Hoffmann designed the Palais Stoclet in Brussels, 1905–1911, street façade. Photograph courtesy Foto Marburg/ Art Resource, NY

Athena (patron of wisdom and the arts) guards the entrance pavilion; and Richard Luksch's sculpted feminine figures grace the garden. Interior decorations include Klimt's monumental mosaic dining room frieze that combined precious stones, metals, and inexpensive materials; Czeschka's elegant folk-art inspired breakfast room furnishings; Ludwig Heinrich Jungnickel's animal frieze for the children's nursery; and ceramic tiles and majolica by Michael Powolny and Bertold Löffler, founders of the Wiener Keramik.

The Cabaret Fledermaus realized Waerndorfer's desire for a theater. This entertainment space, built in the basement of a new building, appears to have been as much an arena for artistic display as for the performances it staged. The walls and bar of the anteroom were decorated with multicolored ceramic tiles of various sizes, patterns, and motifs and complemented by a black-and-white checkered floor. The effect was bold if not overwhelming: one critic derided it as a "ghastly grotto."[9] The anteroom provided a stark contrast to the theater's white space for the audience. Among the contributing artists were Oskar Kokoschka, Egon Schiele, Powolny, Löffler, Czeschka, and Rudolf Kalvach.

Given their commitment to the high-quality production of unique, handcrafted designs and emphasis on artistic experimentation, the Werkstätte's projects were necessarily costly and exclusive. Only a wealthy clientele, largely represented by patrons oriented to the avant-garde could afford their designs. Not surprisingly, projects often went over budget, and the group was chronically faced with financial difficulties. Such economic issues led to the departure of Moser in 1907 after Waerndorfer approached Moser's wife, Editha, for financial assistance without Moser's prior consultation. Waerndorfer also was forced to leave due to mounting debt and in 1914 the group went into insolvency.

Despite this setback, the banker Otto Primavesi became the Werkstätte's new business manager in 1915 and furthered their international profile by opening up branches in Marienbad, Zurich, Velden, Berlin, and New York. The 1915 appointment of Dagobert Peche, who assumed a prominent role alongside Hoffmann, also signaled a stylistic shift. Although Viennese modernism is characterized by stylistic pluralism, the geometric purism pioneered in the early years by Hoffmann and Moser is often regarded as exemplifying the pinnacle of Vienna's modern efforts to combine aesthetics with practicality. In contrast, the later shift toward an increasingly expressionistic mode of representation initiated by Peche resulted in works whose extravagant ornamental qualities often eclipsed their functionality. Although the Werkstätte was not opposed to mechanical production, it relied heavily on handwork and this practice became extreme with Peche, who was completely opposed to industrial production.[10]

Later designs often seem to embody the worst excesses of Viennese Modernist luxury, particularly in light of the immense political and economic difficulties that followed World War I and the dissolution of the monarchy in 1918. The mixed responses to the Austrian pavilion at the International Exposition of Modern Decorative and Industrial Arts in Paris in 1925 reveal the degree to which the Werkstätte was no longer considered a progressive design force. The new, predominantly expressionistic works were perceived as provincial, lacking artistic skill, and unable to inspire deeper intellectual consideration.[11] Armand Weiser observed that Hoffmann's pavilion displayed the same items that had been shown for a decade, and writer Benno Reifenberg complained that the new Austria appeared to be "playing around."[12] The densely packed Paris display would have made it easy to overlook works that still exhibited a modern purpose and sensiblity, as in the area of textile design, but the original principles of the movement seemed to have been sacrificed. In 1932, amidst the debacle following the failure of the world economy and the rise of National Socialism, the Wiener Werkstätte finally closed its doors.

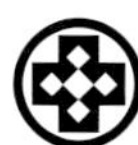

Notes

1. The art critic Hermann Bahr served as a guide for such tours and in a letter to his father commented that these visitors paid a ten Kreuzer entrance fee, which also included a catalogue that otherwise cost thirty Kreuzer. Hermann Bahr, *Briefwechsel mit seinem Vater. Ausgewählt von Adalbert Schmidt* (Vienna: Bauer, 1971), 418. Quoted in Werner J. Schweiger, *Wiener Werkstätte: Kunst und Handwerk, 1903–1932* (Vienna: Branstätter, 1982), 14.

2. Schweiger has made an excellent study of the role of art criticism in the history of the Secession and Werkstätte including the critical response to Hoffmann and Moser's work in the eighth exhibition. See Werner Schweiger, *Wiener Werkstätte: Design in Vienna 1903–1932*, trans. Alexander Lieven (New York: Abbeville Press, 1984).

3. *Vereinigung bildender Künstler Oesterreichs Katalog*...(of the tenth exhibition) (Vienna: Vereinigung bildender Künstler Oesterreichs, 1901). Quoted in Peter Vergo, *Art in Vienna 1898–1918: Klimt, Kokoschka, Schiele and Their Contemporaries* (Ithaca: Cornell University Press, 1975), 65.

4. Schweiger, *Wiener Werkstätte: Kunst und Handwerk, 1903–1932*, 21–22.

5. Josef Hoffmann, Working Program, Wiener Werkstätte, 1905. Quoted in Schweiger, *Wiener Werkstätte: Kunst und Handwerk, 1903–1932*, 42. Translation mine.

6. Schweiger, *Wiener Werkstätte: Kunst und Handwerk, 1903–1932*, 38.

7. Schweiger, *Wiener Werkstätte: Kunst und Handwerk, 1903–1932*, 40.

8. Eduard Sekler, *Josef Hoffmann: Das architektonische Werk: Monografie und Werkverzeichnis* (Vienna: Residenz, 1982), 67.

9. Ludwig Hevesi, *Acht Jahre Secesion* (Vienna: Konegan, 1906), 243. Quoted in Elisabeth Schmuttermeier, "Die Wiener Werkstätte," in *Wien 1870–1930: Traum und Wirklichkeit*, ed. Robert Waissenberger (exh.cat.) (Salzburg: Residenz, 1984), 149.

10. Angela Völker in collaboration with Ruperta Pichler, *Textiles of the Wiener Werkstätte 1910–1932* (New York: Rizzoli, 1994), 111.

11. Völker and Pichler, *Textiles of the Wiener Werkstätte*, 111.

12. Armand Weiser from *Neues Wiener Tagblatt and* Benno Reifenberg, "West-Kunst-Gewerbe. Zur internationalen Ausstellung in Paris," *Frankfurter Zeitung* (5 August 1925), both quoted in Völker and Pichler, *Textiles of the Wiener Werkstätte*, 119.

Recollections and Collecting
An Interview with Barbara Mackey Kaerwer

Joann Skrypzak

JS: What was postwar Vienna like, when you took your first trip in 1953?

BMK: It was sad and gray. People lived with poverty and poor nutrition. The Soviets and the Allies gingerly occupied their sectors in Vienna and all Austria. There were checkpoints and polite harassments, but there were also concerts, families, shabby parks, and cafés. And to find a good bar, one listened for zither music and happy voices floating up cellar stairs to the street. I had the sense of being in a scene from *The Third Man* [a British postwar film noire written by Graham Greene and set in Vienna].

Bomb damage was still very evident nine years after the war's end. There were piles of bricks in what were once streets and now were great cavities. The shops were temporary structures behind fences; behind the shops were half-block-sized holes. Buildings were sheared in half and closed off. Important buildings that were architectural and cultural treasures for the world, not just the Viennese, such as the opera, were in shambles. Many monuments and institutions were still in good shape, however, such as the Schönbrunn Palace and some of the cafés.

JS: Cafés have also been important meeting places for Viennese artists and intellectuals and often exhibit the art nouveau style. What were they like—were many also in ruins?

BMK: My travel companion and friend, Annie, and I knew that these remarkable cafés gave a real flavor to Vienna. This six-month trip was a period of discovery, before I had become an art historian, so I didn't look at things as an art historian might. Many cafés had been carefully maintained, as they had been in the 1890s or pre-World War I. The decoration was mostly Jugendstil, which has a sense of luxury, a sumptuousness not seen as often in the French art noveau and almost never in the German. But Austrians were quite also aware of art deco, and cafés that embraced this style had emerged between the two world wars. The Austrians had always been aware of the French. The Viennese were aware of what was fashionable internationally, and some cafés were trendy. But they also knew the historical importance of their café society and weren't as influenced by American style as Western Europe. I sensed nostalgia for the old days of the Habsburgs.

JS: How did you start collecting Viennese applied arts? What interests guided you?

BMK: I must go back a long way to answer you. I started out collecting early twentieth-century German expressionist art. But before collecting anything, a strong interest must exist, and for this I credit the University of Wisconsin's political science department and my major professor, William Ebenstein, in particular. In his courses I learned much about German and Austrian history and culture. I was also encouraged to explore the political movements in these countries and the Soviet Union.

After I had spent those six months in Europe, I realized I didn't know *one* thing about art. I returned to graduate school to study art history at the University of Minnesota. I later worked at the Minneapolis Institute of Arts across the hall from the prints and drawings department and its curator, Dr. Harold Joachim. He was a noted European and American scholar, particularly revered for his expertise with prints and drawings of Germany, his native country. He encouraged my study of the museum's prints and guided an awareness of connoisseurship. He included me in a tiny group invited to examine the portfolios of dealers who came to the museum. Through his inspiration I began to buy prints. Gradually I discovered that I was not as attracted to gentle and harmonious art as to works that are bold and dissonant, or that failed to resolve the dissonance, a quality that often defines expressionist works like those of *Die Brücke*. I began to collect those things because they challenged me. Harold Joachim fed this interest by directing to me works that were available through dealers bringing art to the museum, which I could often buy.

When I began collecting in 1956, these German expressionist works were still despised in Germany; because there was no local market for them, they were inexpensive. However, about 1965, the prices went up significantly so that I could seldom afford them. Having caught the disease of loving to collect and to have these German things to study, I began to cast about. I discovered that there was a great and interesting contrast between the German and Austrian cultures. So I decided to learn about Austrian culture to see if there was something there I could use as a teacher. Early on I decided to collect works that had didactic as well as aesthetic significance, and I found the works were interesting for both the teacher and the student. At that time there was a small market for Austrian things, so they were still within my modest budget. I began collecting them, although not to the exclusion of German things that were still within my means. But I decided that I would form a collection that had educational value and presented issues of style and technique, as well as the period's social and cultural history. Beyond my teaching objective for the Austrian works, there is the pure luxurious pleasure in looking at and handling such opulent art. I started with the beginning of these artistic revolutions, as the artists thought they were revolutionary, say, around 1890, and stopped with the arrival of the Nazis in the 1930s. For Austria, this took me through the art deco. With both cultures it stopped with the closure of the institutions—the Wiener Werkstätte in Austria and the Bauhaus in Germany.

JS: Have your concerns changed with more recent acquisitions?

BMK: My Austrian collection started out with a remarkable Koloman Moser painting (cat. 3) and, rather conventionally, with two-dimensional things. Because the movement included the whole range of applied arts, I consciously began collecting three-dimensional works. The Wiener Werkstätte aimed to elevate applied arts to the level of appreciation of the fine arts; sixteen years later, the Bauhaus had a similar mission. The Werkstätte had done this without a great deal of political consciousness. The decision was easy for me since these applied arts are so attractive, although not all that available since Austrians are very proud of their own tradition. I have had a shopping list for fine Austrian applied arts much more than for certain prints or drawings. I feel that I have not yet reached that well-rounded picture of the Austrian movement that would make a great teaching collection. So that's still an objective. In my recent collecting I have worked very hard to obtain such things as works that show Hoffmann moving to incorporate art deco into his art. After all he lived until 1956, and the art deco movement was important to him. Wanting to find an example of glass that shows these later characteristics, I found a pair of lovely cobalt blue, sharply geometric, paneled vases (cat. 45). These I bought not just because they are attractive but to add diversity and meaning to the collection. Also I have tried to find works in silver and pieces that have the *Gitterwerk,* or latticework design, because Moser and Hoffmann included this pattern in their earliest tableware, metalwork, books, ceramics, and so on. Elements of this geometric style can be still found in works of the early 1920s that have a more feminine quality. Several objects share a decorative manipulation of silver designs that are an example of this more decorative and feminine early 1920s style. Hoffmann picked it up, but used it with discipline very handsomely.

Of course I am interested in high standards of quality. But I also feel sentimental about Austrian culture. Its long, curious, and complex history has fascinated me. I am interested first in showing style, the consistency of an artist and also his development, the influences upon him, and the times, the interaction with other artists, or materials that caused his style to develop. I have been interested in the cultural pressures that have befallen these movements and the men and women within them. My political science training is still vital in my curiosity about what's happening in the art world.

JS: Was the Koloman Moser Jugendstil Buckle (cat. 34) your first Viennese acquisition?

BMK: In 1953, way before I knew what I was doing, I innocently bought that buckle. It just pleased me. It is astonishing today when I find it is by Koloman Moser and Jugendstil.

JS: Which Viennese work in your collection do you consider the most important?

BMK: Even though this is a didactic collection, I treat these things personally. I think I would have to say that the painting *Fight of the Titans* (cat. 3) by Koloman Moser is one of the most important ones, for anecdotal reasons as well as for its real merit. I think I've seen every Koloman Moser painting, and I think this is one of the best on formal grounds. I value it for that personal judgment, but also because I see that he must have been aware of art history and aware of Antonio del Pollaiolo (Italian painter, sculptor, printmaker, goldsmith, 1431/32–1498). Pollaiolo's engraving *Battle of the Nudes* (ca. 1465–1470) also has a group of fighting men and the same gestures, bodies, body language. Koloman Moser used the same technique with his models, where he shows a body recto, and then verso, you see it right, you see it left, you see it lying down. There are mirror images of the figures from left to right within the picture, just as there are in the Pollaiolo, and this is interesting.

Then it is *Nachlass* (part of the estate); *Moser* valued it. He kept it in his collection, and it is stamped "*Nachlass*" on the canvas on the back. I always salute the flag when I have a *Nachlass*. He also is said to have demanded recognition that this painting be dated 1903. As I look at his work I think this is impossible, that it must date from about 1913. But, what is tempting, in my mind, is whether he was trying to beat Matisse to a discovery of this palette—this pastel, rich, bright, luscious palette? In other words, like a "Wild Beast" (Fauve) coming out of Vienna! He was a man who was aware of contemporary art as well as that going back to the fifteenth century of Pollaiolo. So, he was probably aware of what they were doing in Paris ...

Another thing, I bought this painting from a lovely woman, Inge Asenbaum whose husband was a noted dealer of medieval art. I do not know if she was also an important art dealer, or if she was simply a fine art historian called upon to mount exhibitions. There had been a Jugendstil exhibition prior to this particular visit of mine to Vienna in the early 1970s, and it was disassembled by the time I saw the works of art, which were pretty much collected together in her home. They were mounted as objects. It seemed she was disposing of them as a dealer might.

I bought the Moser painting from her. In about three visits I made to her home, she taught me a great deal. I still treasure her. I bought other things during this visit, and in a sense she seemed loath to give up this Koloman Moser painting, but had to. I felt flattered that I was the one. I think she had a deep affection for the things she had had in this exhibition, which were like her children. I understand that feeling, because these works of art in the collection have become my children, too. But anyhow, I felt flattered that she parted with it, trusted me with it. Those are some of the reasons that that particular work of art is one of the big moments.

JS: Which works have become favorites of yours?

BMK: A glass vase (cat. 30) from Pallme König & Habel is something I love because of the process—you can see *process* involved. I'm a twentieth-century woman enough to value process as an important aspect of a work of art. A shallow, oval, basket-shaped vase has been blown, and while the glass was still malleable, another, darker color was dribbled over it. There was a buckling because of the differential in heat between the two processes of the blown glass, which makes for a rich inner surface that pops out and is constrained by the dribbling that follows. While the two processes of blowing and dribbling have left the glass still malleable, the artist sliced along the top of the vase to make a loose tail. Then he flipped it over and pushed it down solidly against the main body of the vase and he had a handle, a little loop handle. You can see that it was sliced off the top of the original vase and has been turned back upon itself. And he did this on the other side, too. So the little, shallow vase has these two little handles that have this wobbly quality of still malleable glass, see? So again, it is process. I love that.

I have a signed Loetz vase (cat. 25), but I don't value it like this one. With this one you can see the artist having fun. Part of the reason I favor all these pieces of glass so much is because you can see the process of blowing glass. The understanding of one kind of material sinking into another according to their specific gravity, the colors interacting, and the total mystery of iridescence. I just love them. I'm never tired of them, either. They keep intriguing me, and I find new things to like about them.

JS: You have a later piece, a small covered box made of silver and enamel that dates from 1920 (cat. 47). Tell me how you acquired this piece and how it fits into the larger context of the Wiener Werkstätte.

BMK: When I began to collect Austrian work, I was concerned with the stylistic development of and historical impact on a movement; my favorite artists were Koloman Moser and Josef Hoffmann, two of the three founders of the group. They impressed me the as early originators of the geometric style. This spoke to the strong reform attitudes at the beginning of the movement. But along the way, and also when the men went off to war, the style changed. The later style becomes feminized, if you will. There is a new delicacy and, I hate to use the word, prettiness. More women who began to work in ceramics became effective members of the Werkstätte. The works incorporate a certain whimsy. I don't think it weakened the design, although it did change it. In any case, this work is a lovely example by one of the talented female artists, Felice Rix-Ueno. It is small in scale, sumptuous in the choice of materials, fashioned in a labor-intensive manner, and it has this enamel cap that is painted beautifully with flowers in luminous colors. It is a tiny little treasure. It seems too tiny for any real function—maybe you could put in a couple of your favorite rings—but is lovely to look at. It is an important example of the group's later stylistic development.

JS: How did you happen to acquire the collection of textile samples—and why?

BMK: I wanted to find great swaths of textiles to see the grandeur of design. I realized that to present what was going on at that moment of turn-of-the-century Austria, I had to include textiles, both for the industrial aspect and the design aspect within that context. I have a small network of connections and there are textile collections, but available examples are difficult to find. I did manage to find a set of textile samples that are interesting (cats. 60–66). They speak of the interest in material, the choice of fabric and texture for the final textile, and they speak of international influences on design, such as cubism and abstraction. Certainly they were also aware of eighteenth-century design through tapestries that still existed at the time in Austria, and the designers were thinking of issues such as the scale for gowns. So they were bringing in a variety of design ideas and also trying to become industrialized and practical.

They also used these textile designs in ways that were even more commercial and speak to the economic conditions of the time. The group, of course, had financial difficulties during World War I and after, and the situation for Wiener Werkstätte members was just a disaster because of the loss of the war and patronage. One response was the publication of these textiles as postcards (cat. 59). Superimposed upon them is a Jewish New Year's greeting. It was a very practical idea, one by which they could earn money and also publicize their skill and charm at making textile designs that were available to purchase.

Similarly, Koloman Moser published a portfolio of designs that were not just for fabrics, but also for upholstery, wallpaper, tapestries, and all kinds of surface coverings. This is one of my favorites that I acquired years ago, *Die Quelle* (*The Source: Surface Decoration*) (cat. 103, figure 1). He produced these interlocking patterns, amazing visual puns in which ground and surface planes interchange. It astonishes me to think that these were produced back in 1901. Another portfolio is *Mode Wien* with plates of ladies' fashion printed on tissue with gold leaf, extremely fragile and exquisite. One plate (cat. 56) has ladies tripping along a path and in a pretty composition wearing dress fashions from the designers and in the fabrics that were available from the Wiener Werkstätte textile workshop. But the whole portfolio is sumptuous, it is delicate, made for a restricted public and not to endure heavy usage.

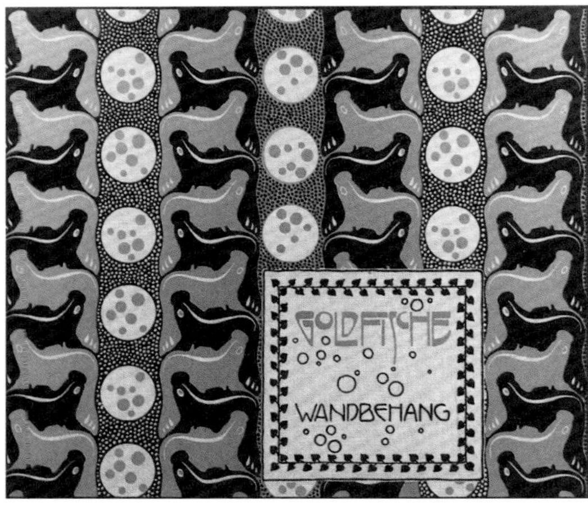

Figure 1. One of Koloman Moser's designs for *Die Quelle: Flachen Schmuck* (1901)

JS: You attended a New Year's Ball in Vienna during a 1988 ski trip with your late husband. You also have ball programs and cardholders in your collection that, in part, fueled your interest in going to the ball. How were these used?

BMK: It seems to me that there is a ball every weekend in the winter in Vienna. The ball programs are often given as favors, or memorials, as they were not always very practical. At the ball we attended, a grand marshal stood on a three-story staircase, in the newer part of the Hofburg. Gentlemen lined this staircase and wore Habsburg military uniforms. As we were leaving at four in the morning, the mayor of Vienna and Fraulein Wien 1988 gave my husband a bottle of superb cognac and me a bottle of perfume. But those things were not used in the sense that favors at the imperial balls were, nor do I know how the favors were presented at imperial balls. But the women would have worn the dance card favors as part of their gowns, so that their hands would be unencumbered. The cards would list each of the dances and the type of dance it was, and there was a space where your partner could write his name. For example, I have one such ball program (cat. 81) that has a set of delicate, thin ivory leaves between two silver repousée covers. It swings open like a fan and attached is a little pen on a silver chain. This one did not have a program, but it has the name of a man, the signature of a dance partner, on one of the leaves. I have tried to protect it, but my friends who have been charmed by the translucent leaves over the decades have swung this dance card open so many times that the signature is now rather smudged.

I also have one curious ball program (cat. 80, figure 2) that surely could not have been worn on the belt of a gown, as it is rather impractical. It has a leather cover embossed front and back with the monogram, AK. This was a ball for the Viennese architect's council—the AK (*Architekten-Kränzchen*)—or architect's gathering. It also has a small metal lectern, with an elaborate Jugendstil design, that can be set up as a tripod. This metal brace ends with an eagle's head and a tiny pencil holds the covers closed. This program is quite fancy, but I think would have been more of a memento that one would receive as a thank-you at the end of the ball and less as a program one could really use. Inside it has the date, in this case 1889 and lists the first part of the program as "before intermission" and includes a program of the dances that were played. There was, for instance, a

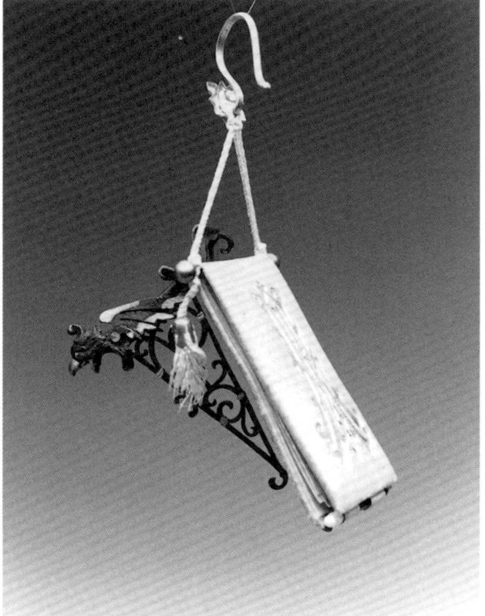

Figure 2. Wilhelm Melzer's 1889 Ball Program, a miniature book with black metal stand

polonaise, a waltz, a polka, and a quadrille. It lists an entire program that may have been as much meant for listening as for dancing. That is, these balls were also meant for showing yourself off. Men wear white tie and tails and the women ball gowns, many of which are reconstructions of eighteenth-century gowns. Even today this is required attire.

The ball venues have spaces for dancing, and other elaborate rooms in the Hofburg are meant for listening. There are stages along each of the four walls and each would offer the same event. It could be the Viennese opera ballet, with eight or ten dancers on each of these four stages, so wherever you were in this crowded ballroom you could see them perform from quite close range. On the walls behind them were elaborate flower arrangements. In another room there would be four music chamber groups playing the same composition, or it could be jugglers or another group of professional performers. The entire New Year's Ball includes the performance of *Die Fledermaus* on December 30, the ball with its ten-course dinner on New Year's Eve, and a performance by the Vienna Philharmonic on New Year's Day. It is this last performance that you can see on New Year's Day on American television.

JS: You have a sizable number of books in your collection. Does the collecting of books differ from collecting in other media?

BMK: I have a shopping list in my mind after decades of going to rare book libraries in this country and elsewhere. I am envious, because I know that these books are extraordinarily beautiful. They were published in small editions, each book numbered, usually by the designer, so they are both hard to find and in museums or private collections that rarely put them up for sale. I have a mental list of books that I'd like to acquire as an educator or because I like pretty things. With prints, however, I tell dealers that I want a specific work because it is going to make the collection more meaningful for students, help complete stylistic development, or reveal something about the culture or an artist's development. But the books are so difficult to obtain I can't do that. It is more a case of serendipity. With an important exception: many rare, fine books were made available to me through the influence and knowledge of the former Kohler Art Library director, Dr. William C. Bunce. He was a dear friend and another mentor. The book arts are sumptuous objects—with their handmade paper, concern with crafting new fonts, handcrafted binding. They were interested in making books as works of art in the sense of William Morris and others who were trying to reform the crafts in the machine age. In that sense the book arts are a statement of the time, both sumptuous objects and reforming agents. But with books there isn't the same developmental quality as there is with prints created by a single artist.

JS: Which of your Austrian books do you like best?

BMK: Let's go from the tiny ball programs to one of my favorites, which is enormous (cat. 76). It is 18 inches tall, 15 wide, about two to three inches in depth, and is extraordinarily heavy. Archduchess Marie Valerie, Franz Josef 's favorite child, commissioned it. Above all it was a flowering reminder for the court of the emperor's life. Notable realist artists were commissioned to represent scenes from his life. My favorite is a scene with the archduchess and her children. The children are walking through the garden room of Schönbrunn Palace, a sunny room with trellises and greenery painted on the walls looking out onto the gardens that sweep up the hill. The emperor is walking through this room with his four little grandchildren, and they are holding his hand and he is looking very pleased, but solemn of course. The other image that I like represents his birthday; the four children are presenting themselves to give him birthday wishes (cat. 76, figure 3). Each child wears a costume that represents a different region of the empire, one is in a Tyrolean costume, one a Hungarian, and so on. They are just adorable, but the costumes again remind us of the grandeur of the empire.

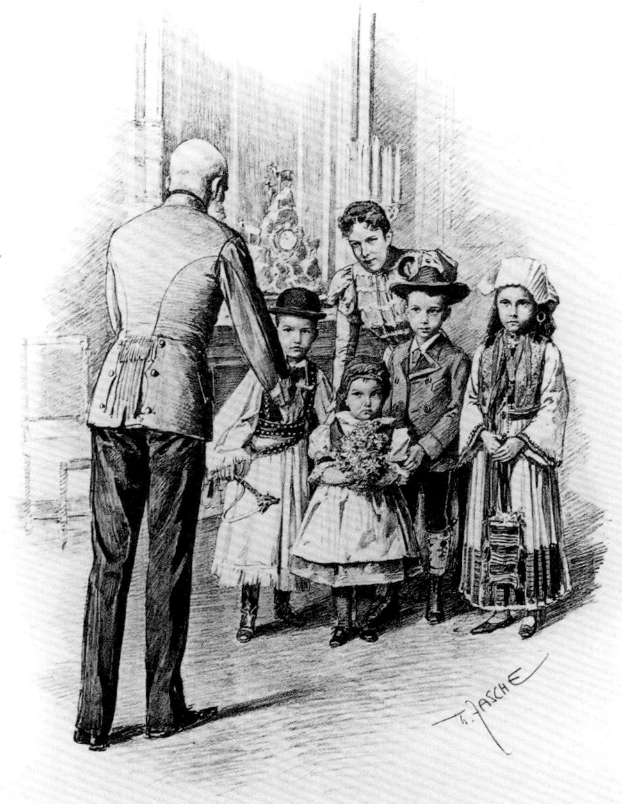

Figure 3. Illustration of children congratulating the kaiser from *Viribus Unitis: Das Buch vom Kaiser*, (ca.1898)

JS: We might say that in a less than subtle way this also represents Josef as the grandfather, or patriarch of these different ethnicities.

BMK: Right. Look at the format. Moser and Hoffmann designed this book, first designing the cover in beautiful leather. This is stamped with Franz Josef's logo, or coat of arms, surrounded by a decorative border that recalls textile design, and inside are beautiful endpapers. Moser produced three gorgeous decorative pages, and I mean gorgeous in the Byzantine sense of the Eastern Church, not derogatorily. Like paintings or mosaics of Byzantine saints they have a richness, with lots of gold and saturated colors.

There is another small, wonderful book with fanciful images of architecture in the city of Karlsbad, the *Bilder aus Karlsbad* (cat. 90). Karlsbad was where the aristocracy historically had gone for their health-baths in the summer time. There is the Ring of Karlsbad where you had to be seen making a promenade in the afternoon, wearing fashionable clothing. The images were done in Jugendstil, not a realistic style. And speaking of the baths, there is image of the Kursalon located in the city park, where, for example, you took your mineral cure baths. The first image is a Dolomites-like mountaintop—the *Hirschensprung*—over which is a rainbow and a wonderful alpine deer. What is significant is the book's gilt brass cover with a beautiful Jugendstil design that incorporates flowers and curling vines. The design is similar to the panels of a fairly newly acquired Wiener Werkstätte case clock at the Art Institute of Chicago designed by the same artist, Carl Otto Czeschka, in collaboration with Josef Hoffmann.

JS: In 1929 the Werkstätte published a monograph of its history, The Wiener Werkstätte 1903–1928 *(cat. 74). Its black and orange-red papier maché cover is meant to resemble a molded tile. As one of the later works by the group, just three years before they had to close business, what does this work tell us about their history and the time?*

BMK: This cover reflects the early impulses of the art deco style. Prior to the acquisition of this piece I had been in Greece, looking at Cycladic marble objects. I was struck by the resemblance between the cover's elongated figures and these early forms. The content of the book is a great distillation of Wiener Werkstätte production in various media that had been achieved over the twenty-five years. We see fashion design and sculpture, small cases, jewelry, tableware, silverware, coffee services, lamps, book design—everything—it is an overview that shows the breadth of their design activities. The group also developed stylized initials, monograms—for the WW itself and individual artists.

This book is a celebration of twenty-five years of the WW and their own sense that they had made a revolution of enormous change in people's admiration for and understanding of applied design, of the decorative arts. It is a matter of pathos from our perspective that they didn't know that they were at the end of their history. We can see this knowing that they were forced to close down in 1932. It is wonderful that we have this monument to their production. By the time the book was published, the Bauhaus (1919–1933) had also come into existence and was also close to its end.

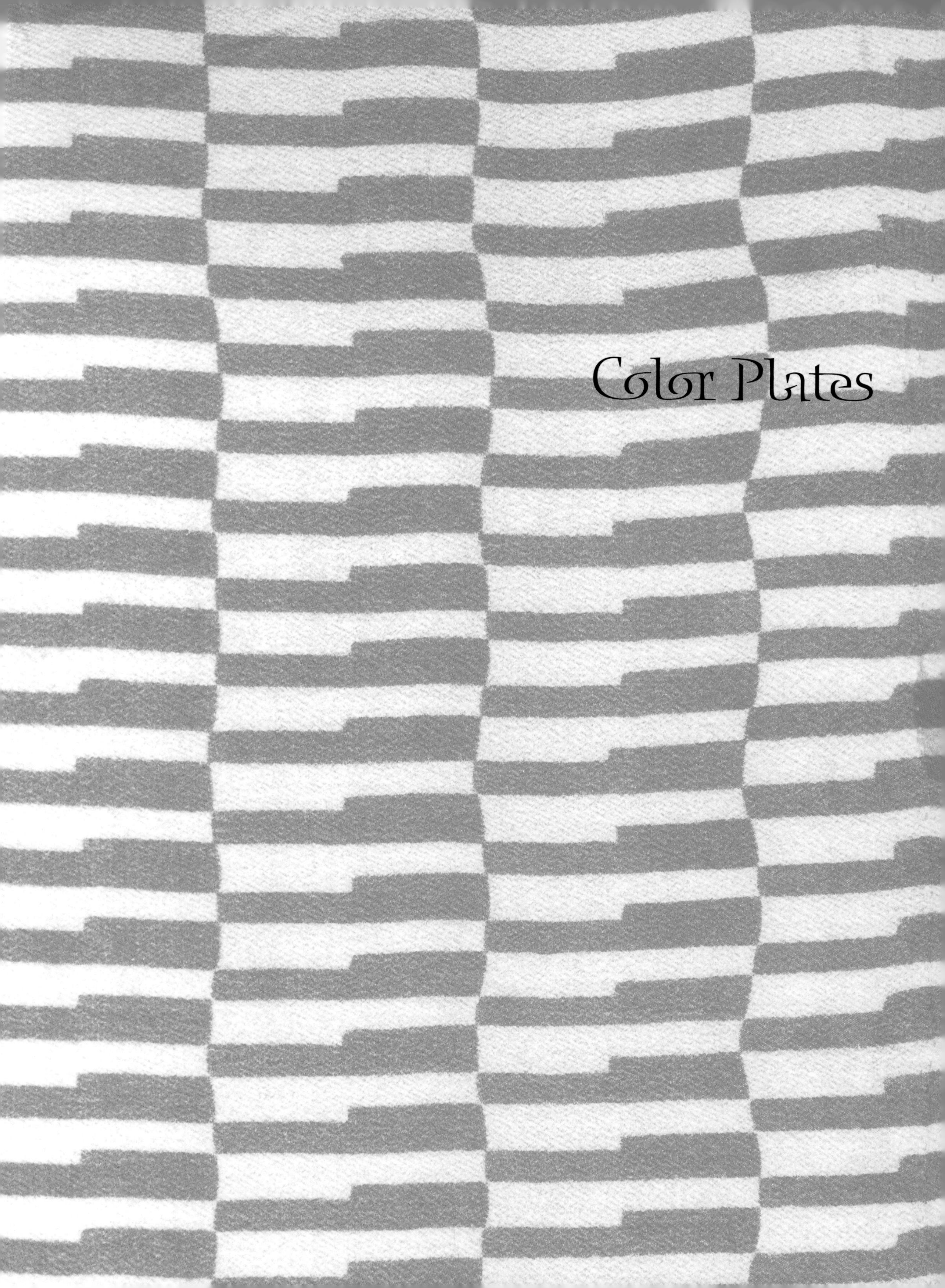

Color Plates

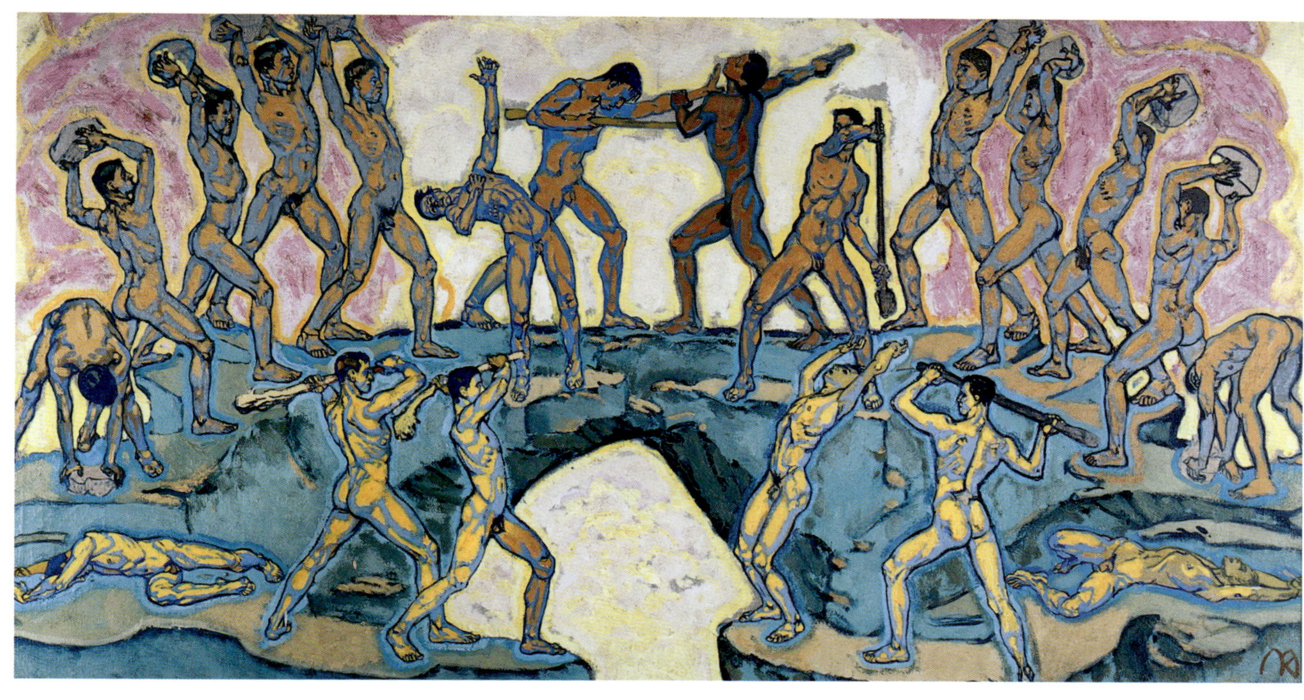

Color Plate 1 (Catalogue 3)
Koloman Moser (Austrian, 1868–1918), *Fight of the Titans* (*Kampf der Titanen*), 1913–1916, oil on canvas.

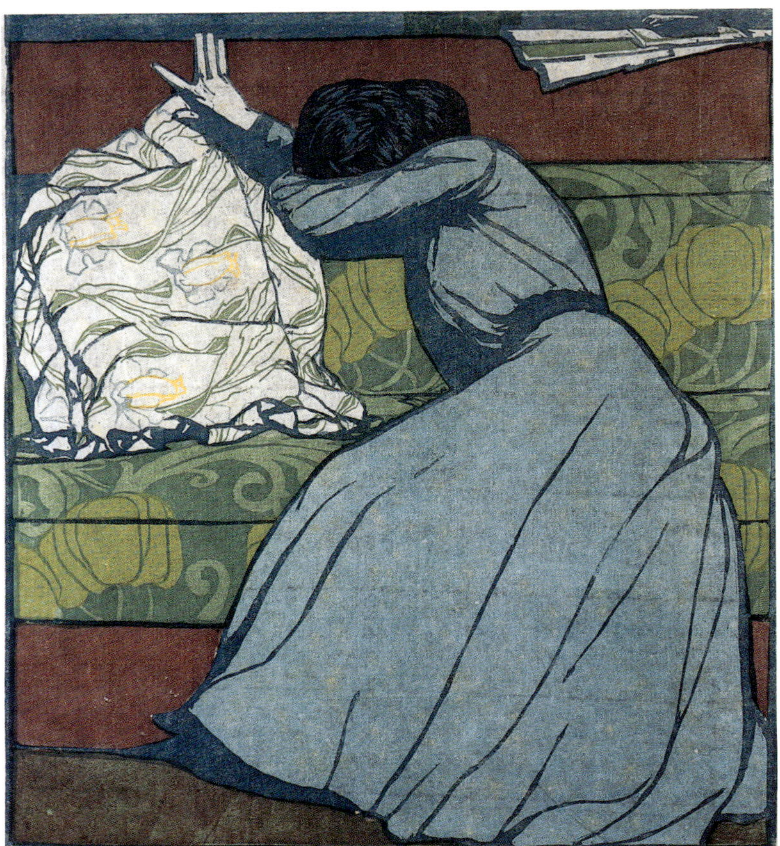

Color Plate 2 (Catalogue 5)
Maximilian Kurzweil (Austrian, 1867–1916),
The Cushion (*Der Polster*), 1903, color woodcut.

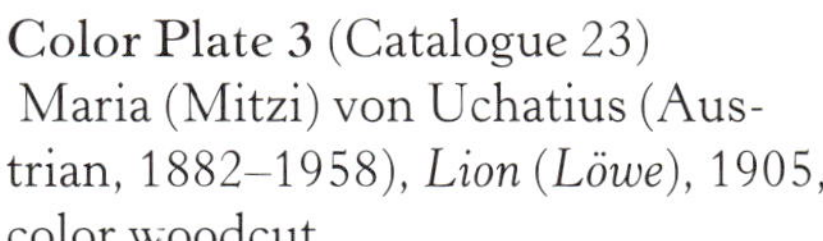

Color Plate 3 (Catalogue 23)
Maria (Mitzi) von Uchatius (Austrian, 1882–1958), *Lion* (*Löwe*), 1905, color woodcut.

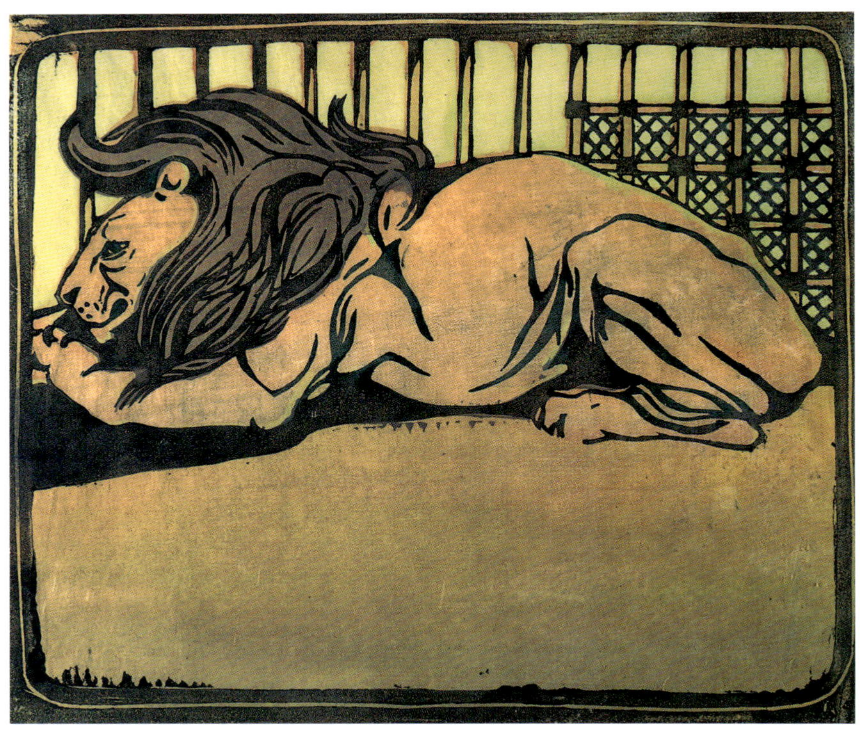

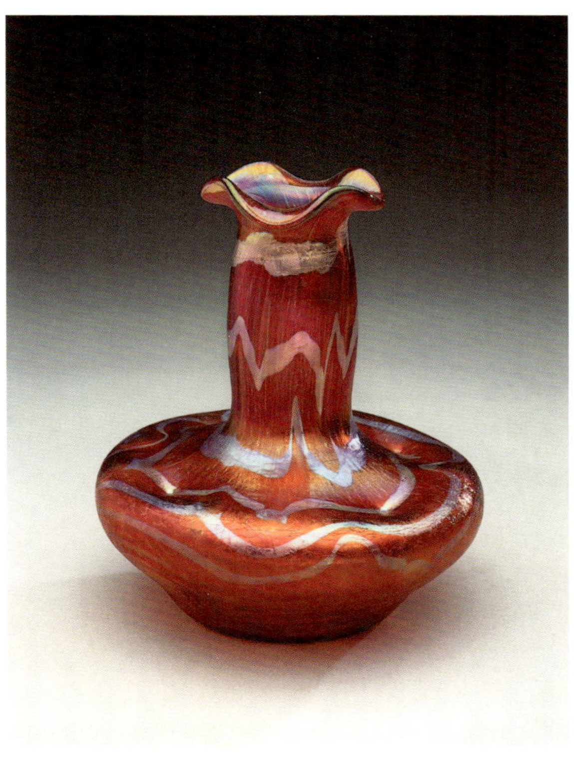

Color Plate 4 (Catalogue 25)
Johann Loetz Witwe designed this iridescent glass vase, about 1900.

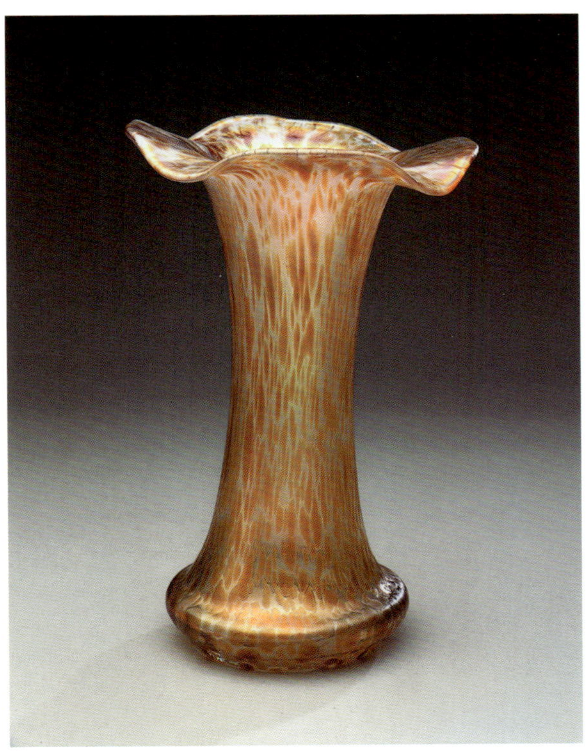

Color Plate 5 (Catalogue 26)
Iridescent glass vase with papillon finish, from about 1900, in the style of Johann Loetz Witwe.

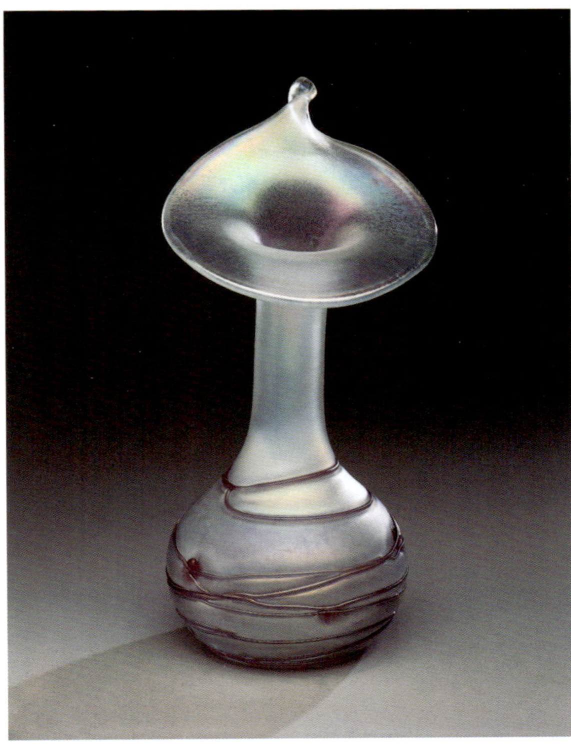

Color Plate 6 (Catalogue 27)
Iridescent glass vase from about 1900, in the style of Pallme König & Habel.

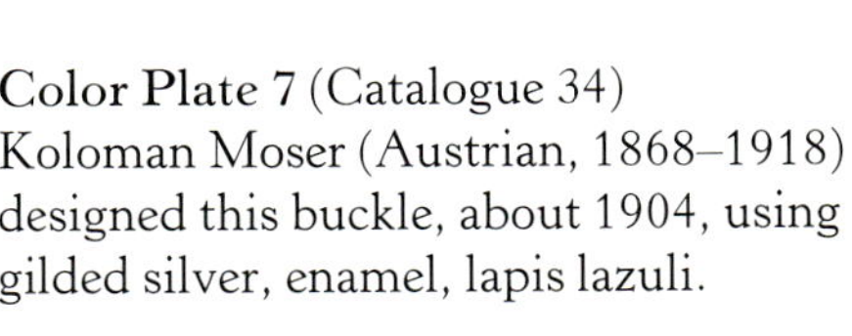

Color Plate 7 (Catalogue 34)
Koloman Moser (Austrian, 1868–1918)
designed this buckle, about 1904, using
gilded silver, enamel, lapis lazuli.

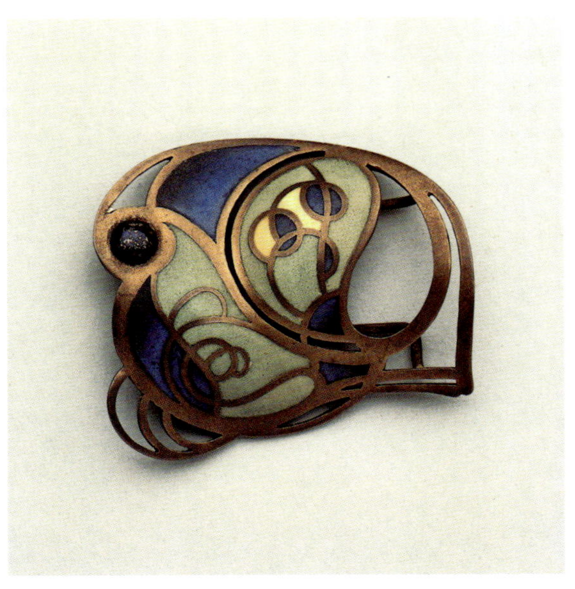

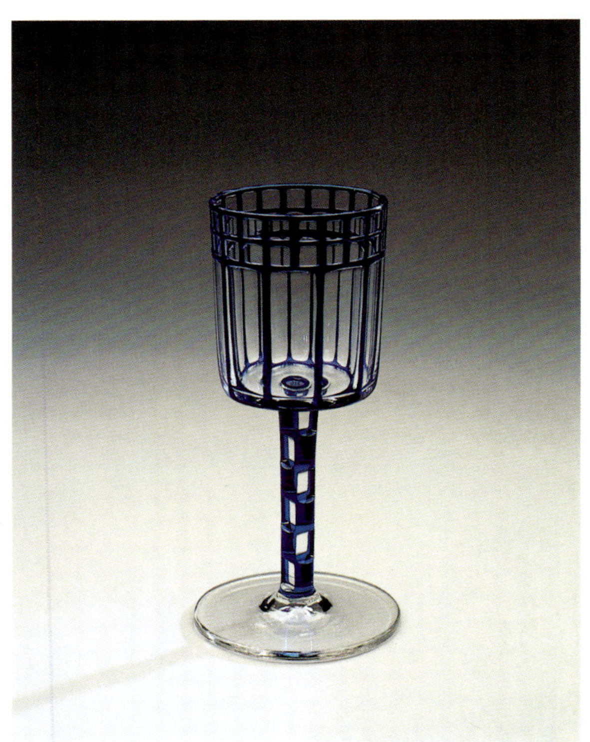

Color Plate 8 (Catalogue 37)
Otto Prutscher (Austrian, 1880–1949)
designed this whiskey glass, about 1907
in clear and blue glass.

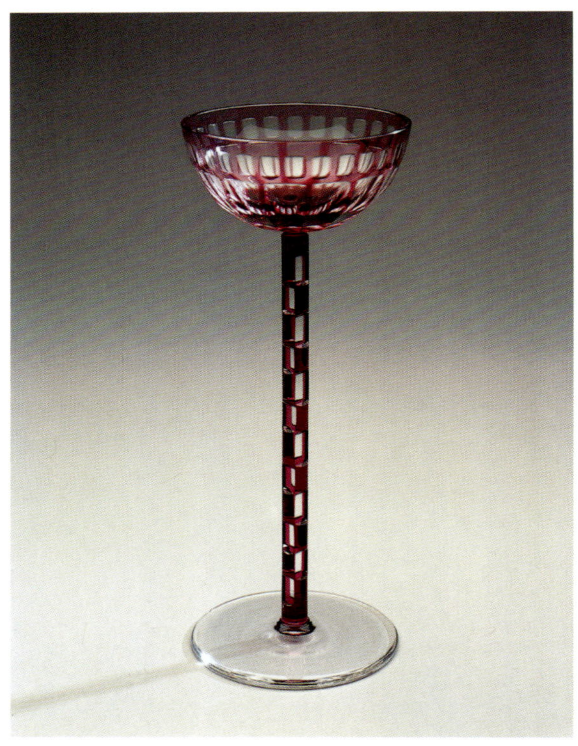

Color Plate 9 (Catalogue 38)
Otto Prutscher (Austrian, 1880–1949)
designed this wine goblet, about 1907,
using clear glass, wheel-cut pink glass overlay.

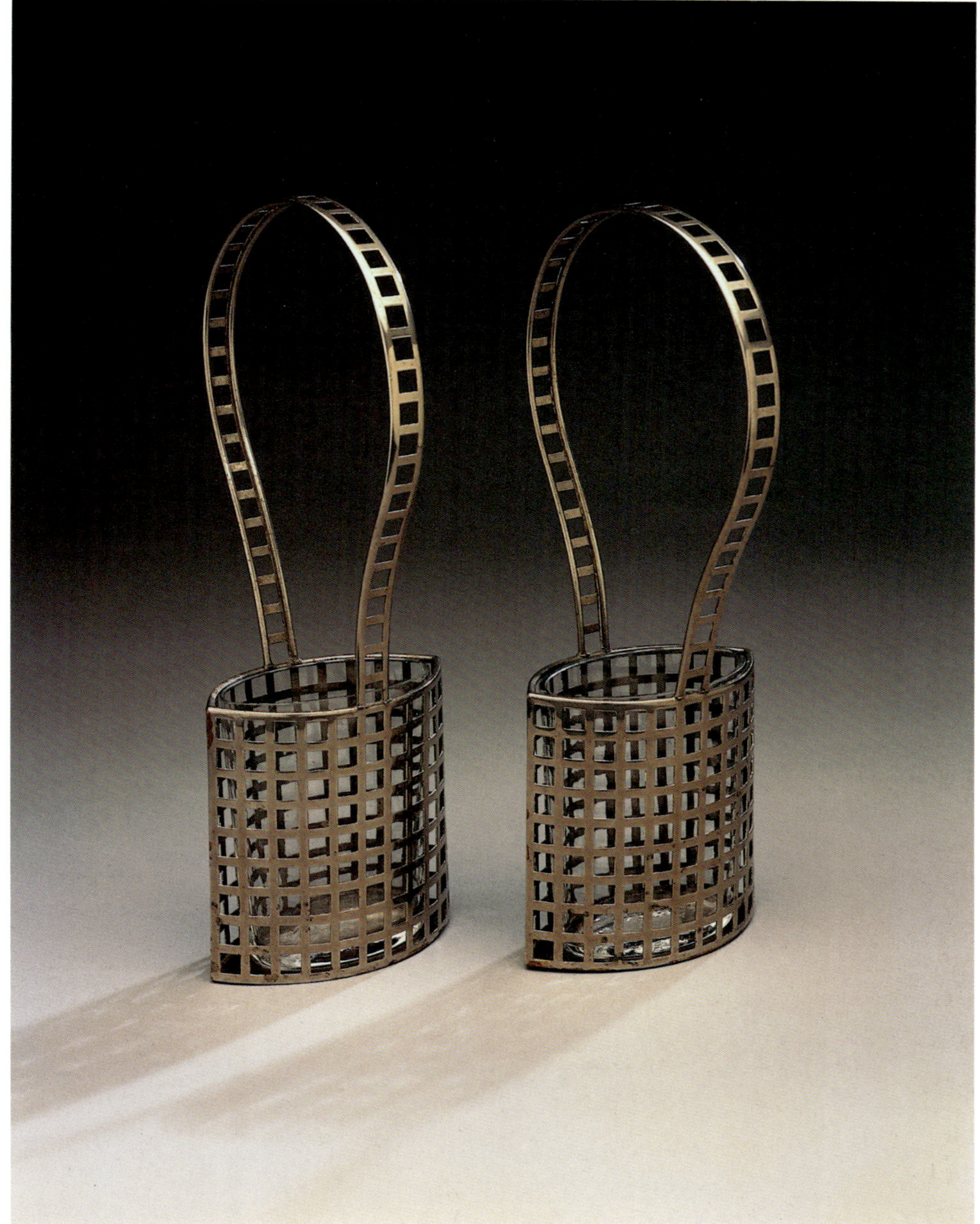

Color Plate 10 (Catalogue 40)
Josef Hoffmann (Austrian, 1870–1956) designed this pair of *Gitterwerk* Baskets, about 1906, executed in silverplate with original glass liners.

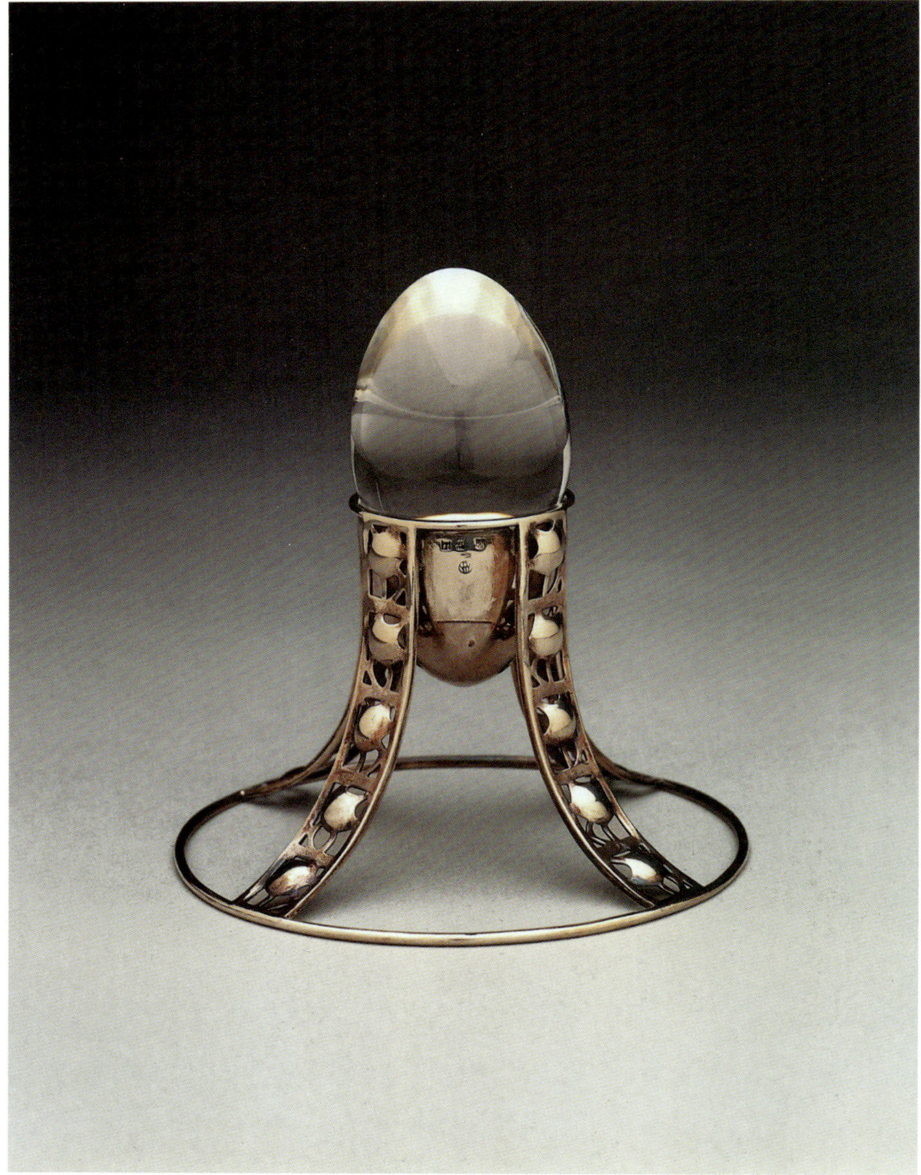

Color Plate 11 (Catalogue 41)
Josef Hoffmann (Austrian, 1870–1956) designed this ivy-patterned eggcup, around 1910, executed in reticulated silver.

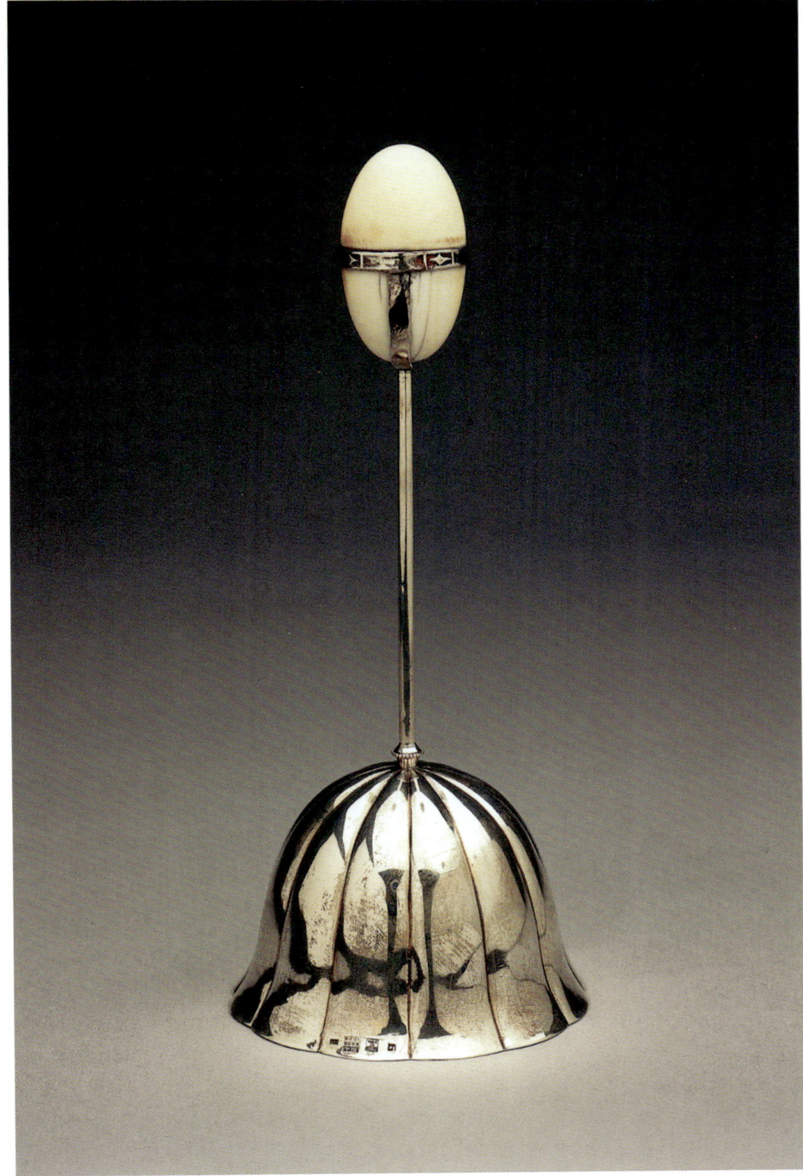

Color Plate 12 (Catalogue 42)
Josef Hoffmann (Austrian, 1870–1956) designed this dinner bell, around 1910, made from silver and ivory.

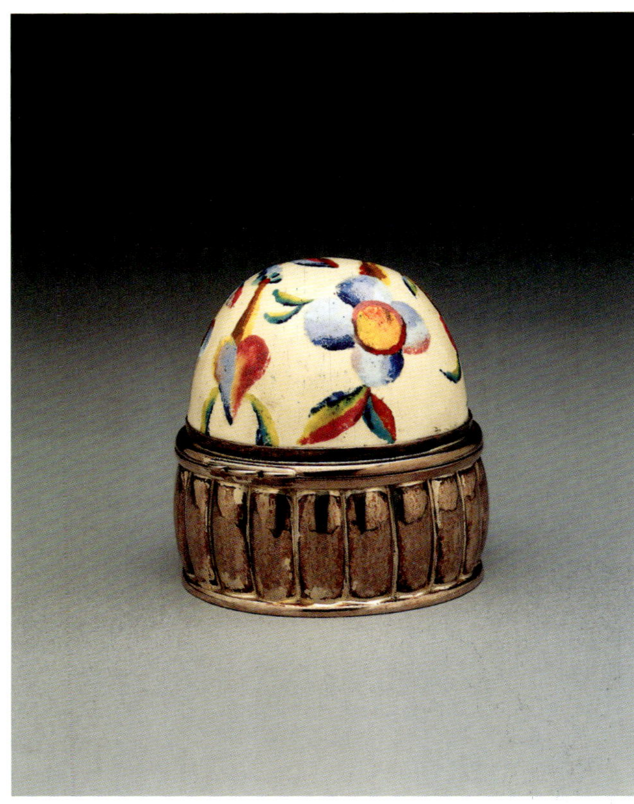

Color Plate 13 (Catalogue 47)
Felice Rix-Ueno (Austrian, 1893–1967) designed this covered box, about 1920, in hand-wrought silver and polychrome enamel.

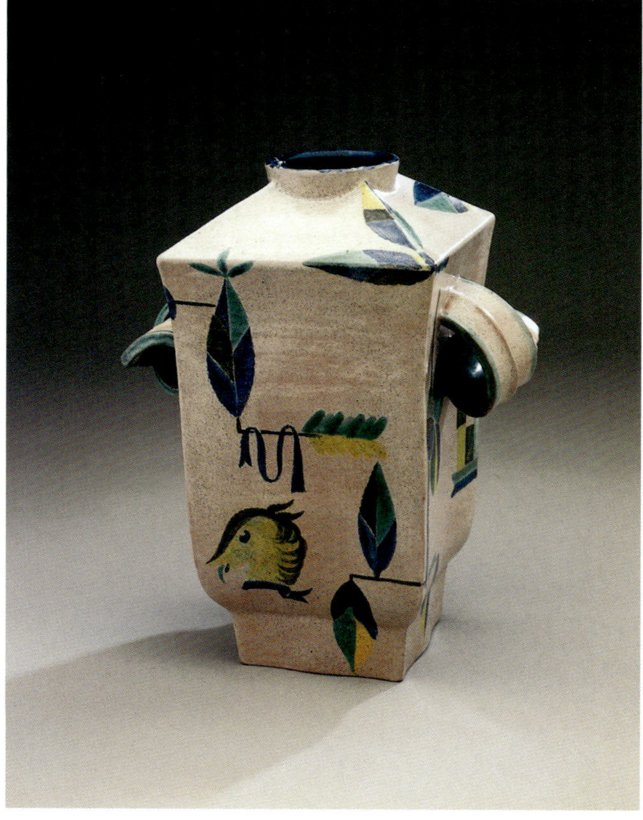

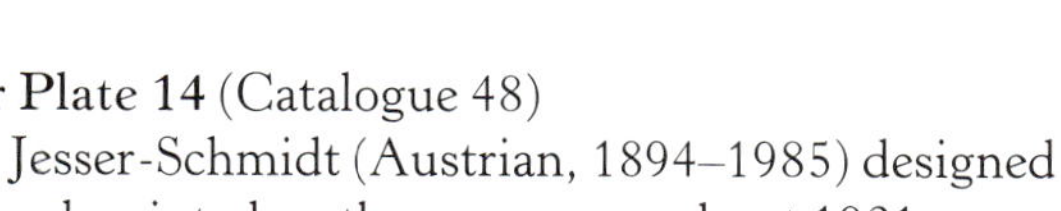

Color Plate 14 (Catalogue 48)
Hilda Jesser-Schmidt (Austrian, 1894–1985) designed this hand-painted earthenware vase, about 1921.

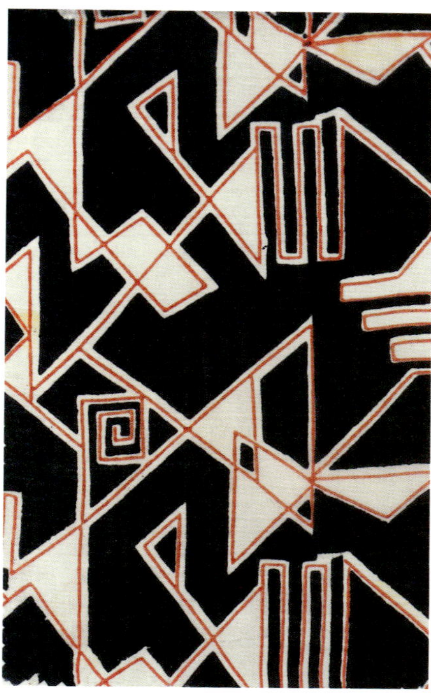

Color Plate 15 (Catalogue 62)
Maria Likarz-Strauss (Austrian, 1893–1956) designed this black-and-red block print on white silk fabric sample, *Ajax,* in 1925.

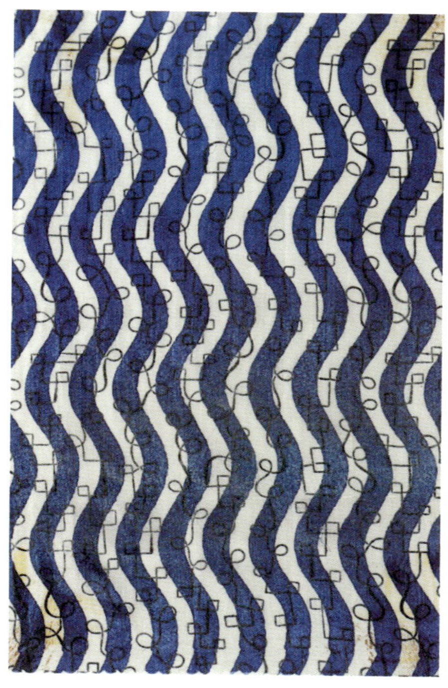

Color Plate 16 (Catalogue 63)
Felice Rix-Ueno (Austrian, 1893–1967) designed this blue-and-black block print on white silk fabric sample, *Biarritz*, in 1924.

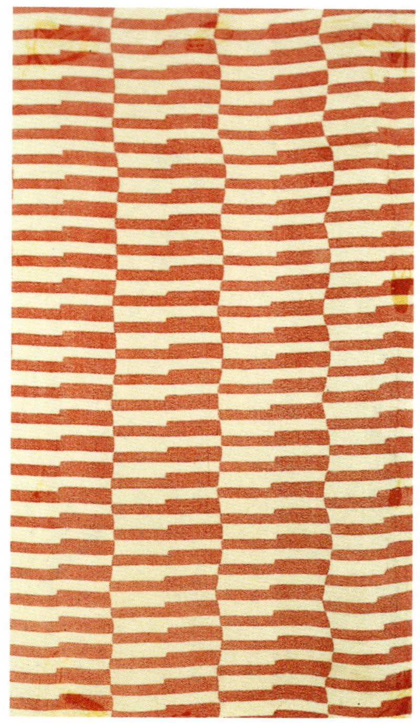

Color Plate 17 (Catalogue 64)
Mathilde Flögl (Austrian, 1893–1950) designed this red-and-yellow block print on crêpe de chine fabric sample, *Clan*, in 1928.

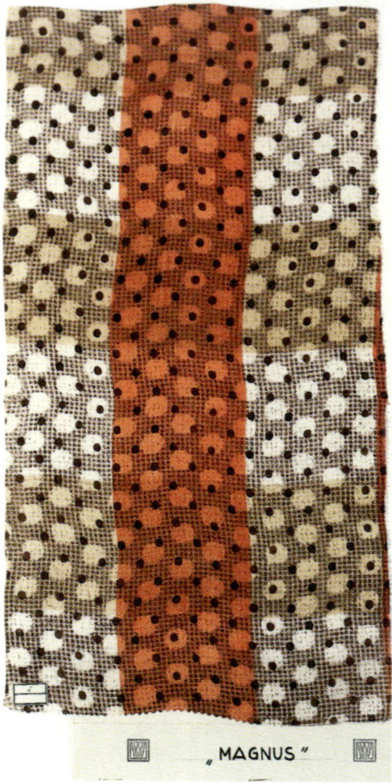

Color Plate 18 (Catalogue 65)
Clara Posnansky (Austrian) designed this fabric sample, *Magnus*, in 1930 with brown, beige, and red on white crêpe de chine.

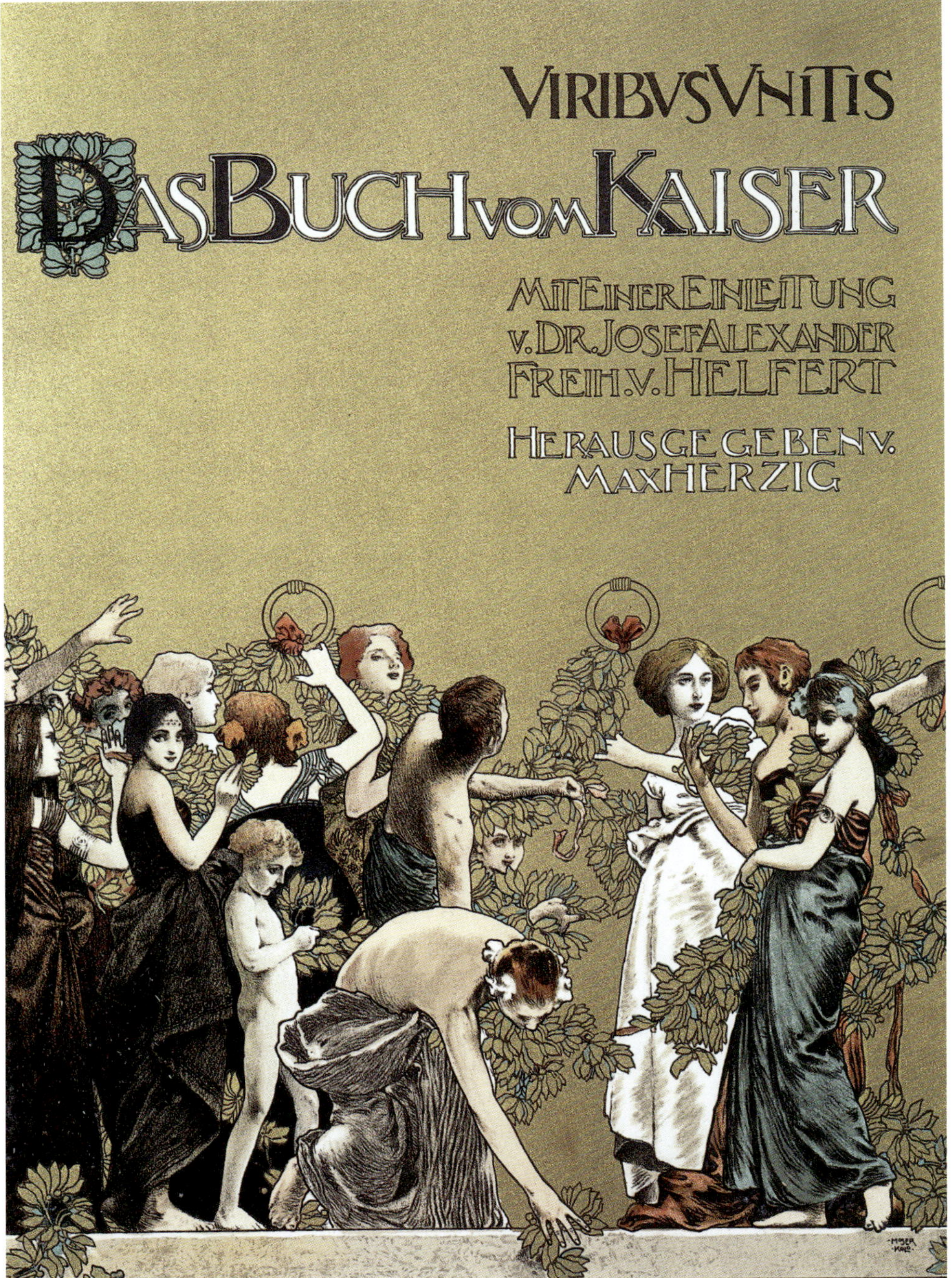

Color Plate 19 (Catalogue 76)
A lavish tribute to Franz Josef I,
emperor of the Austro-Hungarian Empire (1848–1916),
Viribus Unitis: Book of the Emperor (*Viribus Unitis: Das Buch vom Kaiser*),
was published in Vienna about 1898.

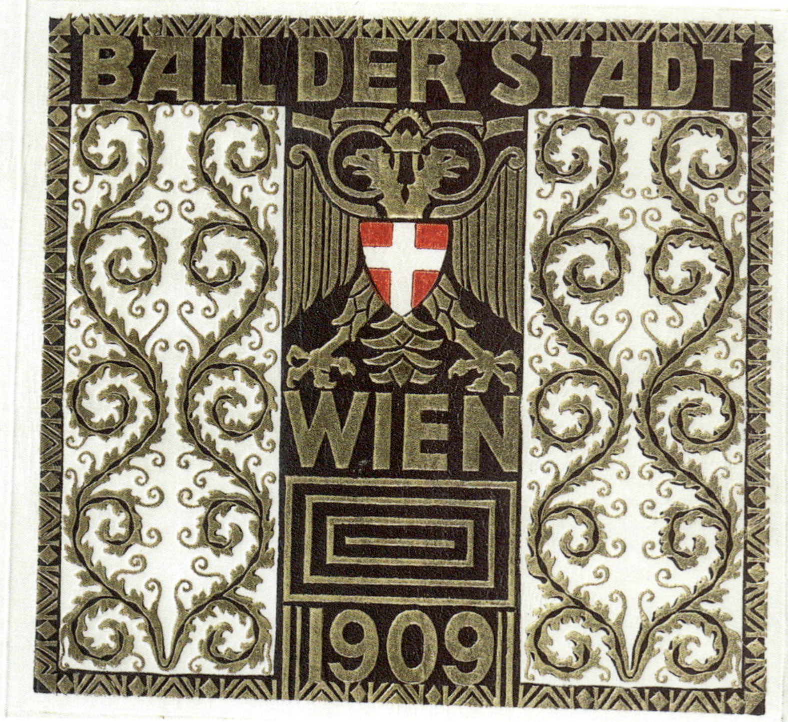

Color Plates 20, 21 (Catalogue 83) Book cover and text page featuring Hadyn from a Viennese ball program illustrated by Remigius Geyling (Austrian, 1878–1974) and bound by Wilhelm Melzer (Austrian, active 1889–1911), City Ball 1909. Jugendstil gold tooling brackets Vienna's heraldic banner on cover.

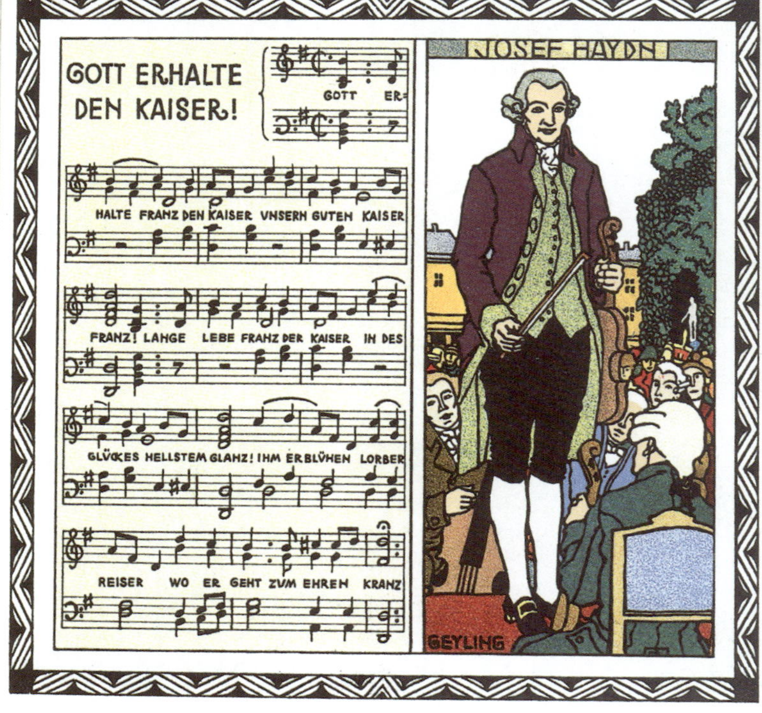

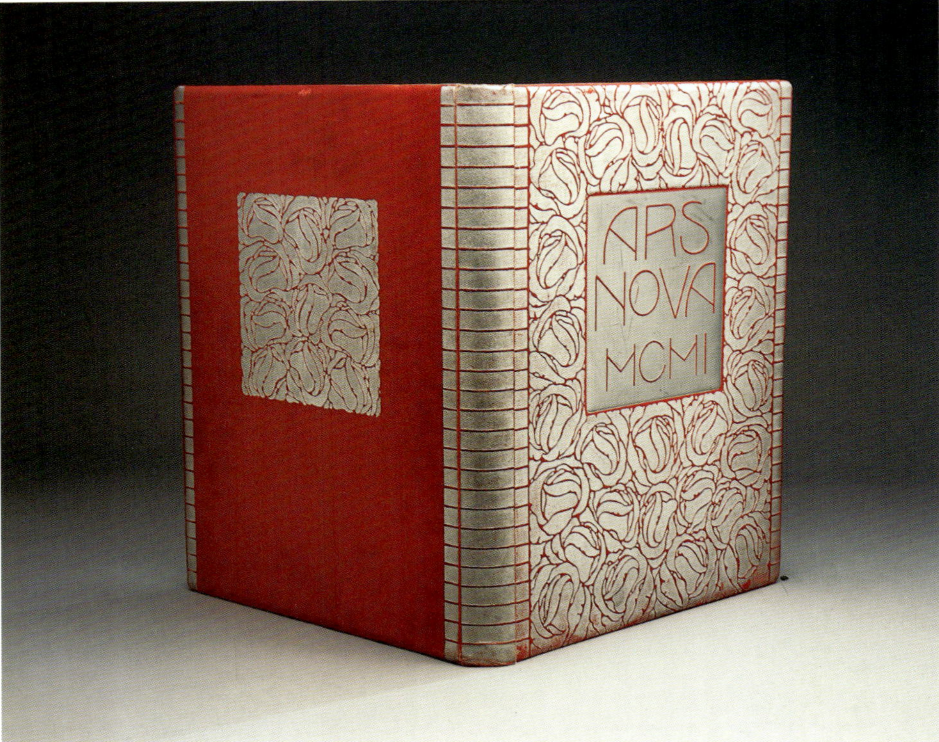

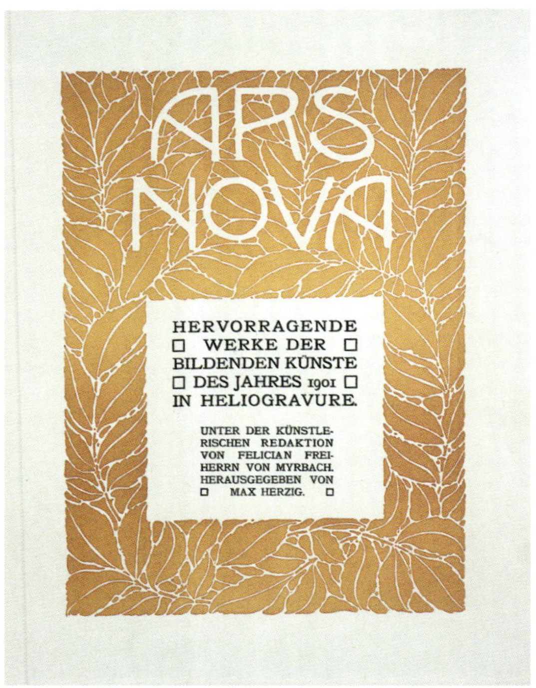

ARS NOVA

HERVORRAGENDE ☐ WERKE DER ☐ BILDENDEN KÜNSTE ☐ DES JAHRES 1901 ☐ IN HELIOGRAVURE.

UNTER DER KÜNSTLERISCHEN REDAKTION VON FELICIAN FREIHERRN VON MYRBACH. HERAUSGEGEBEN VON ☐ MAX HERZIG. ☐

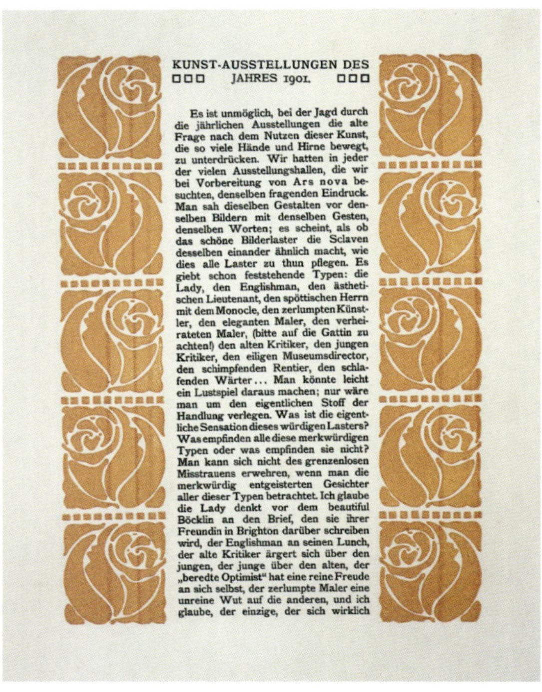

KUNST-AUSSTELLUNGEN DES ☐☐☐ JAHRES 1901. ☐☐☐

Es ist unmöglich, bei der Jagd durch die jährlichen Ausstellungen die alte Frage nach dem Nutzen dieser Kunst, die so viele Hände und Hirne bewegt, zu unterdrücken. Wir hatten in jeder der vielen Ausstellungshallen, die wir bei Vorbereitung von Ars nova besuchten, denselben fragenden Eindruck. Man sah dieselben Gestalten vor denselben Bildern mit denselben Gesten, denselben Worten; es scheint, als ob das schöne Bilderlaster die Sclaven desselben einander ähnlich macht, wie dies alle Laster zu thun pflegen. Es giebt schon feststehende Typen: die Lady, den Englishman, den ästhetischen Lieutenant, den spöttischen Herrn mit dem Monocle, den zerlumpten Künstler, den eleganten Maler, den verheirateten Maler, (bitte auf die Gattin zu achten!) den alten Kritiker, den jungen Kritiker, den eiligen Museumsdirector, den schimpfenden Rentier, den schlafenden Wärter ... Man könnte leicht ein Lustspiel daraus machen; nur wäre man um den eigentlichen Stoff der Handlung verlegen. Was ist die eigentliche Sensation dieses würdigen Lasters? Was empfinden alle diese merkwürdigen Typen oder was empfinden sie nicht? Man kann sich nicht des grenzenlosen Misstrauens erwehren, wenn man die merkwürdig entgeisterten Gesichter aller dieser Typen betrachtet. Ich glaube die Lady denkt vor dem beautiful Böcklin an den Brief, den sie ihrer Freundin in Brighton darüber schreiben wird, der Englishman an seinen Lunch, der alte Kritiker ärgert sich über den jungen, der junge über den alten, der „beredte Optimist" hat eine reine Freude an sich selbst, der zerlumpte Maler eine unreine Wut auf die anderen, und ich glaube, der einzige, der sich wirklich

Color Plates 22, 23, 24 (Catalogue 86)
Cover, title page, and text page from *Ars Nova MCMI,* which represents Jugendstil book design, with its exquisite bindings, endpapers, and decorative borders by Koloman Moser, published in Vienna in 1901. The cover's silver-tooled rose motif is repeated in the gold-colored text borders.

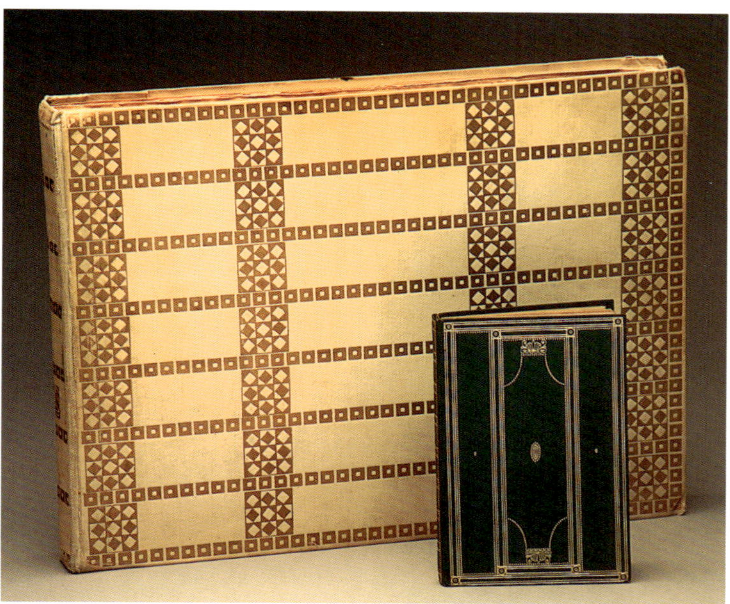

Color Plate 25 (Catalogue 87 and 88)
The larger book shows the back cover of a 1902 luxury edition, *Giovanni Segantini*, designed by Koloman Moser, with its gold-embossed cloth cover dominated by Moser's characteristic checkerboard pattern of alternating squares and diamonds. The smaller 1912 volume of *The Sheperd's Pipe* shows Josef Hoffmann's green leather binding with simple and elegant gold embossing.

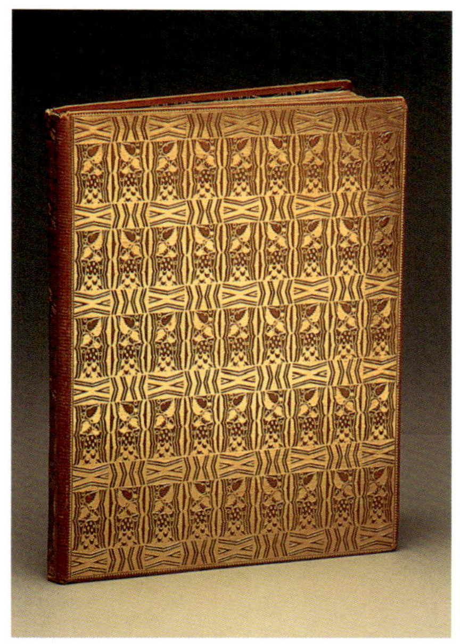

Color Plate 26 (Catalogue 89)
This deluxe edition of *The Poor Fiddler* (Vienna, 1915) is one of fifty examples bound in golden leather by the Wiener Werkstätte. Josef Hoffmann's lavish gilt binding, with a pattern of bell-shaped flowers and leaves, repeats the same motif produced in black and white on the book's endpapers, title page, frontispiece, and text pages.

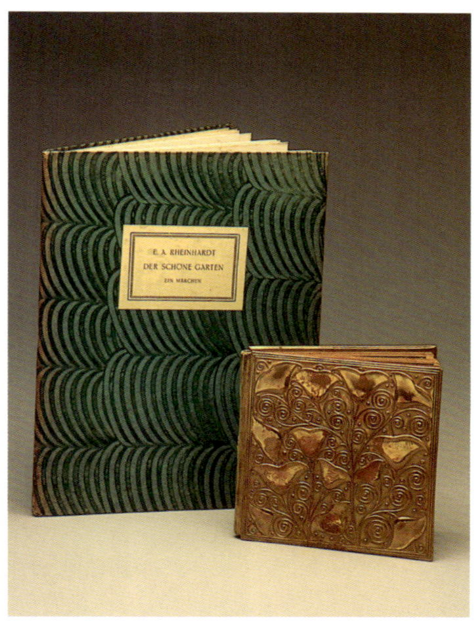

Color Plate 27 (Catalogue 91 and 90)
On the left is *The Lovely Garden: A Fairytale* (Vienna, 1920), one of an edition of 500 printed on japan-type velum. The cover's repeating pattern of curving green and turquoise stripes suggests lush garden foliage. On the right is Carl Otto Czeschka's repousée brass cover for *Pictures from Karlsbad* (1911) decorated with a lively pattern of flowers and scrolling foliage.

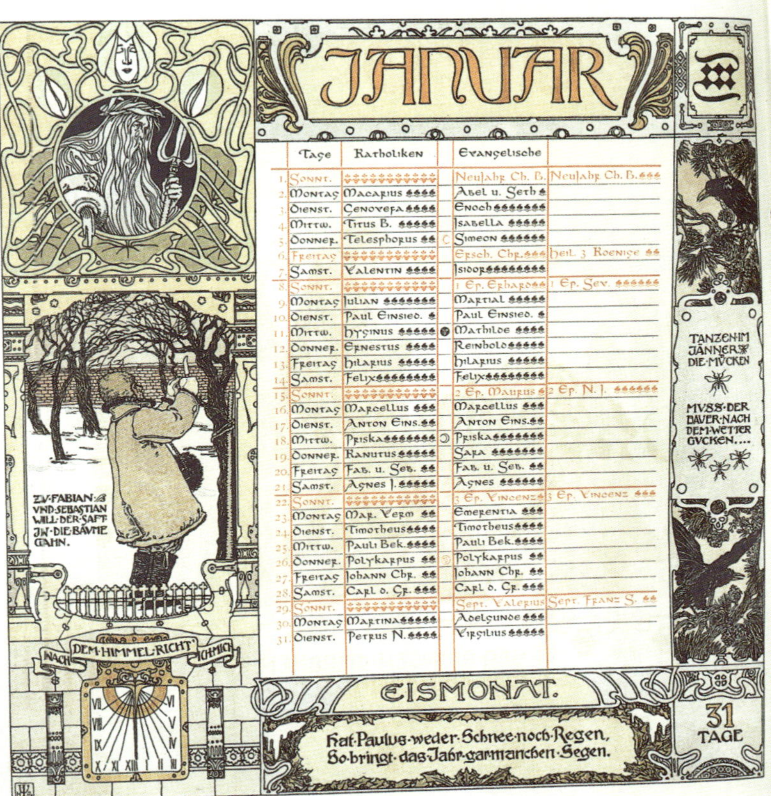

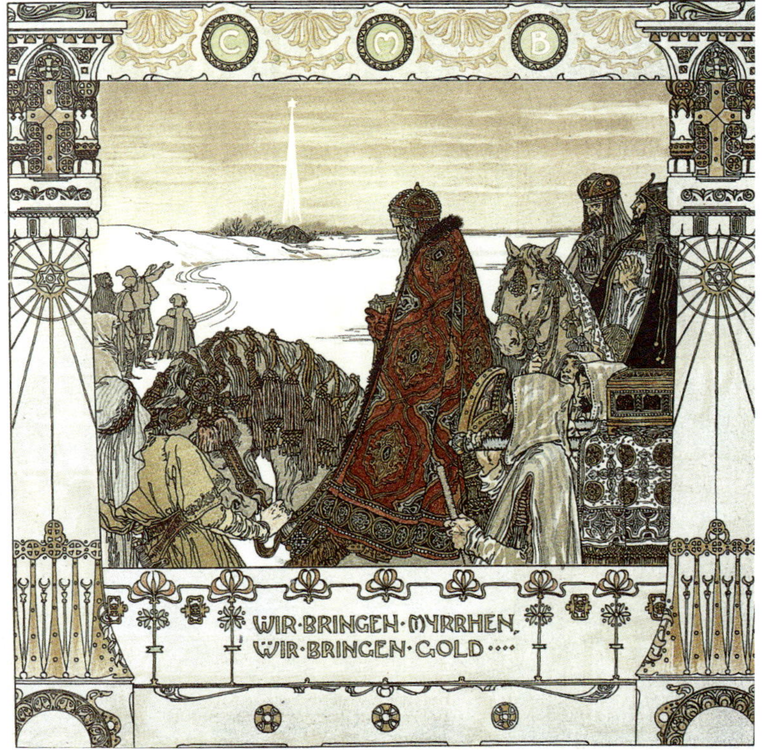

Color Plates 28 and 29 (Catalogue 92) Heinrich Lefler and Josef Urban designed this illustrated calendar for the year 1899 in book format. January's calendar (top) is accompanied by a somber landscape scene of the three journeying Magi (bottom). An ornamental border in the form of architectural structure frames the image. The initials representing the three kings, Caspar, Melchior, and Balthasar appear in the circular vignettes along the top border.

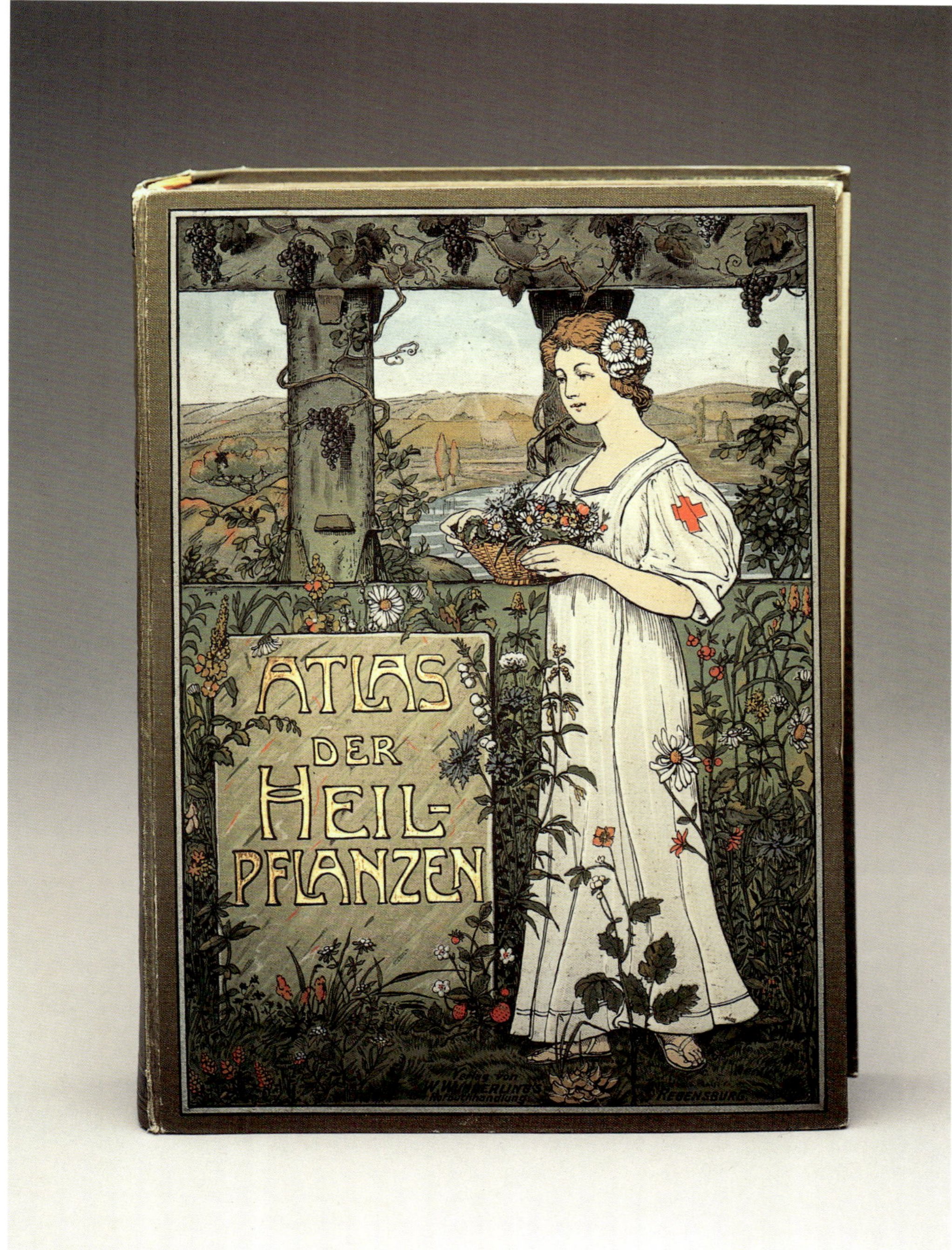

Color Plate 30 (Catalogue 94)
Josef, the archduke of Austria, compiled this 1903 book on medicinal plants, which features naturalistic illustrations by his daughter, Princess Margarethe. This Jugendstil cover shows the sumptuous, organic forms that are also reflected in the book's endpapers, and decorative vignettes.

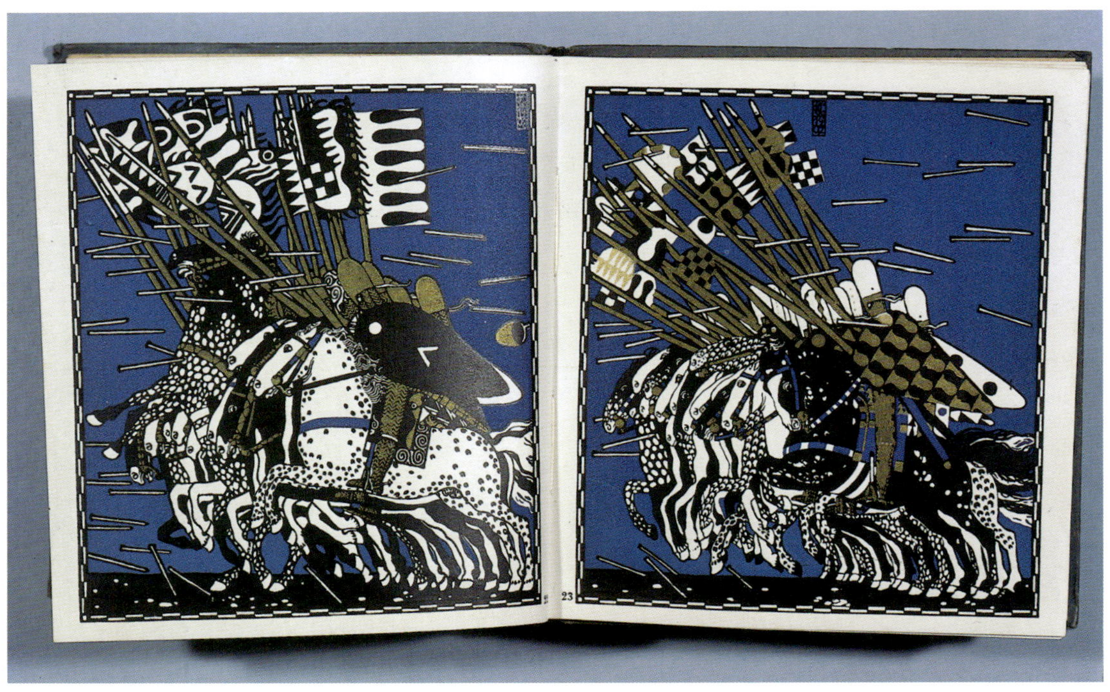

Color Plate 31 (Catalogue 96)
Franz Keim's text and Carl Otto Czeschka's illustrations for *The Nibelungs Retold to the German Nation* (Vienna, 1924) make this book a significant example of the Viennese notion of the *Gesamtkunstwerk*.

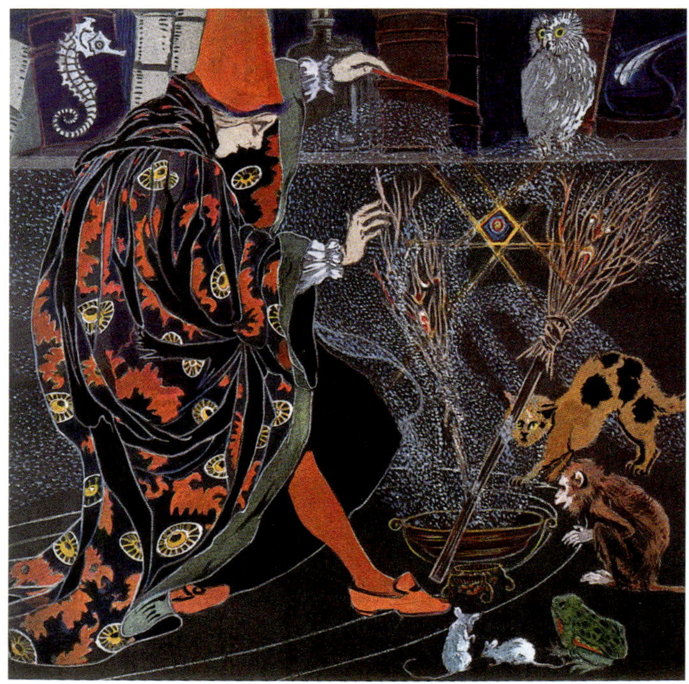

Color Plate 32 (Catalogue 97)
Illona Wittrich's narrative illustrations for Josef Bindtner's *The Spiders: A German Fairytale* (Vienna, 1914) recall nineteenth-century romanticism in which a scene, such as of this magician, appears fantastically alive.

Catalogue

Catalogue

Joann Skrypzak

I. PRINTS, DRAWING, PAINTING

Artists in fin-de-siècle Vienna vigorously explored new stylistic interests and technical possibilities in the decorative arts at the same time that many also continued to use and develop related ideas in the two-dimensional media of painting, drawing, and graphic arts. With the increasing exchange of international artistic ideas during this period, Viennese artists encountered a new wealth of imagery from across Europe and the Far East. Such imagery served as a springboard for them to adapt and experiment with various aspects of style, technique, and subject matter. This inspiration from abroad aided Viennese artists in their search for modes of aesthetic production that broke with the prevailing historicism. It allowed them to assimilate the lessons of international artistic developments, such as art nouveau and Japonisme, and within this context, visually and conceptually articulate works that were simultaneously modern and Viennese in character.

The two-dimensional works presented in this section depict an array of modern styles and themes that appeared in Vienna from the late nineteenth century to around 1930. They provide an indication of the city's contribution to European modernism. Considered against the contemporary blurring division between the fine and decorative arts, they also combine a traditional interest in narrative and symbolic content with a new sense of decorative, graphic possibilities.

Works by the Swiss artists Hermann Gattiker and Ferdinand Hodler exemplify the symbolist movement that emerged in fin-de-siècle Europe. Derived in large part from symbolism, the international phenomenon of art nouveau (literally, new art) and its Germanic counterpart, Jugendstil, came relatively late to Vienna and generally coincided with the founding of the Vienna Secession. Art nouveau signified the broader European desire to forge a new culture, one in which art reflected the concerns and conditions of modern life such as urbanization, industrialization, and expanding knowledge of natural sciences. On an aesthetic level, art nouveau emphasizes forms of nature through a sinuous, organic curvilinearity; stylized floral and vegetal motifs and patterns; and flat, decorative two-dimensional representation. The Viennese artists included in this section, such as Moll, Krenek, Orlik, and Luksch-Makowsky assimilated and explored these elements, and achieved a balance between compositional structure and movement and unadorned and patterned surfaces.

Despite the stylistic overlap between symbolism and art nouveau, on a thematic level, the former pursued more pronounced metaphysical concerns. Originally a literary movement, symbolism wrestled with the period's rising tensions between materialism and spirituality. The movement explored subjective, "inner" states of experience—material and psychological, sacred as well as profane. This led artists to evoke meaning indirectly, suggestively, or symbolically—as in the work of Gattiker, Moser, Kurzweil, and Orlik—rather than to articulate it in a direct, objective fashion.

Other important stylistic trends that characterize the period include Japonisme and expressionism. Japonisme was part of the pan-European and American vogue for things Japanese that followed the opening of Japan's borders in 1854. Japan's striking success in late nineteenth- and turn-of-the-century world fairs and the growing number of western enthusiasts and collectors of its material culture helped ensure the broad popular appeal of Japanese culture. Many saw Japan and other cultures similarly perceived as oriental as having both a more primitive and a more refined culture than that of the decadent and corrupted western world. Western artists also perceived these signs of purity and authenticity in Japanese art and material culture, especially in the ubiquitous color woodcuts to which they looked to cleanse and rejuvenate their own artistic production. The Austrian artists Emil Orlik and Ludwig Jungnickel reflect aspects of Japonisme in their work. This is seen especially in their use of a delicate, painterly or calligraphic curvilinearity and in their treatment of subject matter such as animals and landscapes, which highlight fundamental or essential characteristics and avoid direct references to modernity.

Expressionism, an early twentieth-century movement developed predominantly in Germany and Vienna, is seen in Egon Schiele's *Self-Portrait*. Like symbolism, expressionism explored subjective states of perception. Incorporating a growing interest in Freudian psychoanalysis, however, expressionism often exploited the elements of line and color to convey heightened states of inner psychological tension that lie below the surface appearances of reality.

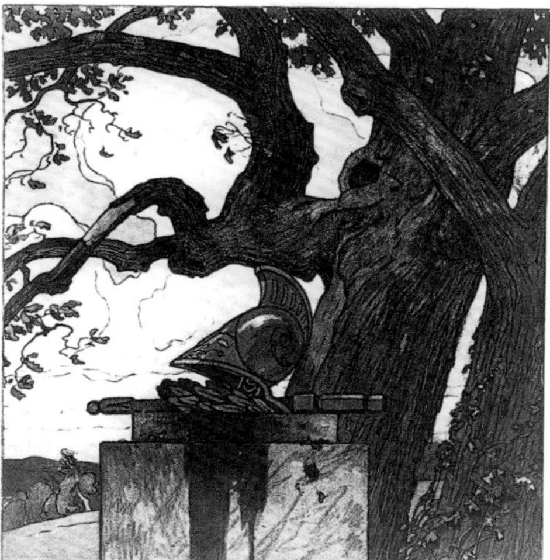

1. Hermann Gattiker (Swiss, 1865–1951)
Hero's Grave (Heldengrab), 1896
Etching, aquatint, plate 13 1/4 x 13 3/16 in. (33.6 x 33.5 cm); sheet 23 5/8 x 17 3/8 in. (60.0 x 44.2 cm)
K.68.2

Contemporary critics recognized Herman Gattiker as representing the new painting in Switzerland in the first decade of the twentieth century. Linked to a constellation of that country's leading past and present artists, such as Hans Holbein and Arnold Böcklin, Gattiker's symbolist landscapes also associated him with Ferdinand Hodler, one of his most celebrated contemporaries. Born in Zurich, Gattiker studied in Dresden and Karlsruhe. He was most prominently successful as an etcher, although he was also skilled in drawing and painting. His late nineteenth-century print *Hero's Grave* exemplifies the melancholy mood, symbolist style, and abstract meaning that characterize much of his work.

On a conceptual level, Gattiker's etching juxtaposes notions of death and life, earthly matter and transcendental spirit, and in doing so, makes a solemnly romantic tribute to heroic sacrifice and patriotism. The hero's stone grave is situated centrally in the foreground of the image. Behind it are the trunks of two large oak trees and part of a vast landscape, each of which continues beyond the limited confines of the square picture frame. Atop the stone monument rests a soldier's gleaming metal helmet, sword, and laurel wreath—the proud and unspoiled accouterments of a fallen hero. The strong, dark branches of the weathered but robust trees frame the helmet. They extend screenlike against the sky and billowing clouds and connect the grave to the background landscape.

Providing a link between the fore- and background, the vital motif of the tree visually ties the grave to the sky. It also suggestively conveys the notion that the heroic spirit embodied in the soldier's sacrifice will survive despite his physical death, an idea that is further symbolized by the ivy that encircles the right tree trunk. Although the helmet falls under the trees' dark shadows, the composition's low horizon pitches its shrouded form against the bright sky. The helmet's metallic crown reflects the brilliance of the sky's illumination and alludes not only to the noble character of patriotic sacrifice, but also to its enduring spirit.

Most symbolist landscapes avoided direct references to a particular time, place, or nationality. As part of the symbolist tradition, Gattiker's image exemplifies the movement's interest in the landscape subject as a vehicle to explore themes of longing, transformation, and nature as a vital means to spiritual transcendence.

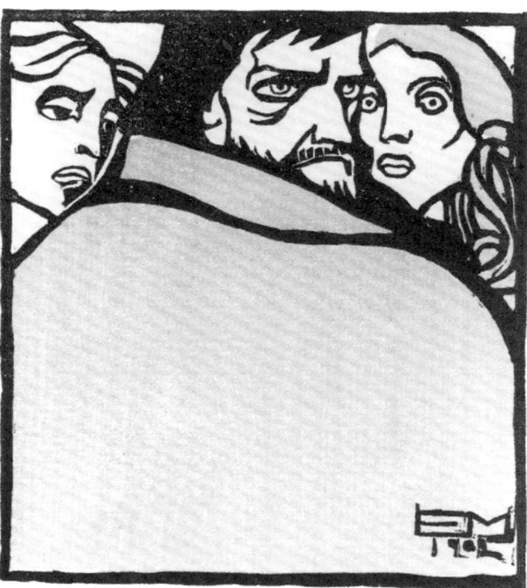

2. Elena Luksch-Makowsky (Austrian, 1878–1919)
Fairytale (Märchen), 1902
Color woodcut, image 5 13/16 x 5 3/8 in. (14.8 x 13.7 cm); sheet 7 x 6 3/16 in. (17.8 x 15.7 cm) sheet
Monogrammed and dated lower right: EM/1902
K.85.11

Elena Luksch-Makowsky's woodcut *Fairytale (Märchen)* appeared in the Vienna Secession's catalogue for its groundbreaking fourteenth exhibition, a *Gesamtkunstwerk* dedicated to Max Klinger and Ludwig van Beethoven. *Fairytale*, like the other works included either in the exhibition or the corresponding issue of *Ver Sacrum* that served as its catalogue, was part of this unified work of art. The works explore related aspects of the show's themes, such as man's longing for happiness and the triumph of the human spirit.

The most prominent of the exhibition's architectural decorations, and the one to which Luksch-Makowsky's print refers, was Gustav Klimt's *Beethoven Frieze*. Comprised of six panels, the frieze extended across the upper half of three walls and was painted in casein colors and decorated with semiprecious stones. Derived from the final movement of Beethoven's Ninth Symphony (*The Ode to Joy*), the program of Klimt's work traces mankind's progress from desire to fulfillment.

On the first wall three nude figures represent weak humanity. They implore an armored Knight, accompanied by the allegorical figures Sympathy and Ambition, in the struggle for happiness. On a narrower wall the next scene depicts the powers that are hostile to man's struggle: the giant Typhon and his daughters, the three Gorgons, who embody sickness, mania, death, desire, impurity, and excess.[1] Above them fly diaphanous female figures, which manifest mankind's longings and desires. Along the final wall, a female with a harp—the personification of poetry—provides relief for mankind in its striving for happiness. Expressing the means of fulfillment through the arts, she also leads the narrative to its culmination, to the Kingdom of the Ideal. An embracing man and woman surrounded by a chorus of female angels represent this realm of pure happiness, joy, and love, which seeks not only to redeem the individual, but all of mankind.

Similar to Klimt's Knight (figure 1), who is supported by the allegories Sympathy and Ambition, Luksch-Makowsky's *Fairytale* depicts a dominant male figure flanked by two females. Although the woodcut reduces its composition to a simplified grouping of forms and exchanges Klimt's delicate rendering and exquisite materials for bold outline and a restricted color scheme, it retains the figures' evocative facial expressions. Echoing the figures' visual characterizations in the *Beethoven Frieze*, Luksch-Makowsky's Knight turns his determined gaze outward to the right, his vision set on a distant goal. Behind his right shoulder Sympathy appears with a bowed head, heavily lidded eyes, and a down-turned mouth; on his left is Ambition, whose wide-eyed gaze conveys a sense of focused aspiration. Luksch-Makowsky distills the figures and the philosophical underpinnings of the heroic struggle down to their most fundamental forms. In doing so, she presents one of the exhibition's central thematic motifs in the fashion of a mythic legend, whereby the narrative's moral is evoked through the most essential of means.

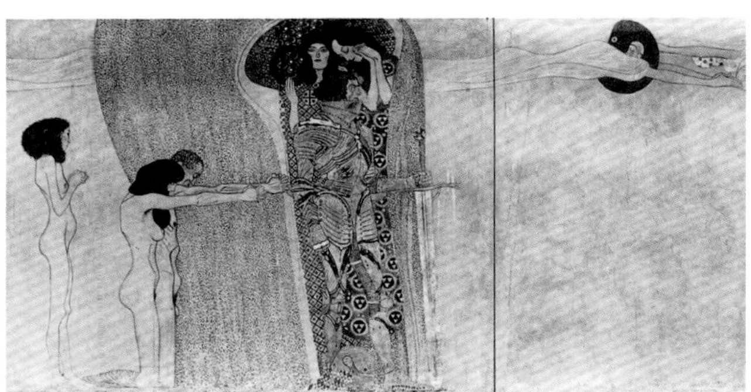

Figure 1. Gustav Klimt. *Beethoven Frieze*. Detail, Well-armed Strong One; Compassion and Ambition (The Sufferings of Weak Humanity), 1902, mural. Photograph courtesy Österreichische Galerie Belvedere

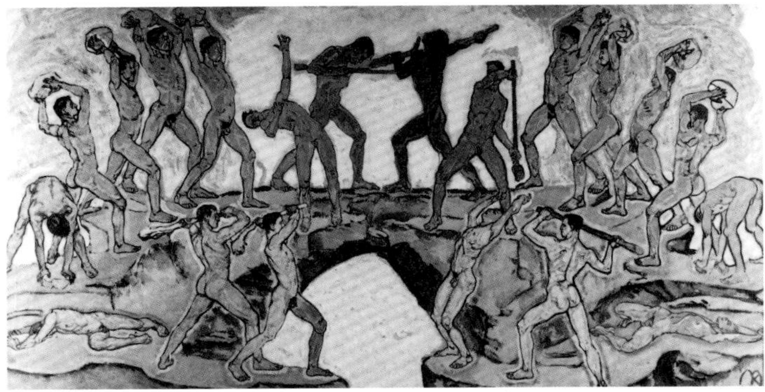

3. Koloman Moser (Austrian, 1868–1918)
Fight of the Titans (Kampf der Titanen), 1913–1916
Oil on canvas, 30 x 59 ½ in. (76.2 x 152 cm)
Signed lower right with monogram: stamped verso, left and right, and on vertical center stretcher supports: *Nachlass* [estate of] Koloman Moser
K.71.2; see Color Plate 1

Koloman Moser was one of the dominant artists of the Vienna Secession. His *Fight of the Titans* suggests his continued interest in the themes presented by the Secession's 1902 Klinger Beethoven Exhibition. One of the paintings installed in the exhibition and related to mankind's struggle for happiness was Ferdinand Andri's *Manly Courage and Joy in Battle (Mannesmut und Kampfesfreude)* that draws on the myth of the Titanomachy. According to Greek mythology, the Titans formed the first divine race, were honored as the ancestors of men, and credited with the invention of the arts. Cast into the depths of the earth by their father, Uranus, the Titans returned after being liberated by their brother Cronos. Hoping to regain the earthly kingdom, they launched an attack against the Olympians. It was only after a terrible battle that Zeus was able to defeat the courageous Titans, bind them in chains, and ultimately cast them far below the surface of the earth.

In Moser's painting, the battle of the Titans and Olympians is arranged symmetrically on a craggy bridgelike rock formation. Ten heroic males appear on each side of the otherwise simplified composition, and their actions closely mirror the figures opposite them. The symmetrical composition and the use of bold outlining and exaggerated, bright colors reflect Moser's interest in the work of the Swiss symbolist Ferdinand Hodler. The aesthetic and conceptual similarity between Moser's Titans and Olympians alludes to Hodler's theory of parallelism, in which the differences between forms of nature and humanity are negligible in light of the similarities that link them to one another. Hodler's figures often articulate the same gesture or motion with slight differentiations. Moser's, however, exhibited a consonant variety from the robust living to the vanquished dead.

Barbara Mackey Kaerwer has noted how Moser's rendering of heroic nudes in a variety of poses might also derive from the Florentine goldsmith and sculptor Antonio del Pollaiolo's engraving *Battle of the Nudes* (ca. 1465–1470). This is particularly evident in the figures engaged in various stages of continuous action, such as those who either pick up or hoist a large stone above their heads. Moser's use of bright colors for heightened emotional effect, such as the vibrant pink of the sky and electric blue shading of the figures, recalls the contemporary movement of expressionism as well as the colorism of Hodler. The combination of such varied elements in *Fight of the Titans* emphasizes not only the strength and determination involved in the Titans' struggle for transcendence, but also the ongoing and particularly masculine nature of such a battle.

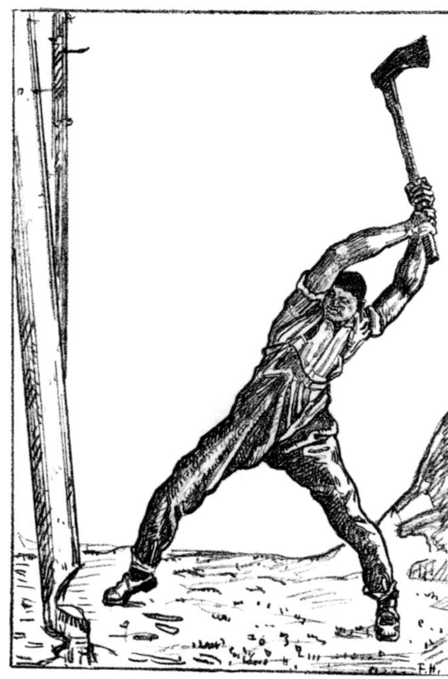

4. Ferdinand Hodler (Swiss, 1853–1918)
The Woodchopper (*Der Holzfäller*), ca. 1910
Lithograph, image 23 3/8 x 15 3/4 in. (59.5 x 40.0 cm)
Signed in the stone lower right: F. H.; signed in graphite lower right: Ferd. Hodler
K.66.2

Between 1898 and 1905, the Vienna Secession organized an important series of exhibitions that brought a range of modern art to Vienna. These shows were intended to introduce artists and the public to the latest in European artistic developments to heighten cultural awareness and encourage further contact abroad. The group devoted their nineteenth exhibition to the work of Swiss painter Ferdinand Hodler, which was mounted in early January 1904. The exhibition was of decisive importance to Hodler and signaled his international breakthrough.

Hodler was a major turn-of-the-nineteenth-century symbolist and much admired by his German and Austrian contemporaries. Many of his supporters, including the Viennese Secessionists, were attracted to his monumental painting style and concept of parallelism. In Hodler's theory of parallelism both art and life related to the notion that all nature and humanity are linked by a greater metaphysical order. He argued in this formulation that "[u]niformity as well as diversity exists within human beings, we are different from each other, but we are even more alike. What unites us is greater and stronger than what divides us."[2] Despite humans' external differences of appearance Hodler maintained that their fundamental similarities bind them to one another and to nature.

Hodler's *The Woodchopper* was one of a pair of images commissioned by the Swiss National Bank in 1908 for two new banknotes.[3] Along with its pendant, *The Reaper*, the figures symbolized the strength and energy of the Swiss people. Situated off-center, the woodcutter occupies the lower right half of the composition. Caught in a powerful, broad-legged stance, the diagonally attenuated figure is extended further by the upraised ax he wields. His bold action against an open ground establishes him as a dynamic, even heroic life force.

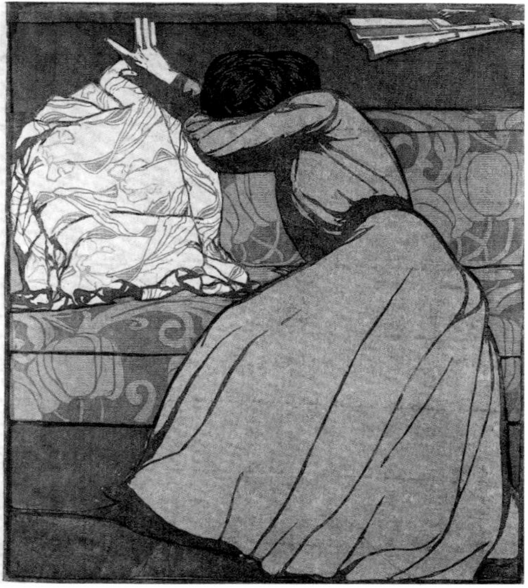

5. Maximilian Kurzweil (Austrian, 1867–1916)
The Cushion (*Der Polster*), 1903
Color woodcut, image 11 1/4 x 10 1/4 in. (28.5 x 26.0 cm); sheet 15 1/4 x 12 1/8 in. (38.7 x 30.9 cm
K.71.3; see Color Plate 2

Domestic interiors, such as the one in Max Kurzweil's *The Cushion*, appear frequently in art nouveau imagery. Such images evoke the symbolist turn toward introspection and interest in a fundamental principle of femininity. In fin-de-siècle Vienna the subject also reflected the withdrawal of artists and intellectuals from the public to the private sphere following their disillusionment at the failure of liberal politics.[4] Moreover, the depiction of interiors reveals the contemporary concern for aesthetic arrangement and applying the *Gesamtkunstwerk* concept to one's personal living environment and way of life. In *The Cushion* the aesthetic interior provides an arena for an unusually bold and tense representation of modern femininity.

The Cushion, the best-known work produced by the Secessionist Kurzweil, features his wife, Martha, seated on a sofa with floral Jugendstil upholstery. It is likely that the setting is their home at Schwindgasse 9, whose interior was designed by Josef Hoffmann. In contrast to other works by Kurzweil in which Martha passively reclines or sleeps, in this image she is tensely seated. Her figure bends at the waist so that the angle of her outstretched torso and right arm counters that of her extended skirts. The position of her gloved hand echoes this taut V-shape, as three fingers grasp the top edge of the sofa while her index finger remains isolated below.

Martha's left arm shields her facial expression and her voluminous blue dress reveals little of the figure beneath it. As a result the significance of her articulated hand gesture, which anticipates those found in the portraits of Egon Schiele, suggests tension and assertion. Michael Pabst has argued that this four-finger gesture might refer to the Jungian idea of Quaternity and the changing social roles of women at the turn of the century.[5] The figure reveals no exposed skin and the image lacks any direct depictions of nature. Kurzweil's subject suggests an emancipated woman loosened—perhaps precariously—from past gender conventions.

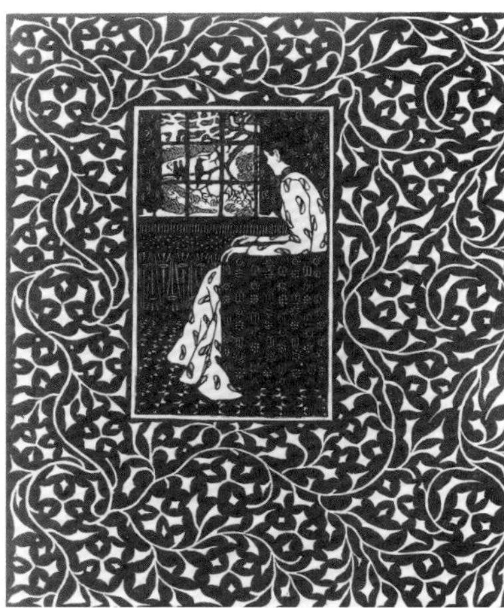

6. Karl Krenek (Austrian, 1880–1948)
Untitled (Seated Woman), from the series *The Four Seasons,* 1906
Hand-colored woodcut, image 10 ½ x 8 ¾ in. (26.7 x 22.2 cm)
Signed with monogram outside border; colophon on back: Geschnitten u. gedruckt von Carl Krenek Wien 1906
K.99.12

The print Seated Woman is one of eight hand-colored woodcuts from Karl Krenek's series *The Four Seasons.* Each work in the series features a central vignette that represents domestic gardens in various seasons and often includes one or two female figures wearing long, patterned reform-style gowns. Framing each central, three-dimensionally rendered vignette is a broad decorative border with a two-dimensional meandering vine-and-leaf pattern, a motif that recalls the book art of British Arts and Crafts designer, William Morris. This vine motif not only visually links the prints in Krenek's series; its curving, rhythmic pattern also alludes to the measured cycle of nature and time that leads from one season to another.

Although none of the prints is titled after a specific time of year, this image's view from a domestic interior onto a snow-covered landscape identifies the season as winter. Krenek depicts a multipatterned interior in which a seated female figure inclines toward a background window through which she gazes. The scene characterizes winter as a time of enclosed withdrawal and longing for nature's rebirth and transformation. In contrast to the more organic forms used to depict the vibrant foliage and bucolic garden settings in the series' other spring and summer scenes, this print abstracts nature and preserves it in artificial form. Krenek, for example, concentrates bright colors and flat patterning in the rendering of the interior, such as in the abstract floral patterns of the wallpaper, the chair's upholstery, and the floor's carpet. As such, even though the woman is at a remove from the exterior world she retains the symbolist association between nature and femininity. The interior scene's static, abstract patterns of nature echo the physical passivity of the seated woman and together they emphasize the dormancy of the wintry exterior.

Rendered by **Carl Moll** in winter, Hohe Warte (cat. 7) was a fashionable residential area on a wooded ridge above Vienna with views of the surrounding countryside. Many Secession artists, including Moll, made their home in this well-to-do region north of the city. They commissioned residences designed by Josef Hoffmann around 1900 and formed a villa colony. Moll was deeply committed to the Secession movement and became its vice president in 1897. He later served as president and in 1904 became director of the Galerie Miethke. The gallery not only represented Gustav Klimt, but also was a leading champion of the Wiener Werkstätte. Seen within this context, *Winter (Hohe Warte in Vienna)* reflects Moll's devotion to the ideas of the Secession as they are projected onto the exterior landscape environment.

Similar to the manner in which Secession residential architecture was intended to present the taste and personality of its owner to the outside world, the boundary between the home's interior and its immediate exterior was often blurred. As a result, a home's interior as well

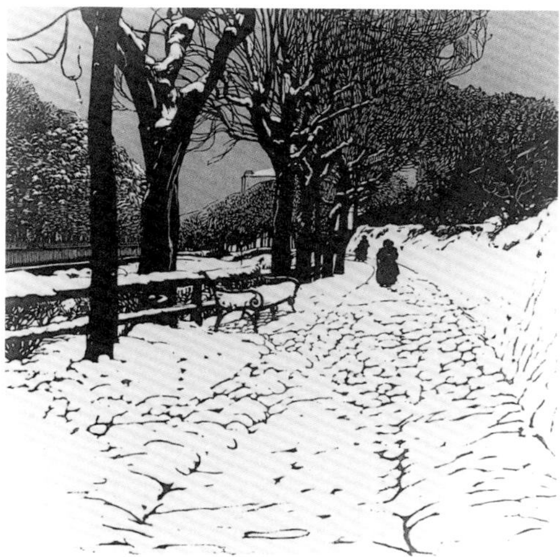

7. Carl Moll (Austrian, 1861–1945)
Winter (Hohe Warte in Vienna) (Winter [Hohe Warte in Wien]), 1903
Color woodcut, image 16 15/16 x 16 15/16 in. (42.9 x 42.9 cm)
Signed outside plate: Probedruck [artist's proof] Carl Moll
Printed outside plate lower left: Winter (Hohe Warte in Wien) Originalholzschnitt von Karl Moll; and colophon at lower right: Verlag der Gesellschaft für Vervielfaltigende Kunst, Wien
K.77.12

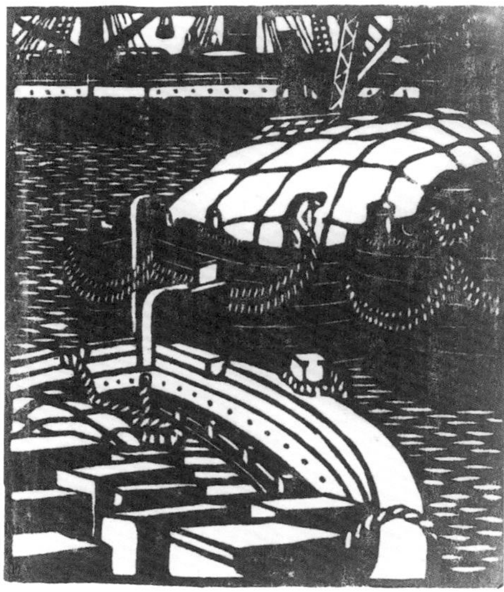

8. Rudolf Kalvach (Austrian, 1883–1932)
On Deck, Trieste Harbor (Auf Deck [Trieste Hafen]), ca. 1908
Woodcut, image 7 11/16 x 6 9/16 in. (19.6 x 16.8 cm); sheet 8 1/16 x 6 7/8 in. (20.4 x 17.5 cm)
K.85.8

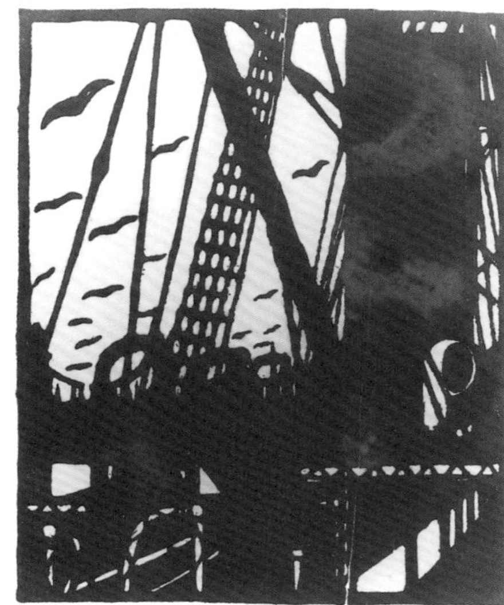

9. Rudolf Kalvach (Austrian, 1883–1932)
Laden Boat, Trieste Harbor (Beladenes Boot, Triester Hafen), ca. 1908
Woodcut, image 8 5/8 x 7 in. (22.0 x 17.8 cm)
K.85.9

as its surrounding environment became an expression of this personal sensibility. Hohe Warte was not only the geographical location of the villa colony; it also represented the Secessionists' desire to articulate a new culture through the environment in which they lived.

As in Moll's other prints of Hohe Warte made around the same time, he presents his well-known *Winter* in the square format preferred by the Secessionists. Seemingly far removed from the bustle of Vienna's city center, this scene depicts a snow-covered park walkway bordered on the left by a wooden railing, a single park bench, and a row of dark barren trees. The path is also enclosed on the right by a high embankment of snow. Two silhouetted female figures stroll in the midground of the image as the main pathway curves to the left and recedes into the distant background. From the viewer's foreground entry into the scene, the empty expanse of the path evokes a sense of stillness. Along with the path's lateral enclosures, the blue-gray overcast sky above and the print's muted gray tones further enhance the mood of melancholic quiet and suggest Hohe Warte's separation from all that lies beyond. Although the composition is measured and undramatic, Moll organizes the receding pathway to heighten the viewer's spatial awareness of the distance between the immediate foreground and distant background. As in the symbolist transcendent landscape (see cat. no. 1), the viewer of this image is led into the Secessionist scene but also conscious of the path's remote end.

Trieste played a significant role within the Austro-Hungarian Empire prior to World War I, even as it maintained its linguistic and cultural ties with Italy. In the fourteenth century the city came under Austrian protection; in the seventeen century it was championed by Prince Eugene of Savoy (see also cat. 98) and flourished as Austria's one port city. Like his contemporary Egon Schiele, who had painted Trieste in 1907, Kalvach also admired the city's vital harbor. His family moved from Vienna to Trieste in 1901, and in 1908 he produced a series of black-and-white woodcuts that featured various harbor scenes of the city. Despite this move to Trieste, however, Kalvach and his brother Max maintained close ties with Vienna, where he attended the city's Applied Arts School. As Kalvach's career as an artist developed, he continued to divide his professional and family lives between Vienna and Trieste. This separation provided rich subject matter for his work, but also, as Hanna Egger has suggested, produced a difficult divide within his daily life.[6]

In contrast to Carl Moll's depiction of the comfortable middle-class residential area of Hohe Warte (cat. 7), Kalvach's harbor images represent a place in which heavy work takes place. The works in Kalvach's series move away from the symbolist concern with spiritual transcendence to show the physical world of boats, water, cargo, and the men who marshal such elements into productivity. They not only turn to the industrial subjects of the Trieste harbor, but monumentalize them as well.

Kalvach's woodcuts contrast solid and patterned planes of black and white and imbue his scenes with a sense of measured industriousness. In *On Deck, Trieste Harbor*, a prow of a boat in the left foreground draws the viewer diagonally into the center of the scene where the small figure of a man works the heavy ropes of a second boat. The length of a third boat extends across the background horizon and leaves only a hint of sky above. This compositional arrangement situates the ships to dominate the image as well as the viewer's sense of place. In *Laden Boat*, dense black forms are contrasted with open white sky, and the birds approaching overhead counter the diagonal plank that recedes from the center foreground into the right background. In both prints, the compositions work to place the viewers actively within the immediate scene rather than leave them passively perched on its edge. Combining a wealth of varied patterning and dense, curving forms, Kalvach's images evoke the rhythm, strength, and authority of a harbor whose vitality depended on the activity of its workers.

A member of both the Vienna and Berlin Secessions, **Emil Orlik** was born in Prague, studied at the Munich Academy, and is considered an important rejuvenator of the modern color woodcut. As a student he was inspired by the work of Rembrandt and Millet and developed into an avid sketcher, able to capture movement, outlines, and atmospheric tones quickly and effectively.[7] Around 1900 he made his first trip to Japan and this encounter with the culture of the Far East proved decisive for his stylistic development.

Orlik's woodcut *Figures under Trees* demonstrates the manner in which he adapted Japanese-inspired motifs and stylistic elements such as simple, elegantly composed landscapes and flat, ornamental surfaces to European

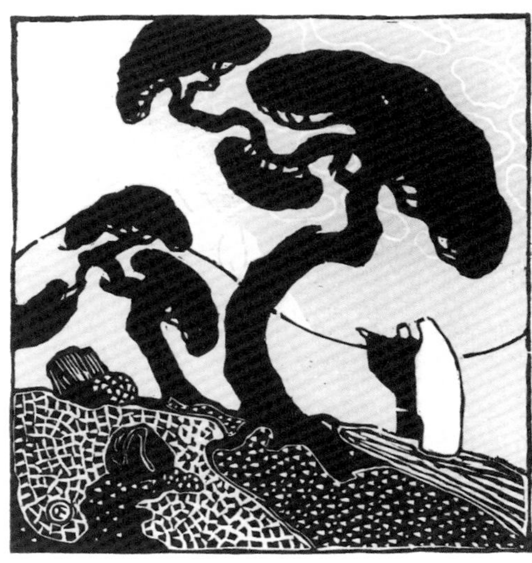

10. Emil Orlik (Austrian, 1870–1932)
Figures under Trees (Gestalten unter Bäumen), 1902
Color woodcut, 5 1/2 x 5 3/16 in. (14.1 x 13.2 cm)
Monogram lower left: E within O
K.84.2

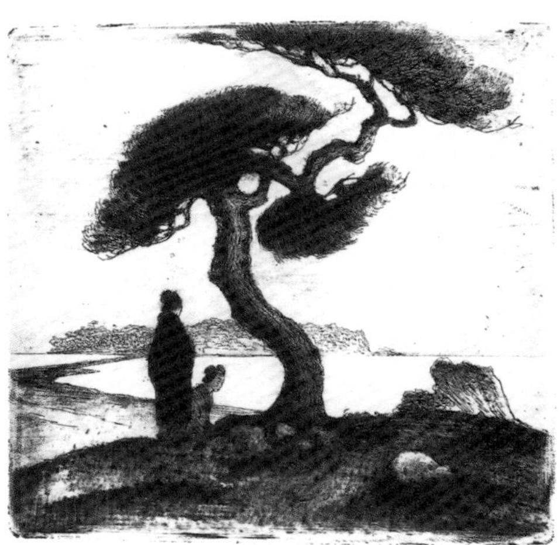

11. Emil Orlik (Austrian, 1870–1932)
Japanese Scene, ca. 1925
Etching, plate 4 x 4 1/2 in. (10.1 x 11. 4 cm); sheet 8 1/4 x 7 1/8 in. (20.9 x 18.0 cm)
Signed graphite lower right below plate mark: Orlik
K.90.11

subject matter. The print is composed of a boldly colored series of layers that begin with a variously patterned foreground, curving silhouetted trees above, and pair of shrouded figures on the right. In the midground rises a gently sloping hill behind which a sharp, snow-covered alpine profile juts into the golden, cloud-decorated sky above. The gesturing figure's raised arm counters the down- and rightward curve of the dark trees and the sweeping slope of the yellow hill in the midground. This small but dynamic signal effectively redirects the viewer's attention leftward and toward the distant mountain in the composition's background. This narrative device, in combination with the figures' generalized, cloaked forms that imply a semireligious, even medieval character, suggests a scene in which the pair engage in a type of spiritual pilgrimage through the mountainous landscape.

Orlik produced his related *Japanese Scene* more than twenty years after *Figures under Trees* and after further travels to Japan, China, India, and Egypt as well as throughout Europe. Although the landscape motif is fundamentally the same as in the earlier print, its stylistic treatment and resulting mood have an entirely different effect and underscore Orlik's direct observation of east Asian subjects. The delicate, even wispy rendering of the landscape in this etching lends it a more atmospheric sensibility. The earlier woodcut's bold patterns and colors, and sunny alpine setting are replaced with an array of hazy gray tones and subtle textures, a placid body of water, and an expansive sky. The two cloaked figures likewise have been altered. They now have more distinct facial features and wear traditional Japanese hairstyles and costumes. Rather than seeming to engage in conversation, the two women in *Japanese Scene* alternately stand and sit and gaze meditatively offshore toward the distant horizon.

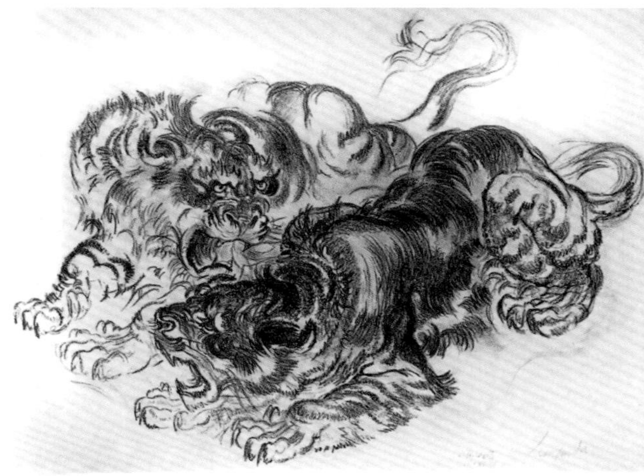

12. Ludwig Heinrich Jungnickel (Austrian, b. Germany, 1881–1965)
Hissing Predatory Cats with Elfi Opitz (Fauchende Raubkatzen, mit Elfi Opitz), 1928
Charcoal, image ca. 14 1/4 x 20 in. (36.3 x 50.9 cm)
Dated and signed lower right: 11.XI.28 Jungnickel
K.88.6

Ludwig Jungnickel was drawn to the Vienna Secession as early as 1898 and participated in a number of its exhibitions at least until 1918, including the 1908 *Kunstschau*. He also contributed a decorative frieze of animals for the nursery of the Palais Stoclet in Brussels, in association with the Wiener Werkstätte. Despite this involvement, however, Jungnickel was never a member of the Secession. He was attracted to the work of Klimt and Moser but remained on the group's periphery and in general tended to avoid the highly stylized and cultivated forms of Jugendstil. In contrast, his later travels through the Balkans and contact with its rural inhabitants helped him solidify his aesthetic aspirations to articulate a direct harmonious relationship to nature. As part of this interest, he also sought inspiration in nonwestern art and became well known for his images of landscape and animal subject matters and skill as a printmaker.

Produced during the interwar period, *Hissing Predatory Cats* demonstrates Jungnickel's masterful handling of line. Although executed in charcoal, the drawing is similar to the ink paintings of the sixteenth-century Japanese artist, Kanō Eitoku, which he likely saw through reproductions. In Japan, Eitoku had ushered in a new monumental style of painting known as *taiga*, which used an expanded range of colors and gold-leaf backgrounds and was widely adopted by later Japanese artists.[8] Eitoku's folding screen of *Chinese Lions,* formerly in the Imperial House Collection, might have been a model for Jungnickel's drawing (figure 2).

In *Hissing Predatory Cats,* Jungnickel eliminates background elements entirely and allows the lions to fill the picture plane. As in the screen painting, the tussling lions are oriented to the left, and advance toward the center foreground from the right midground. Jungnickel renders his animals' bodies with great detail and emphasizes an intense dynamism. In particular, the lion's ferocious expressions, bared teeth and claws, taut muscles, bristling fur, and billowing tails convey a sense of their fierce struggle with one another. In contrast, Eitoku's lions are depicted in a more stylized fashion, seen in the decorative patterning of the hair and generally heavier consistency of line. Jungnickel uses various linear textures from long, sinuously curving strokes used for the tails to shorter, smudgy layered ones used for the fur. As a result, both the lions' spirited poses and their sensuous rendering convey fleeting, wildly playful movement.

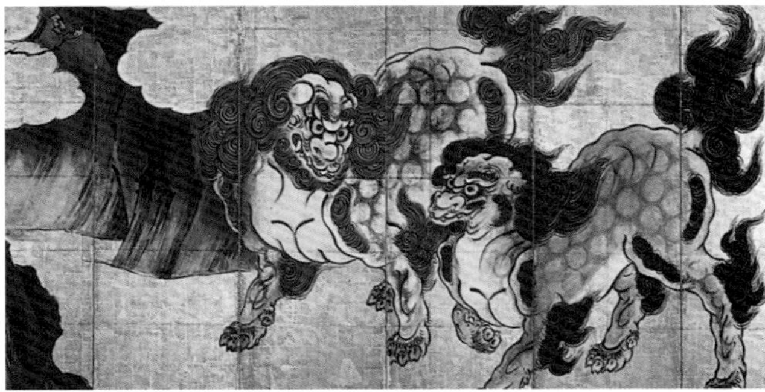

Figure 2. Kanō Eitoku (Japanese, 1534–1590), *Chinese Lions,* six-panel screen, ink and colors with gold-leaf ground. Photograph courtesy Museum of the Imperial Collections, Tokyo

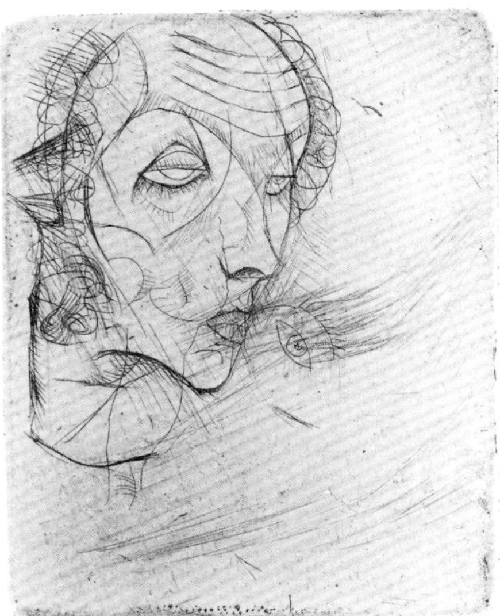

13. Egon Schiele (Austrian, 1890–1918)
Self-Portrait (Selbstbildnis), 1914
Drypoint, plate $5\,^{1}/_{8}$ x $4\,^{1}/_{2}$ in. (13.0 x 11.0 cm)
K.77.7

Egon Schiele was a precocious artist who had early mastered the traditional skills of the fine arts. In late 1906 at the age of sixteen he entered the Academy of Fine Arts in Vienna (*Akademie der bildende Künste*). By 1909, when he departed from the institution, he had made connections with fellow students, established friendly contact with Gustav Klimt, and met critics and collectors who would become his patrons. With the virtuosity and oftentimes moving and disturbing quality of the works that followed, Schiele became a leading proponent of Viennese expressionism.

The etching medium Schiele used for his self-portrait exploits the element of line to convey a sense of psychological agitation. Schiele represents his face and neck in three-quarter profile facing right. Together the furrowed brow, heavily lidded eyes, and hollow cheeks convey an overall sense of tense, psychological exhaustion. The thin, brittle, linear and spiral patterns that frame the face present a heightened state of nervous energy that exemplifies the type of subjective representation emphasized by expressionists. Adjacent to the figure's lips appears a disembodied eye that seems to float either to or from Schiele's mouth. In sharp contrast to art nouveau's use of curving, rhythmic lines and pattern to evoke states of spiritual longing and transition, Schiele's expressionistic treatment suggests a spirit at a crisis point.

Like many of his avant-garde contemporaries, Schiele was interested in Sigmund Freud's writings on psychoanalysis. His works focus largely on the human subject—a motif that allowed him to investigate psychological and sexual themes rigorously. Foregoing more conventional representations of the erotic, however, Schiele chose to explore more primal and awkward aspects of sexuality and psychology. This *Self-Portrait* is one of the artist's many penetrating personal examinations of what the exterior human facade reveals of the inner psyche.

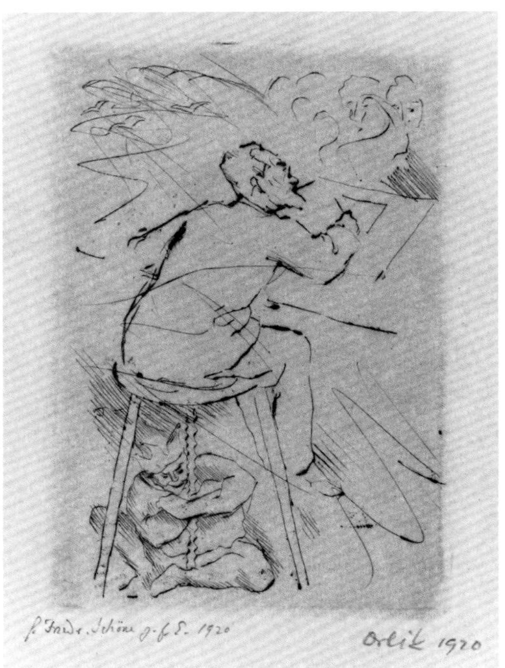

14. Emil Orlik (Austrian, 1870–1932)
Self-Portrait at the Easel with Fools (Selbstbildnis an der Staffelei mit Narren), 1920
Drypoint, plate $4\,^{3}/_{4}$ x $3\,^{3}/_{16}$ in. (12.1 x 8.1 cm); sheet $9\,^{3}/_{8}$ x $6\,^{3}/_{8}$ in. (23.9 x 16.3 cm)
Signed and dated lower right in graphite below plate mark: Orlik 1920
K.93.3

Working in a realist style that became internationally popular during the interwar period, Orlik depicts himself in the role of the artist drawing busily at his easel. Seated under his stool is the smirking figure of a jester or fool, and in the upper right background are three figures with grotesquely distorted features. It is not clear if the group represents the artist's models or studio visitors, but together with the jester they appear belligerently poised to disrupt the intently working artist.

The alert and actively engaged character of Orlik's artist presents a sharp visual contrast to Schiele's image of himself (cat. 13). Whereas Schiele alludes to the individual's internal conflicts as the psychological manifested as physical distress on the body, Orlik's scene pre-sents the artist's demons in the guise of disruptive others. On a stylistic level, the delicate drypoint reflects Orlik's well-honed ability to capture his subjects' characters in a quick sketch. It recalls, moreover, the skillful manner in which cartoons and caricatures achieve succinct expressive impact with minimal means. Reminiscent of the fairy-tale drawings of romantic writer and artist E. T. A. Hoffmann, Orlik's fools even suggest fantastic or allegorical representations. Interpreted on this level, the mischievous characters seem to be humorous, fictive spirits who embody forces that vex and trouble the artist's creative lucidity.

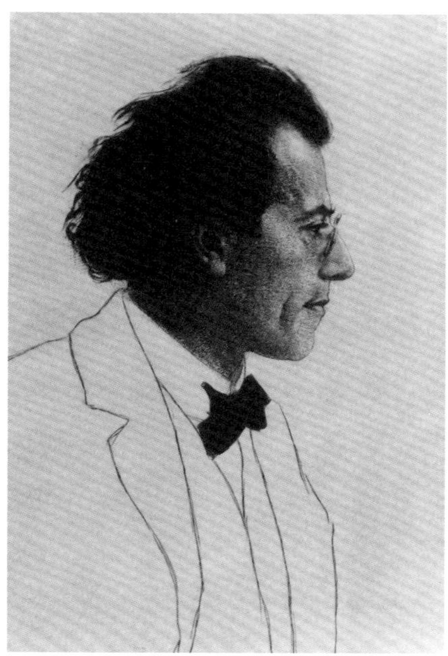

15. Emil Orlik (Austrian, 1870–1932)
Portrait of Gustav Mahler, 1902
Drypoint, roulette, mezzotint, 11 9/16 x 7 7/8 in. (29.4 x 20 cm)
Lower right: signature and date in graphite
K.99.23

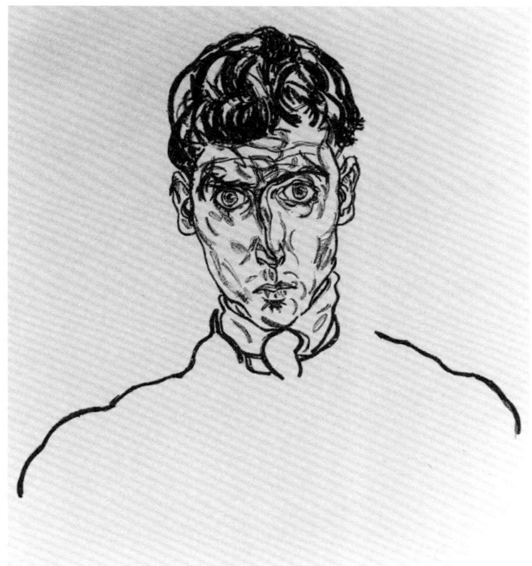

16. Egon Schiele (Austrian, 1890–1918)
Portrait of Paris von Gütersloh (Porträt Paris von Gütersloh), 1918
Lithograph, 10 1/2 x 11 7/8 in. (26.8 x 30.1 cm)
K.67.3

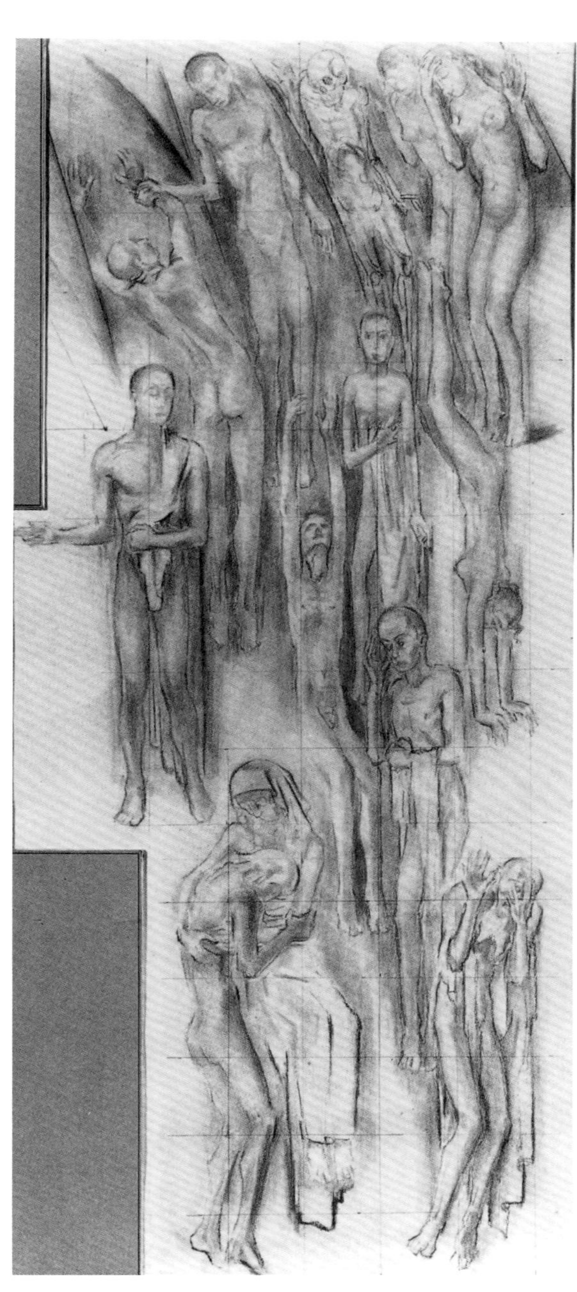

17. Robert Philippi (Austrian, 1877–1959)
Souls with Seated Virgin (Design for the Crematorium at the Vienna Cemetery), ca. 1921
Red and black chalk, 31 1/2 x 14 1/2 in. (80 x 36.8 cm)
With graph lines for enlargement
K.88.1

II. APPLIED GRAPHICS AND ILLUSTRATION

Around 1900, new technical advances in mechanical reproduction allowed Viennese artists to develop further the aesthetic potential of the graphic arts in the areas of advertising, illustration, and design. Artists were better able to integrate image and text on the same page, and along the lines of the *Gesamtkunstwerk*, to produce a harmoniously synthesized totality for a variety of purposes. A dominant model of this type of applied graphics-as-artwork was the Vienna Secession's short-lived periodical, *Ver Sacrum* (Sacred Spring) (see cats. 68, 69, and 70). Published between 1898 and 1903, the periodical was conceived of as a unified, refined, and polished work of art in which each page could theoretically stand alone as a complete work of art. It was the designers' aspiration that the aesthetic coordination of text, image, and other graphic components achieve the larger philosophical purpose to bring about the spiritual renewal of the viewer.

The prints in this section range from a page designed for *Ver Sacrum* and children's book illustrations to a theater advertisement and holiday cards. To varying ends each work exemplifies the conceptual and aesthetic ambitions of the *Gesamtkunstwerk*.

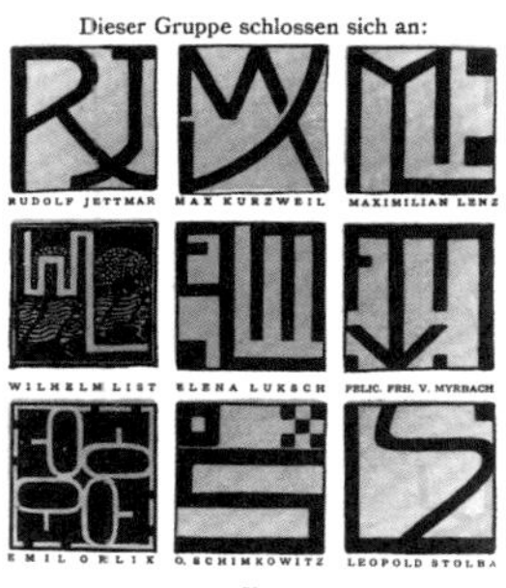

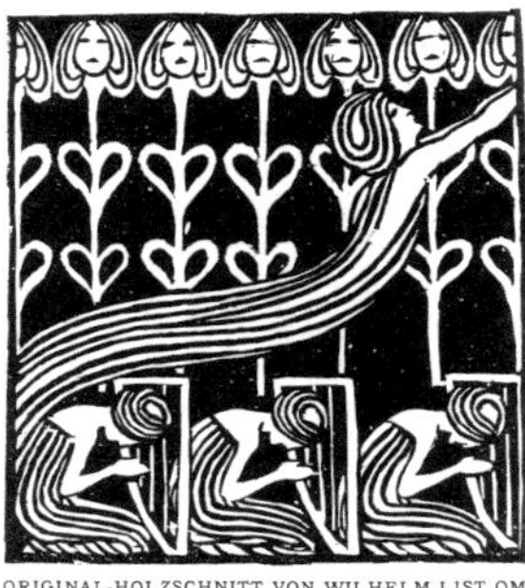

18. Wilhelm List (Austrian, 1864–1918)
Untitled (page 76 from *Ver Sacrum* 4 [1902]) recto: (page 75) color woodcut of Vienna Secession artists' monograms;
verso: Frieze with flowers, harpists, and angel;
Woodcut, 5 1/2 x 5 1/4 in. (13.9 x 13.4 cm)
K.73.3

Wilhelm List was both a member of the Vienna Secession and an editor of its periodical, *Ver Sacrum*, to which he made numerous contributions. He designed this untitled woodcut for the 1902 edition of the periodical that served as the catalogue for the Beethoven/Klinger exhibition. Similar to Elena Luksch-Makowsky's woodcut, *Fairytale* (*Märchen*), 1902 (see cat. 2), List's black-and-white image relates thematically to the main works in the exhibition. In particular, List derived the motifs for this decoratively patterned image from Klimt's "Poetry" and "Floating Forms," which appear in the third and final mural of the *Beethoven Frieze*. The print combines two adjacent mural scenes that are separated by approximately four meters, and thus condenses the path of mankind's quest for spiritual fulfillment, from the solace provided by poetry to its approach to ultimate deliverance.

Along the bottom of List's square format woodcut is a row of three women in identical profile formation. Each wears a long, flowing gown that bares her shoulders and arms, kneels toward the right, and plays a lyre with her head bowed forward. Above their heads soars the figure of a fourth woman who inclines her head upward and extends her arms before her, a posture that draws the viewer's attention to the background figures. Dressed similarly to the lyrists, this woman's diaphanous gown trails behind her; its columnlike form indicates the curved diagonal trajectory of her upward flight from the lower left to upper right of the image. Together, this group of four women is based on the lyrist and multiple flying figures of mankind who appear in Klimt's "Poetry," section of the mural (for image, see Peter Vergo, p. 74) the narrative scene in which mankind finds fulfillment and solace in poetry. In contrast to the mural, however, List's print repeats Klimt's single lyrist to form a trio, and reduces the group of soaring figures to one.

Behind this quartet of women is a row of seven highly stylized figures. Composed of thin, vertical, plantlike stems decorated with pairs of rounded leaves at the top of which simplified faces serve as blossoms, these figures echo Klimt's female choir that surrounds the embracing couple, who appear in the culminating scene of his narrative. Klimt's floating figures also have their eyes meditatively closed and hold in their upraised hands the flowers suggested by List's floral figures. The ascending diagonal thrust of the soaring woman links together the foreground lyrists and the background figures. Her arms, which extend beyond the right edge of the print, also suggest to the viewer that ultimate fulfillment lies beyond the immediate present and is achieved only through a continual upward progression of endeavor.

On the reverse of the page appear nine square format monograms of artists who participated in the exhibition. They include Rudolf Jettmar, Max Kurzweil, Maximilian Lenz, Wilhelm List, Elena Luksch, Felician von Myrbach, Emil Orlik, Othmar Schimkowitz, and Leopold Stolba.

Orlik produced this striking portrait of Henrik Ibsen for the program of German-language premiere of Ibsen's *Peer Gynt* (cat. 19) that took place in May of 1902 at Vienna's German Volkstheater. Four small squares, a characteristic Secessionist graphic symbol of totality, mark the outer corners of the page and simultaneously unify the portrait and the text below it. Dominating the

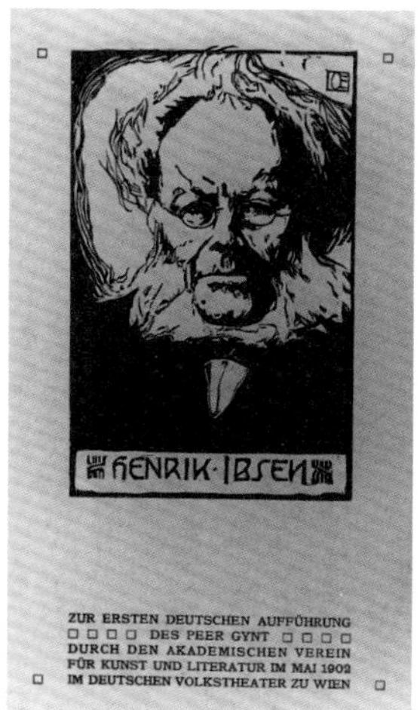

19. Emil Orlik (Austrian, 1870–1932)
Program for the first German performance of [Ibsen's] *Peer Gynt*, 1902
Woodcut, sheet 15 1/16 x 9 in. (38.3 x 22.9 cm)
K.77.6

page, however, is the dark gray-green and white image of Ibsen, which resembles contemporary photographs of the Norwegian playwright taken around 1900 when he was seventy-two. Orlik translates into woodcut Ibsen's bespectacled penetrating gaze, sternly set mouth, high forehead, bushy white hair, and broad, wiry beard. In doing so, he brilliantly matches the stately yet gruff appearance of the writer to a medium also associated with a vigorous, enduring authenticity as well as Germanic-Nordic ethnicity. The circular, open white space that encircles Ibsen's head suggests an aura of creative inspiration and also functions as a type of honorary halo.

Since the late nineteenth century, Vienna's intellectuals had celebrated Ibsen. He not only helped forge the path to a naturalist style of modern drama in Scandinavia and Germany, but also was widely influential as a founder of symbolist drama. He was particularly honored among Vienna's group of young, modern writers—known as Young Vienna (*Jung-Wien*)—who were interested in bringing about a renewal of literature. Especially in the wake of Ibsen's visit to Vienna in 1891 for the premiere of his *Kronprätendenten*, this group considered him, in the words of writer and critic Hermann Bahr, an esteemed "godfather."[9]

Ibsen completed *Peer Gynt* with remarkable speed in four months, and the play was published in November 1867. The drama presents as its theme the conflict between the spirit of compromise and decisive committal to a course of action. This conflict is embodied in the character of Peer Gynt and thus proposes that the question of self-actualization lies solely within one's self, rather than in a confrontation with others or one's environment. Ibsen drew the play's characters from Norwegian folklore. Through them he presents a general satire on human nature, on the religious and political nature of life in Norway as a nation, and on specific local customs.

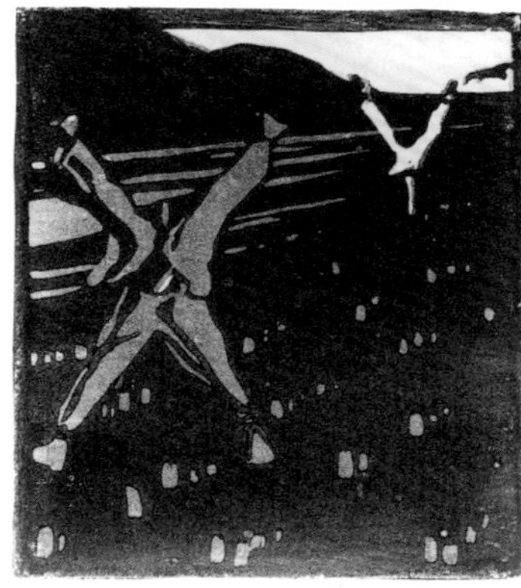

20. Nora Exner von Zumbusch (Austrian, 1879–1915)
Scarecrow (*Vogelscheuchen*), 1903
Color woodcut, image 7 1/8 x 6 7/16 in. (18.2 x 16.2 cm)
K.85.5

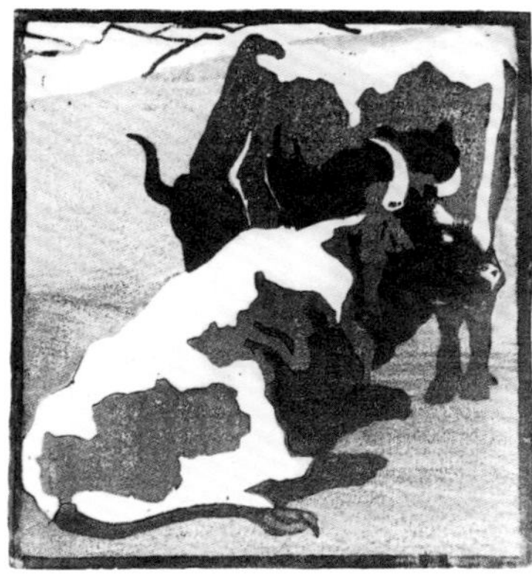

21. Nora Exner von Zumbusch (Austrian, 1879–1915)
Cows (*Kühe*), 1903
Color woodcut, image 7 x 6 5/16 in. (18.0 x 16.1 cm)
K.85.6

Within the state-sponsored system of applied art school training, late nineteenth- and early twentieth-century art programs in the Austro-Hungarian Empire provided many opportunities for artists-in-training to illustrate and publish children's books. Children's ABC books, for which the playful prints by Exner von Zumbush, Fiebiger, and Uchatius were intended, were especially popular within the context of late nineteenth-century educational reform before compulsory education was instituted. It is likely that the Austrian practice of using of large blocks of contrasting colors was derived from English models such as Sir William Nicholson's *The Square Book of Animals* (1900) as well as from Japanese woodblock prints.[10]

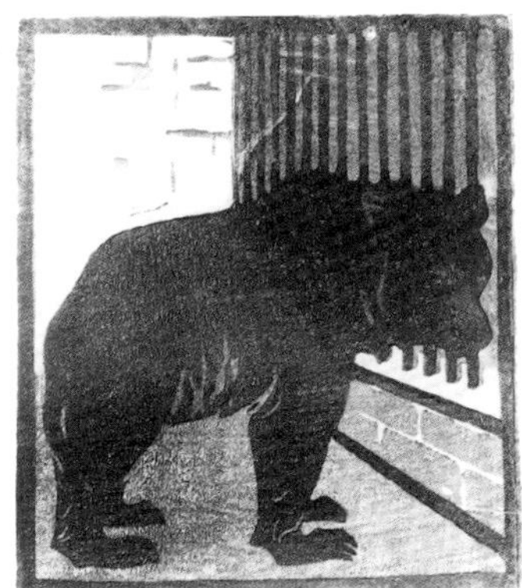

22. Franz Fiebiger (Austrian, 1880–ca. 1955)
Bear (*Bär*), 1903
Color woodcut, image 7 1/4 x 6 3/8 in. (18.4 x 16.3 cm)
K.85.7

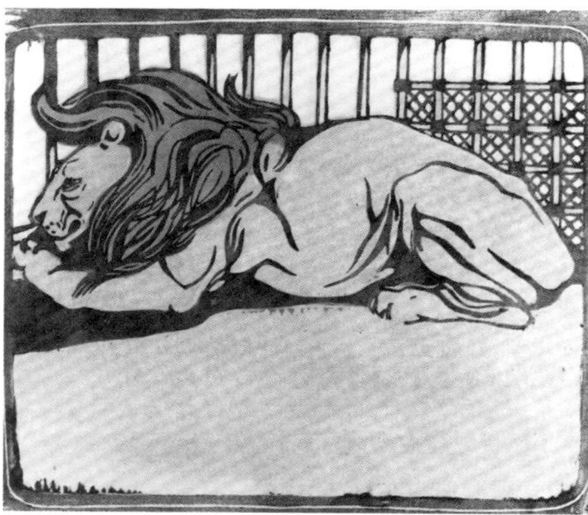

23. Maria (Mitzi) von Uchatius (Austrian, 1882–1958)
Lion (*Löwe*), 1905
Color woodcut, image/sheet 7 5/8 x 9 1/8 in. (19.4 x 23.2 cm)
K.85.15; see Color Plate 3

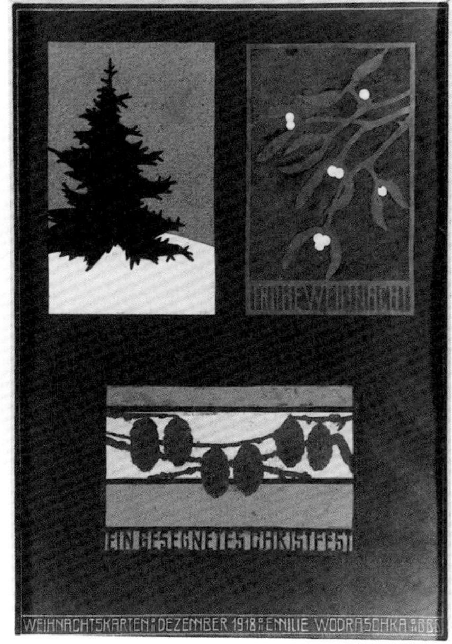

24. Emilie Wodraschka (Austrian, active 1918)
Three Christmas Postcards, 1918
Decoupage with colored papers, 12 5/8 x 9 in. (32.1 x 22.9 cm)
Inscribed bottom edge in white: Weihnachtskarten Dezember 1918. Emilie Wodraschka
K.90.20

Exner's *Scarecrow* and *Cows* (cat. 20 and 21) and **Fiebiger's** *Bear* were reproduced in a 1903 edition of *Ver Sacrum* and were to be included in a hand-printed *Tier ABC*, or animal picture book.[11] The three square-format 1903 woodcuts as well as **Uchatius's** *Lion* of 1905 were meant to engage children didactically through visual means. Each print uses a limited range of contrasting colors and a simplified yet dynamic composition. The scarecrow and animals, however, are not arranged in the typical fashion to form a letter of the alphabet—such as "B" for Bear, for instance. Without additional information regarding their conception, it is possible to speculate that the subjects are presented in a setting that corresponds logically to lived experience. In this fashion, children could learn to recognize the scarecrow, for example, as associated with a late summer field, the cows with a green pasture, and the domesticated bear and lion with a cage in a zoo.

Beginning with the Vienna Secession around 1900, postcards became a relatively inexpensive medium for Viennese artists to publicize new ideas, themes, artistic activities, and events to a sizeable audience. The Wiener Werkstätte continued this practice. As historical documents, such Viennese postcards provide an excellent scope of commercial graphic design tendencies that extend from the Secession into the 1920s.

Emilie Wodraschka's Three Christmas Postcards exhibit a reductive design sensibility typical of the interwar period. Each design presents a single subject rendered in a restricted range of unmodulated colors, such as the dark pine tree set on a snow-covered hill and silhouetted against a blue sky. Wodraschka's compositions have neither the refined curvilinearity of art nouveau nor the spiky effervescence of expressionism. Her subjects are pared down to an essential form. Arranged in subtly dynamic, asymmetrical compositions placed on a diagonal or framed by horizontal band of stripes, they convey a simple and bold elegance.

III. APPLIED ARTS AND DESIGN

A. *Jugendstil Glass*

As a result of royal patronage the central European region of Bohemia has a long glass-making history. In the nineteenth century, the dominant Bohemian tradition of cut and engraved glass looked westward to France, and adapted the technologies and aesthetics of layered and etched glass inspired by the glassmakers Emile Gallé and the Daum Frères. Following the art nouveau trend to render nature-inspired forms, fin-de-siècle Bohemian glass developed organic, swelling, and curvilinear shapes, ethereal colors, and iridescent finishes. Whereas French art nouveau glass is dominated by motifs from the natural world such as insects, fish, reptiles, and varieties of plants, Austrian Jugendstil designs reflect a more abstract interpretation of nature. In fact, Austrian vessels often suggest living, if at times otherworldly, flora themselves, such as the Kaerwer collection's calla lily-shaped vase in the style of Pallme König & Habel (cat. no. 27).

In the 1880s the Loetz Witwe firm (est. 1836 in Klášterský Mlýn) began to specialize in an iridescent type of Jugendstil vase known as *Lusterglas*. The contemporary taste for iridescent decoration derived from a historicist interest in excavated Roman glass, the surfaces of which developed an iridescent finish after being buried.[12] The phosphorescent qualities of animal and plant organisms, known to artists through popular science literature, may also have provided modern inspiration for this type of finish. Following the success of the U.S. glassmaker Louis Comfort Tiffany, Loetz was among the first to exploit the decorative potential of iridescent glass. By 1900 Loetz was considered one of the best glassmakers in Europe, which contributed greatly to this style's popularity among contemporary collectors.[13] Pallme König & Habel was among the many Bohemian glass firms that also began to produce iridescent glass around 1900.

In general, most Bohemian glass manufacturers produced their own designs. They also commissioned well-known artists to design works that they would then manufacture and, in some cases, retail. The firms E. Bakalowits & Söhne (est. 1845) and J. & L. Lobmeyer (est. 1822), for instance, both opened retail shops in Vienna around the time of their founding.[14] Bakalowits began to commission works by modern Viennese artists in the nineteenth century, including Josef Hoffmann and Koloman Moser, and also served as a liaison to facilitate production between artists and other glass manufacturers.[15] The well-established system of Bohemian glassmaking thus provided Vienna Secession and Wiener Werkstätte artists an important and fruitful arena in which to realize their designs well into the twentieth century.

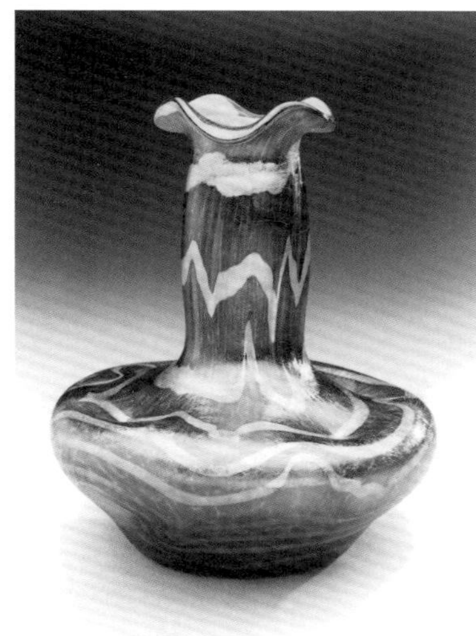

25. Johann Loetz Witwe
Vase, ca. 1900
Iridescent glass, 6 3/4 x 5 11/16 in. top diam. 2 5/8 in. (16.8 x 14.5 cm. top diam. 6.6 cm)
Etched in base: Loetz/ Austria
K.70.19; see Color Plate 4

This piece of clear, dark pink glass has yellow stripes, spotting, and iridescent silver line decoration. The form's low, wide body is strikingly contrasted with a long neck and wavy mouth.

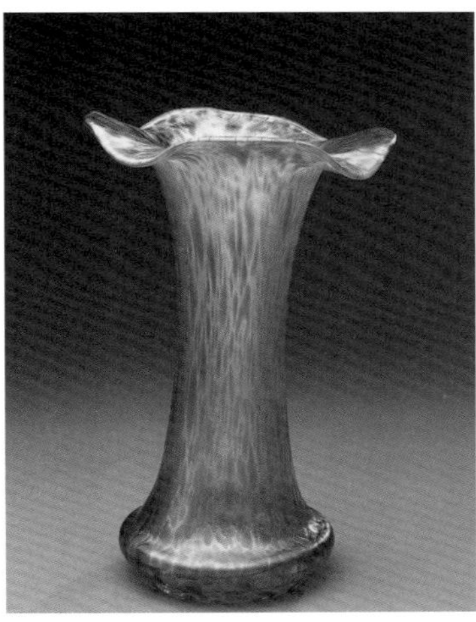

26. In the style of Johann Loetz Witwe
Vase with Papillon Finish, ca. 1900
Iridescent glass, 9 3/4 x 7 5/16 in. (24.8 x 18.6 cm)
K.88.9; see Color Plate 5

Characteristic of Bohemian Jugendstil glass, the shape of this vase evokes exotic, plantlike forms. The tall vessel has a slender body that broadens into a mouth with a wide, wavy flange. The allover splotchy-patterned gold finish is known as "papillion" and refers to the French term for butterfly. This type of artistic glass decoration, patented by Max Ritter von Spaun, is aptly named after the spotted, velvety iridescence of butterfly wings.

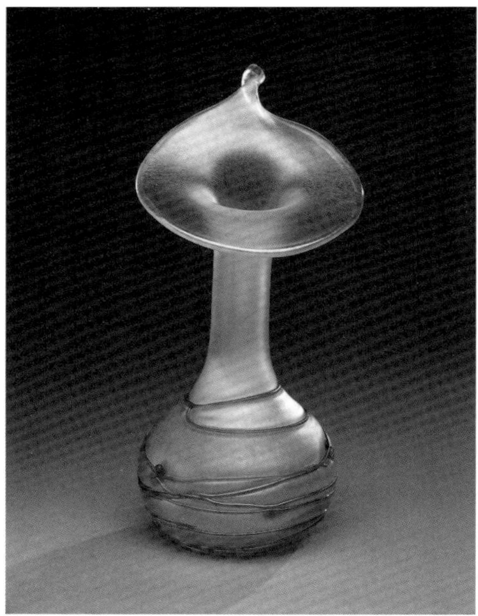

27. In the style of Pallme König & Habel
Vase, ca. 1900
Iridescent glass, 11 x 5 in. (28 x 12.8 cm)
K.88.12; see Color Plate 6

This flowerlike design has a low, round body that tapers into a slender neck. The flanged-mouth opening is set at an angle and resembles a calla lily. The white glass used for the vase is finished with a pale pink iridescent glaze; narrow pinkish-purple banding encircles the base.

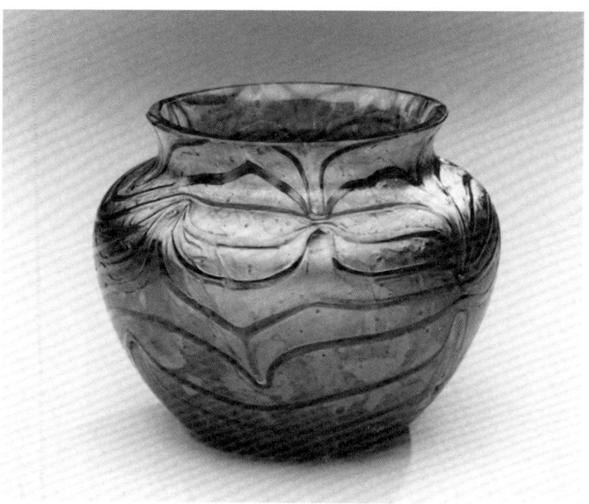

28. Johann Loetz Witwe
Vase, ca. 1900
Iridescent glass, 3 3/8 x 4 1/2 in. (8.6 x 11.4 cm)
K.70.18

Small, low vases with a short-mouthed opening like this one were a vessel type commonly produced by the **Loetz** firm. This variation combines olive green glass layered with an iridescent surface glaze and dark blue banding.

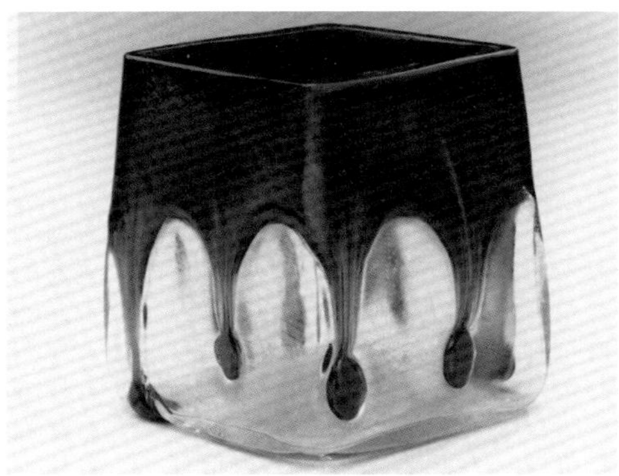

29. In the style of Maria Kirschner (Austrian, 1852–1931)
Vase, ca. 1905
Clear and iridescent glass, 4 x 3 5/16 x 4 1/4 in.
(10.2 x 8.2 x 10.9 cm)
K.66.10

Contrasting regular forms and irregular patterns of process, this rhomboid-shaped clear glass vase is decorated with a dark, iridescent teal and purple enamel "drip" design that extends from the top rim onto the lower half of the vessel. The simple, bold, geometric form recalls similar designs produced by Maria Kirschner, a painter and applied arts designer originally from Prague. From around 1903 to 1914 Kirschner collaborated with the Loetz firm, and designed vases and other glass works that combined colored and uncolored glass.[16]

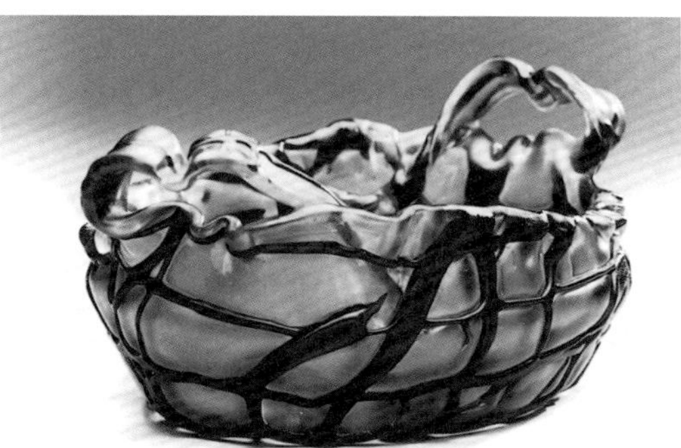

30. Pallme König & Habel
Basket Vase, ca. 1900
Green and dark purple iridescent glass, 3 9/16 x 8 15/16 x 5 3/8 in.
(9 x 22.5 x 13.7 cm)
K.36

The shape and layering of materials in this vase draw attention to the process of its construction. The exterior surface of the low, oval-shaped basket of green glass has been overlaid with a crisscrossed pattern of dark purple glass bands. As the vessel and decorative banding cooled at different rates, pockets of green glass expanded to fill the spaces between the purple bands. Along the undulating top rim of the basket, the glassmaker cut two thin strips of glass, one on either side. Looping these backward and then refastening them to the vase, the strips were fashioned into irregularly shaped handles at the far ends of the vessel.

B. *Applied Arts, 1901–1910*

Around 1899, the Loetz Witwe glass-making firm began to produce the designs of Josef Hoffmann and Koloman Moser. After the Wiener Werkstätte's founding in 1903, it further developed this production association and licensed firms such as Bakalowits, Lobmeyer, Loetz, and Meyr's Neffe to produce its glass designs. As a result, the firms manufactured not only designs by Hoffman and Moser, but also those by other leading Werkstätte artists such as Dagobert Peche, Michael Powolny, and Otto Prutscher.

By 1904, the iridescent style of Jugendstil glass with its fluid, organic forms and soft, romantic colors was replaced by the more classical, rectilinear design sensibility of the Wiener Werkstätte, often referred to as constructive Jugendstil. Strongly informed by the designs of Moser and Hoffmann, this purist style emphasizes clean, architectonic forms, simple geometric patterns, and bold colors.

The works in this section reflect an array of stylistic production in the applied arts that range from Kolo Moser's Jugendstil buckle to the purist Wiener Werkstätte designs derived from architectural forms. Josef Hoffmann's *Quadratstil* (square style) metal vases and baskets and striped porcelain cup and saucer exemplify this latter style, as do Otto Prutscher's stemmed glasses.

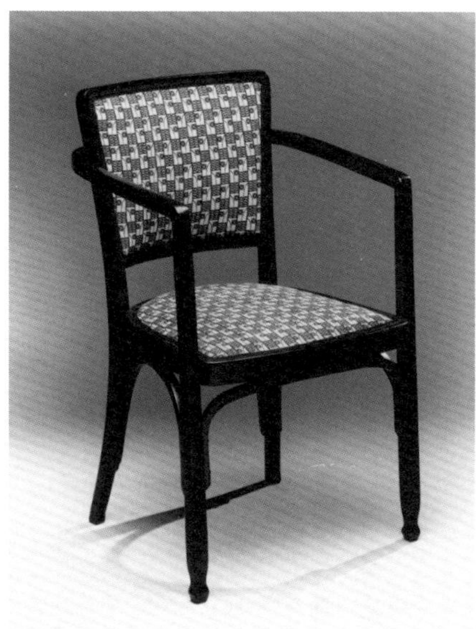

31. Koloman Moser (Austrian, 1868–1918), designer; executed by Jacob & Josef Kohn
Arm Chair, 1901
Bent beechwood with 1985 reproduction of 1905 Hoffmann fabric, 34 1/4 x 21 1/8 x 22 3/4 in. (87.0 x 53.7 x 57.9 cm)
K.87.9

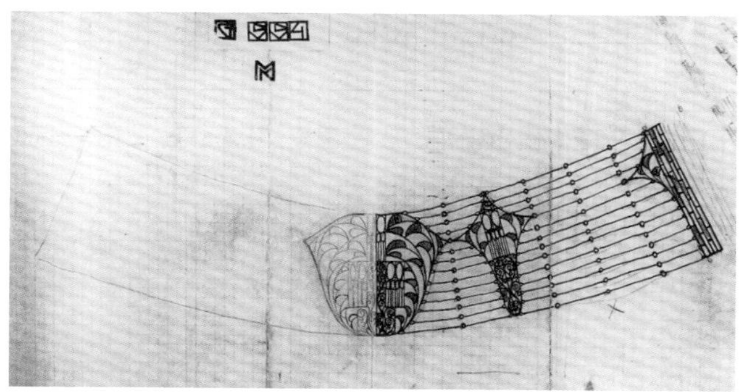

32. Koloman Moser (Austrian, 1868–1918)
Design for Choker Jewelry, 1903
Recto: pen and ink, graphite; verso: graphite, 9 13/16 x 15 5/8 in. (24.9 x 39.7 cm)
Stamped upper left edge: K.M.
K.2000.2

Viennese Jugendstil jewelry is generally more abstract, geometric, and stylized than its European counterparts. Much of the inspiration for these designs derived from the architectural forms associated with the Vienna Secession. Most Wiener Werkstätte designs were produced on a small scale and used semiprecious stones. In the institution's working program, Josef Hoffmann explained such choices on this basis:

> We use many semi-precious stones, especially in our forge; they make up in colorful beauty and infinite variety what they lack in value by comparison with diamonds. We love the silver of silver, the gold of gold in themselves; to us the artistic quality of copper is just as valuable as that of precious metals. We must confess that jewelry of silver can be equally as valuable as one of gold and precious stones. The value of artistic work and inspiration should be recognized and prized once again. The work of the artisan should be evaluated with the same measure as that of the painter and the sculptor.[17]

Typical of many of Moser's jewelry designs, this work combines a delicate, lacelike linearity with stylized floral and leaf forms. In 1905 a completed version of Moser's choker, produced in gold and set with opals, was illustrated in the periodical *Deutsche Kunst und Dekoration* (figure 3).[18]

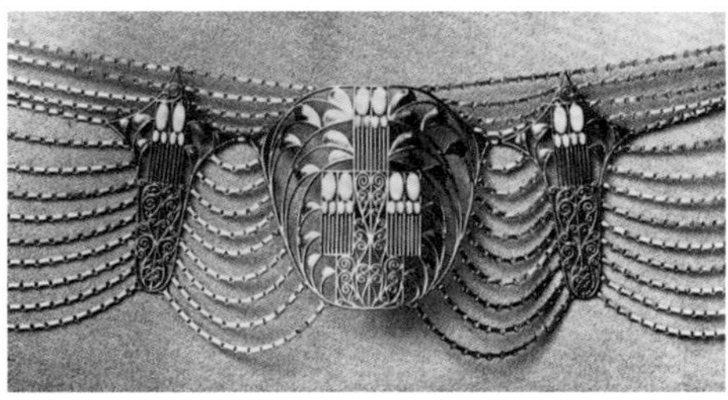

Figure 3. Kolomon Moser, Gold Choker with Opals, after *Deutsche Kunst und Dekoration* 18 (1905–06): 192.

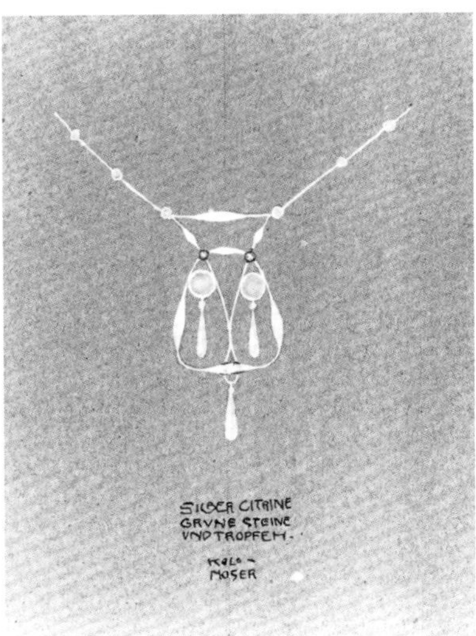

33. Koloman Moser (Austrian, 1868–1918)
Design for Pendant of Silver Citrine, Green Stones, and Drops (*Silber Citrine, Grüne Steine, und Tropfen*), 1903
Gouache, graphite, and pen and ink, 9 x 13 in. (22.9 x 33.0 cm)
Verso upper right corner graphite: XXXIV
K.2000.1

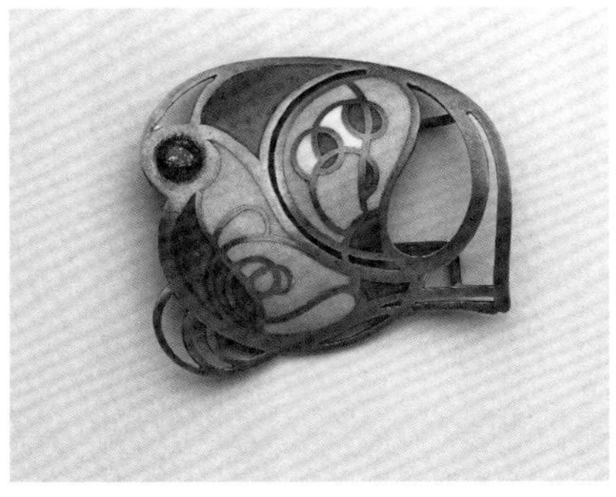

34. Koloman Moser (Austrian, 1868–1918), designer; executed by the Wiener Werkstätte
Silver-gilt Buckle, ca. 1904
Gilded silver, enamel, lapis lazuli, H. 2 5/8 x 2 3/8 in. (6.6 x 6.0 cm)
Stamped verso: G·A·S· with hexagram below
K.53.1; see Color Plate 7

Moser's buckle balances delicacy and rhythm. He further enlivens a meandering asymmetrical silver framework with elegant patterns of line and color. Negative space is contrasted with flat, decorative surfaces of blue and green enamel, curvilinear designs, and a round bead of lapis lazuli.

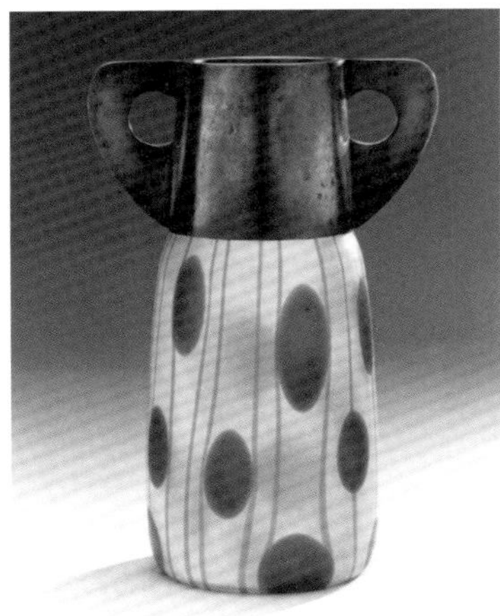

35. Koloman Moser (Austrian, 1868–1918), glass designer; **Jutta Sika** (Austrian, 1877–1964), mount designer; executed by Johann Loetz Witwe
Vase, ca. 1905
Silver-plated brass mounts, white and blue glass, H. 9 1/4 in. (23.5 cm); diam. 4 1/8 in. (10.4 cm); handle width 6 1/4 in. (15.9 cm)
K.99.48

As a professor at the Vienna Applied Arts School, Moser began around 1900 to design porcelain coffee and tea services with his students, including Jutta Sika and Therese Trethahn. Moser and Sika collaborated on this silver and glass vase, which draws on the clean, reductive shapes of their tea and coffee vessels, particularly in the use of flat, triangular handles pierced by a circle. The body has an ornamental pattern of blue circles framed between vertical lines on a contrasting white background. This decorative motif appeared as early as 1900 in other vases by Moser that similarly incorporate his taste for simple, geometric shapes.

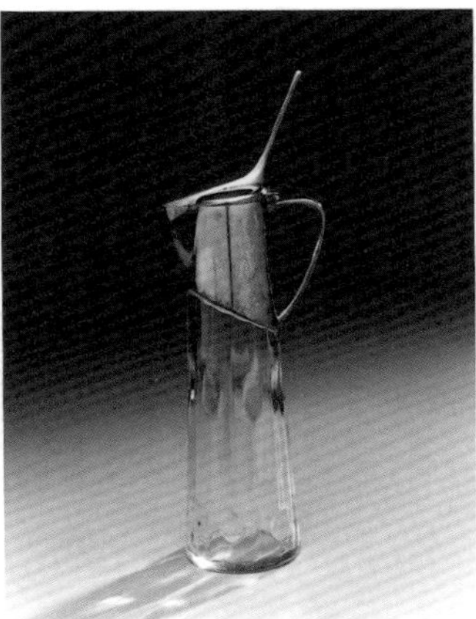

36. Koloman Moser (Austrian, 1868–1918), designer; executed by E. Bakalowits & Söhne
Pitcher (*Krug*), ca. 1905
Hand-wrought silver, glass, 8 13/16 x 3 3/8 x 2 1/4 in. (22.4 x 8.5 x 5.7 cm)
K.99.41

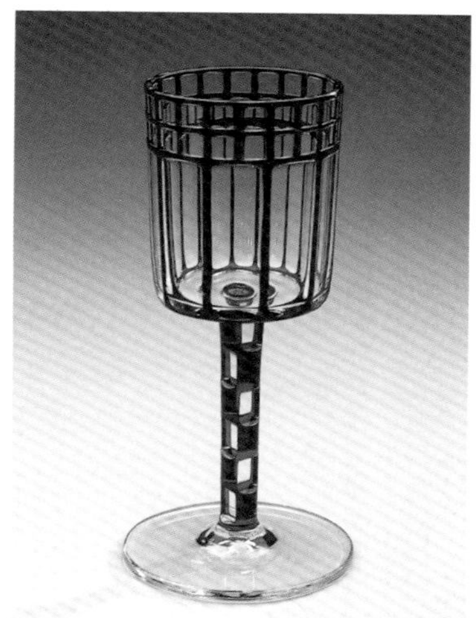

37. Otto Prutscher (Austrian, 1880–1949), designer; executed by Meyr's Neffe
Whiskey Glass, ca. 1907
Clear and blue glass, H. 6 1/4 in. (15.9 x 7.8 cm)
K.2000.12; see Color Plate 8

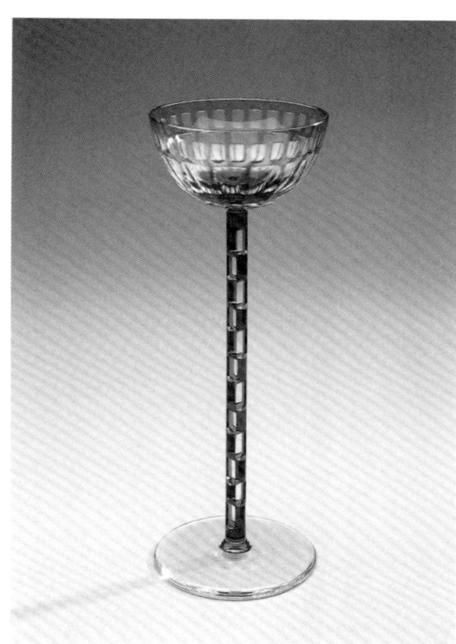

38. Otto Prutscher (Austrian, 1880–1949), designer; executed by Meyr's Neffe
Wine Goblet, ca. 1907
Clear glass, wheel-cut pink glass overlay, 8 3/16 x 3 1/4 in. (20.8 x 8.3 cm)
K.2002.7; see Color Plate 9

Hallmarks of Austrian Jugendstil, such as the taste for abstract, cubic, and rectilinear forms, emerged in the 1890s. These characteristics derived from the progressive architectural designs of Otto Wagner. His students such as Josef Olbrich and Josef Hoffmann later assimilated these qualities in their work, as did many of Hoffmann's students at the Applied Arts School in Vienna.

Otto Prutscher, who studied and in 1910 became a professor at the school, designed bold, architectonic works of cut glass for the Wiener Werkstätte. His whiskey glass and wine goblet synthesize the Bohemian technique of colored and cut glass, the classic and robust forms of early nineteenth-century Biedermeier glassware in an elegant, three-dimensional rendering of Hoffmann's *Quadratstil*.

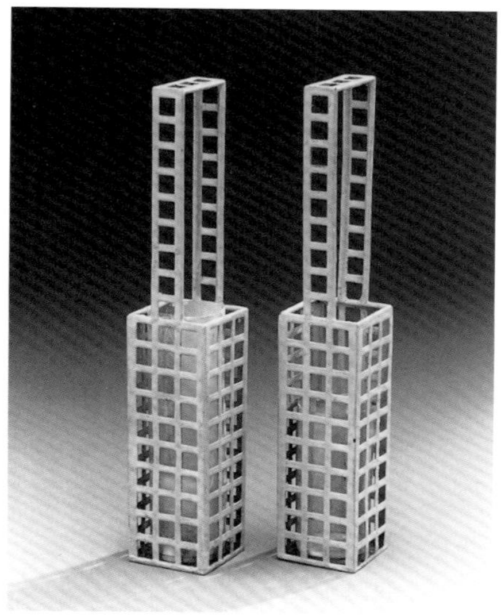

39. Josef Hoffmann (Austrian, 1870–1956), designer
Pair of "Skyscraper" Bud Vases, 1905–1907
White painted latticework sheet metal, 9 1/4 x 1 3/4 x 1 3/4 in. (23.5 x 4.4 x 4.4 cm) ea.
K.97.5

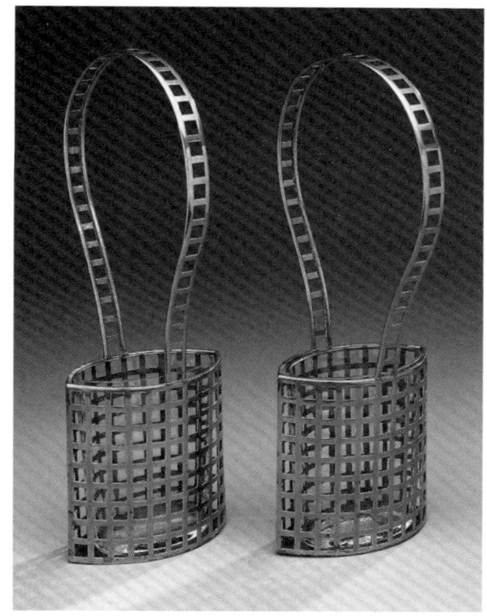

40. Josef Hoffmann (Austrian, 1870–1956), designer; executed by the Wiener Werkstätte
Pair of *Gitterwerk* Baskets, ca. 1906
Silverplate with original glass liners, 9 7/8 x 3 5/8 x 4 3/4 in. (at handle) (25.7 x 9.0 x 12.1 cm)
Punched bottom of base: WW and Rosemark)
K.99.49; see Color Plate 10

Hoffmann's architectural *Quadratstil* designs became a signature element of his early geometric style. His interest in the reductive decorative motif of the square was probably inspired by the work of Scottish architect Charles Rennie Mackintosh. Hoffmann and Moser met Mackintosh in 1900 at the Vienna Secession's eighth exhibition, which displayed works by the Glasgow Four. Subsequent contact between the two groups was quite close, and the influence on each other's work seems to have been mutual. Hoffmann, for instance, incorporated the square motif into the façade of the Purkersdorf Sanatorium; it also appeared in the building's furniture and furnishings and was used in later works as well.

Of the metal works issued by the Wiener Werkstätte, flatware, small vessels and boxes, and *Gitterwerk* (latticework) were the leading products. Hoffmann's original *Gitterwerk* designs were intended for more affordable distribution and, like these painted bud vases, were made of sheet metal finished with white lacquer. Around 1906 Hoffmann also began to produce similar pieces in silver, exemplified by the pair of mandala-shaped baskets. *Gitterwerk* was also used in the design of other domestic items such as candleholders, trays, storm lamps, cruet holders, and plant stands. These pieces appeared both in silver plate and white-painted finishes.

A variety of works for the domestic interior appeared in the October 1906 exhibition, *The Laid Table*. The exhibition inaugurated a new Wiener Werkstätte showroom that had opened at the Neustiftgasse premises in the summer. Moreover, it also exhibited some sixty different table settings produced by the institution. The main concept behind the design of such objects for everyday use was the integration of aesthetics and practicality. The works displayed an array of decorative elements, could be variously coordinated, and, according to one contemporary assessment, were simultaneously "ornamental, elegant, and sensible."[19]

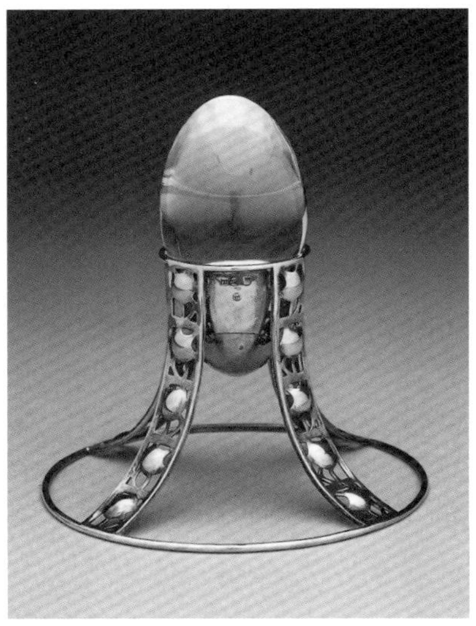

41. Josef Hoffmann (Austrian, 1870–1956), designer;
Adolf Wertnik, silversmith
Ivy Pattern Eggcup, ca. 1910
Reticulated silver, 2 7/8 x 4 5/8 in. (7.3 x 11.7 cm)
Stamps on side of egg cup: JH monogram, WW monogram, WW Rosemark, AW monogram, Vienna 800 silver assay mark
K.99.42; see Color Plate 11

The ivy pattern used for this eggcup is a variant of Hoffmann's *Gitterwerk* that incorporates stylized plants or flowers.

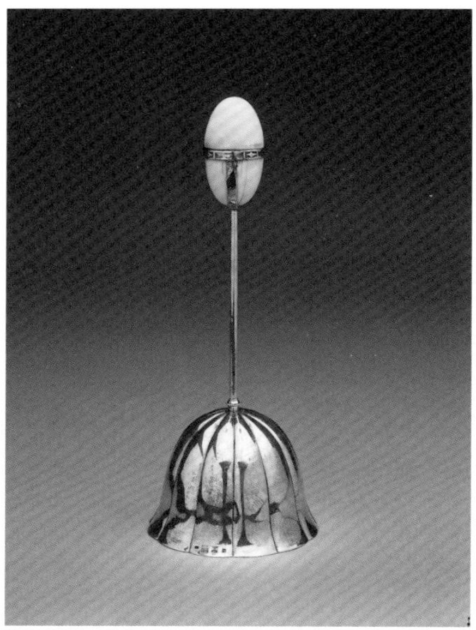

42. Josef Hoffmann (Austrian, 1870–1956), designer;
executed by the Wiener Werkstätte
Dinner Bell, ca. 1910
Silver, ivory, 8 7/16 x 3 9/16 in. (21.5 x 9.1 cm)
Stamped on rim of bell: 900/ WIENER / WERK / STÄTTE in a square; MADE / IN / AUSTRIA in a square; and JH monogram
K.2001.8; see Color Plate 12

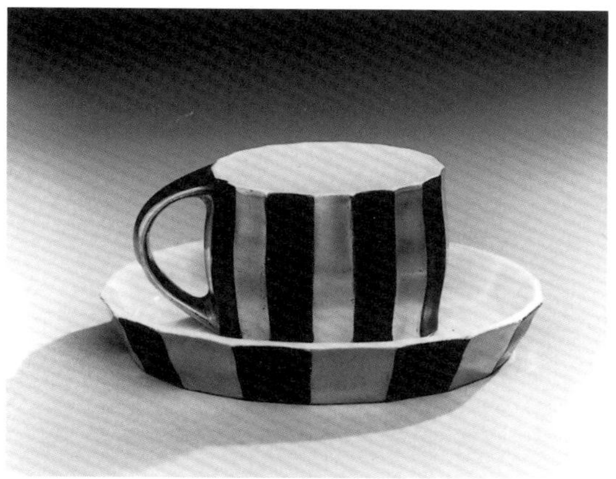

43. Josef Hoffmann (Austrian, 1870–1956), designer; executed by Pfeiffer & Löwenstein
Cup and Saucer, ca. 1910
Hand-painted porcelain, cup: Diam. 1 5/8 in. (4.1 cm); saucer: Diam. 4 1/2 in. (11.43 cm)
Logos on bottom of cup and of saucer: W.P.M. / JOS. BÖCK / WIEN in brown glaze within rectangle of brown squares; IMPERIAL / PSL in green glaze with brown in center
K.99.44

This cup and saucer are part of a standard coffee-service designed by Hoffmann. The completed services were decorated in a variety of simple geometric, black and gold patterns.

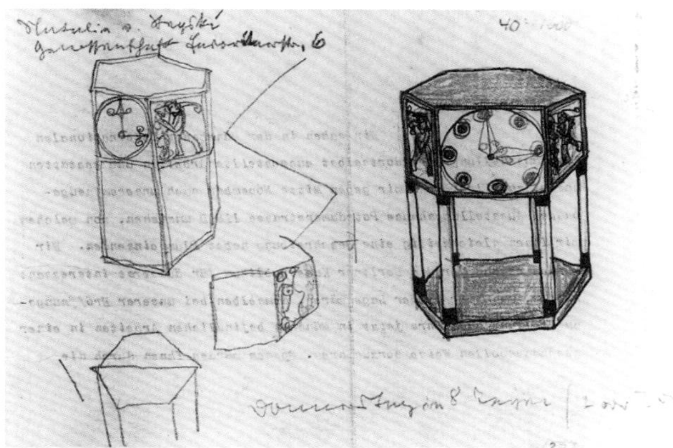

44. Bertold Löffler (Austrian, 1874–1960)
Design for Clock, n.d.
Black ink and graphite with yellow, blue, and brown crayons, 5 1/2 x 8 13/16 in. (14.0 x 22.4 cm)
Graphite upper right: 40-1600, graphite upper left: Natalia V. Reyski Genossenschaft [cooperative] Favoritenstr. 6
K.94.2

Bertold Löffler's association with the Wiener Werkstätte is perhaps best represented by his work in the area of ceramics. He and Michael Powolny contributed ceramic decorations to the Cabaret Fledermaus in Vienna and the Palais Stoclet in Brussels and in 1906 founded the Wiener Keramik. Löffler's undated clock design was possibly intended for use as a *Tischuhr*, or table clock. On the reverse of Löffler's design appears a typed, unaddressed letter from a Berlin official asking for works exhibited in Munich to be lent to a new exhibition hall on Potsdamer Strasse in Berlin. The typeface is visible through the paper.

The face of the relatively small clock is set in a hexagonal pedestal supported by an open base. To each lateral side of the central clock façade is a decorative panel with a figural motif. Although the size of the design makes it difficult to identify these figures clearly, their youthful proportions suggest they bear a similarity to Löffler's and Powolny's well-known ceramic putti. These chubby three-dimensional figurines often represent allegories of the year's various seasons, and for the clock panels they may have been intended to function on a similar symbolic level.

C. *Applied Arts, 1920–1938*

Around 1905 to 1906, Wiener Werkstätte designs began to depart from the purist geometric and rectilinear forms. In turn, they incorporated a greater degree of floral and vegetal ornamentation, although this is still stylized and abstract. The often *völkisch* quality that appears in the work of this period derived from ethnic and peasant sources from around the Austro-Hungarian Empire as well as from an interest in the naïveté of children's art.

On a more abstract level, the work of the Vienna Secession and the Wiener Werkstätte purist phase echoed the state-supported emphasis on developing an international style of modern cultural expression. This was motivated to an extent by a desire to assert Austria's cultural authority within an international arena, and in an attempt to surpass issues of ethnic differentiation and the rising potential for conflict. In contrast, by assimilating various ethnic forms of expression, the later, postpurist stylistic phase appears to embrace the plurality of national identities that comprised the Austro-Hungarian Empire by adapting regional aesthetic characteristics.[20] This stylistic shift, however, did have significant consequences. In particular it led to the international perception that Austria was no longer a progressive modern design force, but rather increasingly ideologically regressive and unresponsive to contemporary sociocultural concerns.

Around 1915, after Dagobert Peche joined the Wiener Werkstätte and assumed a prominent position along with Hoffmann, designs in general took on more voluptuous character and shape. Peche's work in particular eschewed an interest in practicality all together and instead celebrated a more expressionistic style characterized by attenuated, whimsically sculptural forms.

With the founding of the Wiener Keramik by Löffler and Powolny in 1906, this more ornamental style gained additional ground. The Wiener Werkstätte began distributing the Keramik's works in the following year and also commissioned them to produce tiles and mosaics for the Cabaret Fledermaus as well as other residential projects such as the Palais Stoclet. The Wiener Werkstätte began producing its own ceramics in 1917. This late start resulted from on-going financial difficulties and poor political and economic conditions during the war. Many of the figurines and other ceramic wares executed during this period are charming, capricious, and at times even gaudy. They often also display a rougher finish and include a greater degree of ornamental decoration and natural motifs, generally posing a strikingly fanciful contrast to the stately sophistication of the earlier designs.

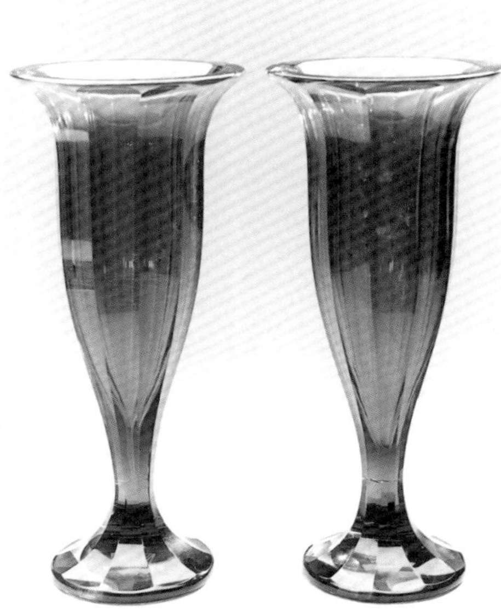

45. Josef Hoffmann (Austrian, 1870–1956), designer;
executed by Ludwig Moser & Söhne for the Wiener Werkstätte
Pair of Paneled Glass Vases, ca. 1920
Cut cobalt glass, 12 1/2 x 5 9/15 in. (31.8 x 14.2 cm)
Acid-etched in square on base: WW
K.2001.7

With this pair of paneled vases, Hoffmann, like Otto Prutscher (see cat. no. 37), draws on the tradition of Bohemian colored and cut glass. The regularly patterned design of the tall, elegant vessels and the stress on linearity has an affinity with Hoffmann's earlier geometric style. The deep blue color of the glass also lends a cool, rational sensibility to the design. In contrast, however, the rounded, swelling profile of the vases indicates the sensuous character of his designs beginning around 1915.

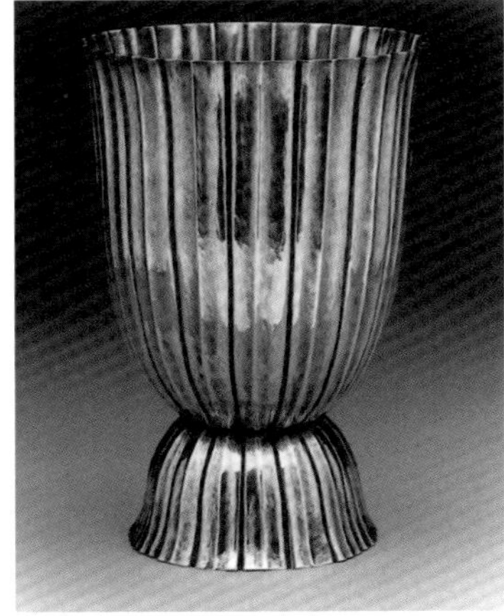

46. Josef Hoffmann (Austrian, 1870–1956), designer;
executed by the Wiener Werkstätte
Fluted Vase, ca. 1920
Hand-wrought, silver gilt alpaka (nickel, zinc, and tin),
7 1/2 x 5 1/2 in. (19.0 x 13.5 cm)
Stamped on foot: encircled JW, Rosemark, WW, JH
K.2000.5

Like Hoffmann's cobalt paneled vases, the sinuous shape of this fluted vase made of alpaka—a combination of nickel, zinc, and tin—reflects his turn toward more feminine and baroque designs during the interwar period.

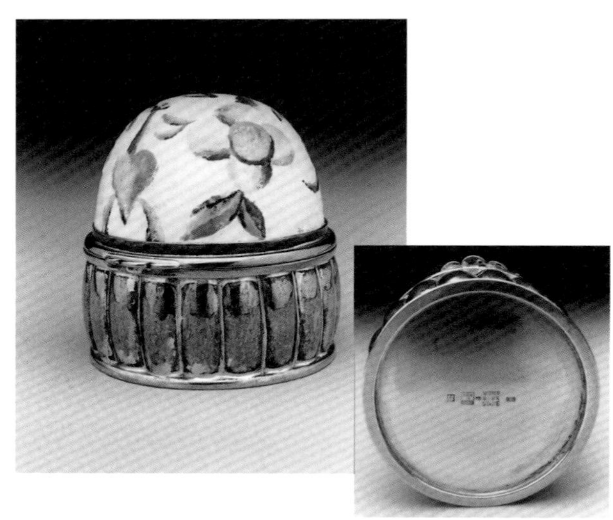

47. Felice Rix-Ueno (Austrian, 1893–1967), designer;
executed by the Wiener Werkstätte
Covered Box, ca. 1920
Hand-wrought silver, polychrome enamel, silver foil,
2 1/4 x 2 1/4 in. (5.7 x 5.7 cm)
Stamped on base: FR, 900, WIENER WERKSTÄTTE, MADE IN AUSTRIA; hand painted in cartouche under lid: WW
K.99.43; see Color Plate 13

This charming small box, perhaps meant for a woman's vanity table, combines a silver base and spherical ceramic cover. Whimsical hand-painted motifs, such as flowers and hearts, in predominantly pastel colors, enliven the otherwise smooth white surface of the cover. The hand-crafted style of the motifs and the somewhat rough, crude, expressionist manner in which they are applied are typical of Wiener Werkstätte design after Dagobert Peche assumed a prominent design role along side Josef Hoffmann.

In addition to the Wiener Werkstätte and artist monogram impressions stamped on the bottom of the box, Rix-Ueno painted a small blue and pinkish-purple square on the inside of the cover that enclosed the workshop's initials, "WW."[21]

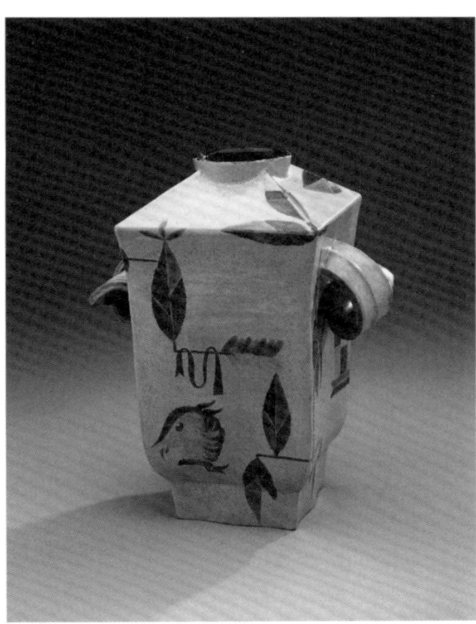

48. Hilda Jesser-Schmidt (Austrian, 1894–1985), designer; executed by the Wiener Werkstätte
Vase with Handles, ca. 1921
Hand-painted earthenware, 9 1/4 x 7 1/4 in. (with handles): diam. 5 1/8 in. (23.5 x 18.5 x 13.0 cm)
Stamped on bottom: WW / Austria / 874
K.2000.7; see Color Plate 14

Hilda Jesser-Schmidt studied with Oskar Strnad and Josef Hoffmann at the Applied Arts School before joining the Wiener Werkstätte in 1916. Later in 1922, she became an instructor at the school, a position she held for forty-four years. Her training was closely tied with Hoffmann and the school rather than with the ceramic workshops of Powolny and Löffler. According to Jesser-Schmidt's own account, her broad-ranging work includes designs for embroidery, fabric, tapestries, and decoration for etched and painted glass, porcelain, leather goods, and commercial graphics. She also produced ceramic work and painted furniture and wooden boxes with her own designs.[22]

Jesser-Schmidt's ceramic designs, including this vase with handles, are closely linked with the painterly decoration of her fabrics and tapestries. They also exhibit a taste for oriental motifs, such as exotic flora and fauna. On a formal level, this oriental sensibility takes on an angular, art deco quality seen in four-sided vessels with stepped, folded, or sharply creased corners and playful, curving handles. In this work, the form of the vase evokes the shape of Japanese paper lanterns. Its decoration combines a speckled ground that suggests the texture of raw silk painted with fanciful plant and animal motifs.

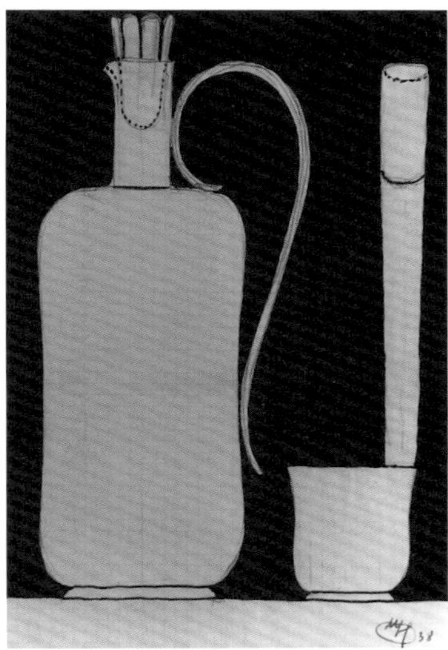

49. Josef Hoffmann (Austrian, 1870–1956)
Design for Decanter and Ladle, 1938
India ink over graphite, image 10 5/16 x 7 3/16 in. (26.3 x 18.3 cm); sheet 13 7/16 x 8 1/4 in. (34.2 x 21.1 cm)
Encircled monogram in brown ink lower right, dated: JH 38
K.91.1

This decanter and ladle were probably meant to be produced in glass or in metal, the material that comprises the greatest volume of Hoffmann's output. The date of the design, 1938, indicates that it appeared after the Wiener Werkstätte closed its doors in 1932. Stylistically it bears the hallmarks of Hoffmann's late design phase, such as the fluid, swelling forms apparent in the curved handle and sloping shoulders of the decanter. The classicizing and somewhat biomorphic character of the design also recalls the style of art deco.

D. Textile and Fashion Design

Textile and fashion design were other significant areas in the Viennese realization of an architectural environment as a *Gesamtkunstwerk*. As designers thoroughly coordinated interior spaces and envisioned the consumer—especially women as arbiters of domestic taste—as an integral component in a unified work of art, forays into textile and fashion design were logical extensions of their aspirations. Already around 1900, the Viennese textile manufacturer Johann Backhausen & Söhne (est. 1849) produced Vienna Secession designs by Hoffmann and

Moser.[23] The prominent Secession painter Gustav Klimt also designed women's robelike garments for the fashion salon owned by his companion, Emilie Flöge, and her sisters Pauline and Helene. Along with fashion design, the modern Viennese textiles produced by the Applied Arts School, various workshops, and manufacturers included patterned fabrics, tapestries, upholstery, lacework, and embroidery. They also generated a whole range of related accessories such as hats, fur goods, jewelry, enamels, artificial flowers, batik, shoes, and leather goods.[24]

On the heels of the Wiener Werkstätte's founding of a textile division around 1909–10 came the opening of the fashion department, which was one of the most prominent means to distribute fashion design. The opening officially took place around 1911, although in all likelihood, design and production had begun well before this date.[25] The first Wiener Werkstätte salon opened in the resort city of Karlsbad under the direction of Eduard Wimmer-Wisgrill, and other branches were added later. In addition to the Viennese showrooms for fashion and textiles that were added in 1916 and 1917, the group opened branches in Marienbad and Zurich in 1917, New York in 1921, Velden in 1922, and Berlin in 1929.[26]

The Kaerwer Collection includes textile and fashion designs in a range of media and stages of realization. Among these are drawings for textile patterns, lacework, finished textiles, postcards based on textile designs, and fashion design illustrations. The linocut fashion plates from *Mode Wien 1914–15* (Vienna Fashion) represent the style of garments advanced during the fashion department's early experimental phase.

The Austrian fashions of this period sought to develop a distinct Viennese look and also assimilated a number of contemporary trends such as the reform dress, a taste for the oriental, and the work of the French fashion designer Paul Poiret. Beyond the loose, empire-waist dress and the harem pant, what most characterizes the "new Viennese dress" is an adaptation of fashions from the late nineteenth century. Typical of this retrospective trend are long, voluminous dresses, swinging skirts, and charming, often stately, feminine silhouettes that emphasize an hourglass shape.

In contrast, the textile samples exhibit some of the more progressive forms of Austrian modern design. Spanning the years 1911 to 1931, their patterns range from the peasant-style floral pieces of Peche to the dynamic combinations of bold, abstract forms and striking colors in the designs of Maria Likarz-Strauss, Felice Rix-Ueno, Mathilde Flögl, and Clara Posnansky.

Seen in a broader context, this Viennese interest in fashion and other small decorative media announced more ephemeral, even trivial manifestations of artistic conception in contrast to the type of monumental presentations possible in such traditional fine arts as architecture and painting. Indeed, the tendency of Wiener Werkstätte works toward frivolity received increasingly critical attention, particularly in later years, when its products appeared especially out of tune with the times.[27] Nevertheless, in bringing art to these most intimate levels of life, Viennese designers and craftspeople managed to generate not only a desire for their products, but also to disseminate an all-encompassing taste for an aesthetic way of living.

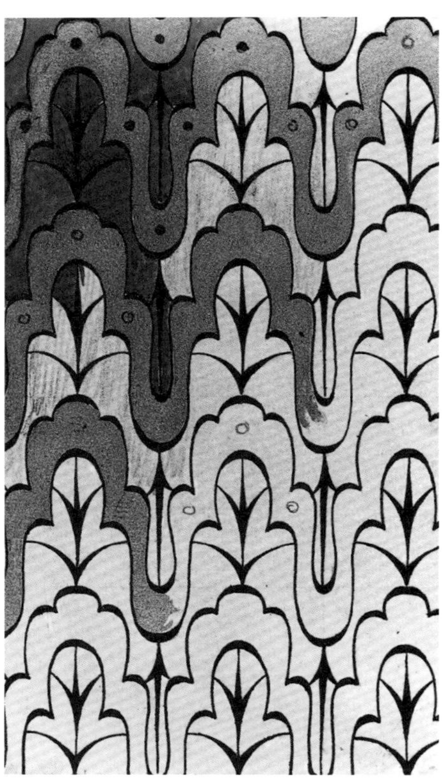

50. Karl Krenek (Austrian, 1880–1948)
Pattern with Silver and Red, n.d.
Black ink and watercolor, 6 3/4 x 3 7/8 in. (17.0 x 9.8 cm)
K.94.1

This pattern designed by Karl Krenek is undated although it is possible that he produced it as early as 1896–1898, when he studied at the Royal Educational Establishment for the Textile Industry (*königliche und kaiserliche Lehranstalt für Textilindustrie*). From 1898 to 1906 he studied at the Applied Arts School in Vienna and later at the Academy of Fine Arts. The bold patterning and crisp, bright colors of red and silver suggest heraldic forms contrasted with stylized plantlike motifs in black.

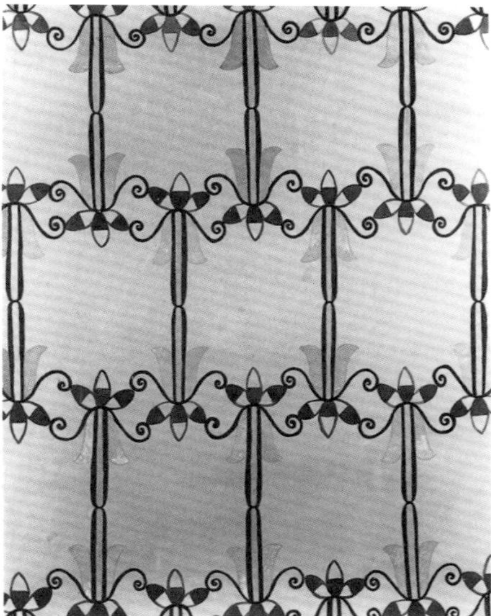

51. Artist unknown, Wiener Werkstätte
Pattern for a textile, n.d.
Pen and india ink, with lavender, green, and yellow gouache, 22 5/8 x 19 3/8 in. (57.9 x 49.4 cm)
Labels on mount read: K9006. Design for fabric no. 38. Wiener Werkstätte and no./ O 38
K.2000.9

With the establishment of its textile division in 1909, the Wiener Werkstätte produced hand-printed and painted fabrics. These were mostly of silk, although also included cotton, voile, linen, and woven fabrics.

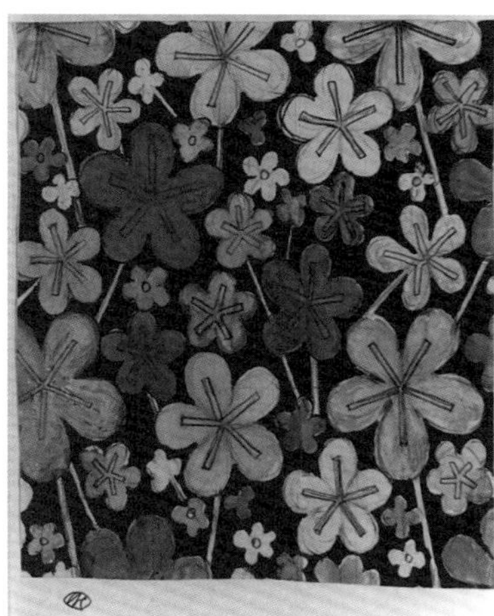

52. Josef Hoffmann (Austrian, 1870–1956)
Design for Fabric, ca. 1920
Watercolor and graphite, image 9 3/8 x 8 in. (23.8 x 20.3 cm) (irreg.); sheet 11 11/16 x 8 1/4 in. (29.7 x 20.9 cm)
Lower left on white sheet: encircled initials in blue ink
K.99.2

As we see in other applied arts by Hoffmann, this work reflects his turn away from the purist Wiener Werkstätte style around 1906 and toward more floral, though nonetheless still abstracted, ornamental imagery.

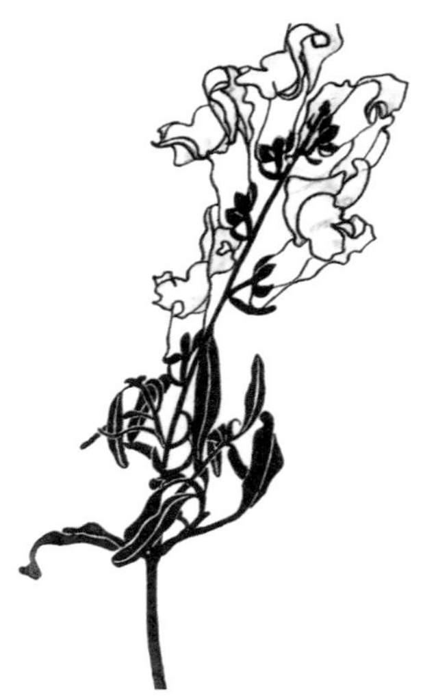

53. Angela Piotrowska-Wittmann (Austrian, 1898–1934 or after)
Snapdragon, n.d.
Black ink, watercolor, and graphite, 8 5/8 x 6 5/8 in. (22.0 x 17.0 cm)
Signed lower right in graphite: A. Piotrowska
K.94.3

Angela Piotrowska-Wittmann trained at the Art School for Women and Girls and later, from 1914 to 1921 studied at the Applied Arts School in Vienna. She produced textiles for the Wiener Werkstätte and also formed the workshop "Piowitt" with Michael Wittmann and became a ceramic decorator. Block-printed textile designs by Piotrowska appeared around 1914–1915. *Snapdragon*, which is more a watercolor study than specifically related to textile or ceramic design, likely also dates from around 1915 or later.

Similar to the style of Emilie Wodraschka's Three Christmas Postcards (see cat. 24), *Snapdragon* is rendered in a reductive realistic style. Piotrowska-Wittmann's flower vertically dominates the clean expanse of the white ground, and its slight diagonal curve to the right enlivens the composition. Although the fundamental forms of the flower are retained, Piotrowska-Wittmann limits her colors to a flat, deep orange and warm yellow for the petals and complements these with a dense black for the foliage. The petals' graphic outline and unmodulated colors emphasize the *Snapdragon*'s flat, two-dimensionality and the elegant rhythm of curving forms.

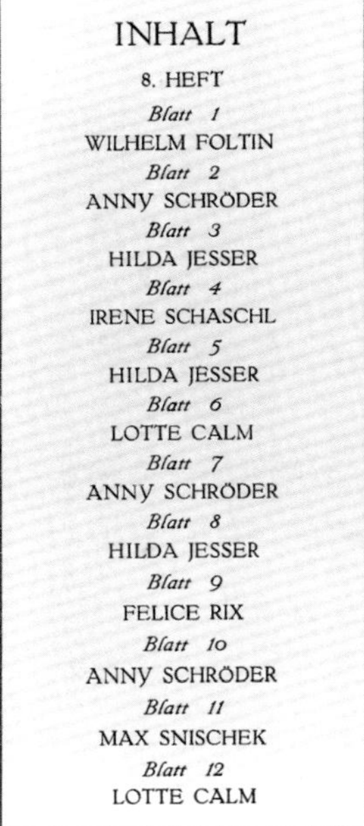
INHALT
8. HEFT
Blatt 1
WILHELM FOLTIN
Blatt 2
ANNY SCHRÖDER
Blatt 3
HILDA JESSER
Blatt 4
IRENE SCHASCHL
Blatt 5
HILDA JESSER
Blatt 6
LOTTE CALM
Blatt 7
ANNY SCHRÖDER
Blatt 8
HILDA JESSER
Blatt 9
FELICE RIX
Blatt 10
ANNY SCHRÖDER
Blatt 11
MAX SNISCHEK
Blatt 12
LOTTE CALM

54. Wiener Werkstätte, Various Artists,
Table of contents from *Vienna Fashion* (*Mode Wien*) no. 8, 1914–1915
Portfolio of hand-colored linocuts (includes 7 of the 12 original prints), gold leaf liner, 12 1/8 x 9 in. (30.8 x 22.8 cm)
K.99.47

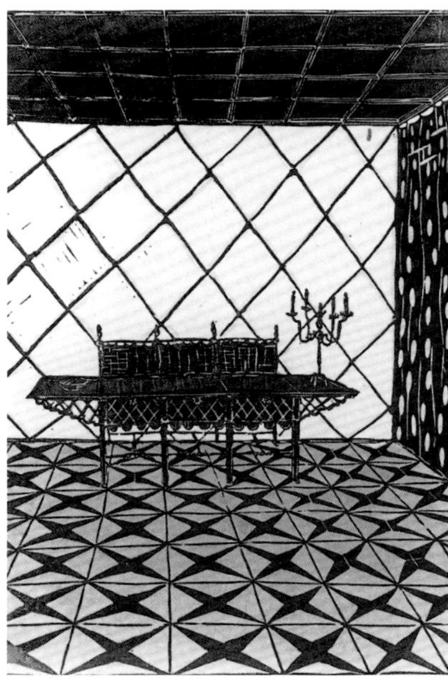

55. Wilhelm Foltin (Austrian, 1890–?)
Portfolio Plate 1 from *Vienna Fashion* (*Mode Wien*), no. 8, 1914–1915)
Hand-colored linocut, sheet 11 1/2 x 8 3/8 in. (29.2 x 21.3 cm)
Plate number stamped upper right
K.99.47.1

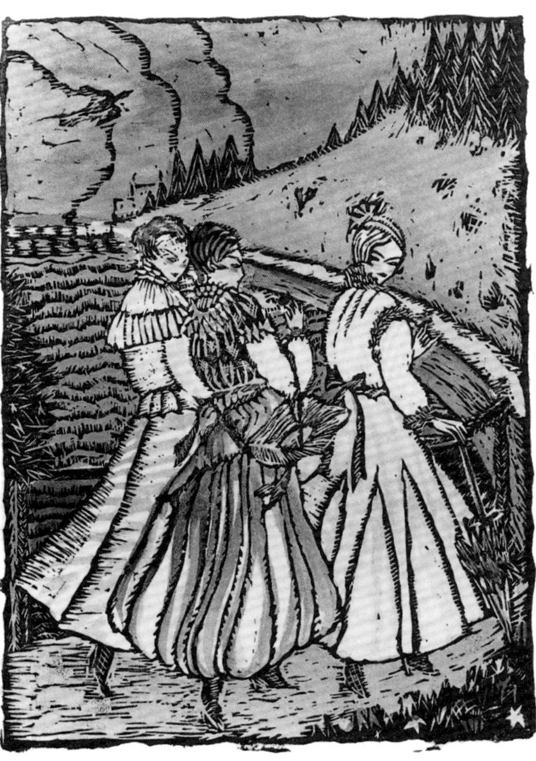

56. Lotte Calm (Austrian, 1897–1927)
Three Women Strolling in a Park, portfolio plate 12 from *Vienna Fashion* (*Mode Wien*), no. 8, 1914–1915
Hand-colored linocut, image 10 x 7 5/16 in. (25.5 x 18.6 cm); sheet 11 1/2 x 8 1/4 in. (29.2 x 20.9 cm)
Inscribed in graphite lower right edge: LOTTE CALM; plate number stamped upper center edge
K.99.50

The years 1911 to 1914 were an experimental phase for the Wiener Werkstätte fashion department during which it worked to establish a distinct Viennese silhouette. The culmination of this development is seen in the *Mode Wien* (Vienna Fashion) fashion plates. This publication was a series of twelve portfolios, each comprised of twelve fashion plates and printed with the title "Mode Wien 1914/15." The illustrations exhibit a range of detail and understanding of garment construction and were intended as primary impressions to be translated into a final garment. These linocut plates are from the eighth portfolio and display a somewhat fuller cut of garment than their French counterparts, particularly in their long dresses and voluminous skirts.

Rejecting the sleek exactness of conventional photography, the linocut medium was a means to approximate the quality of woodcuts, despite its lack of a wood grain texture. Nonetheless, the primitive, folk-art quality suggested by the prints, along with the expressionistic, even crude style of their execution give them a charming, ethnic authenticity that helped characterize the "new Viennese look" of the fashions themselves. Such a distinction was particularly desirable, given the increasingly patriotic outlook and frowned-upon attitude toward foreign fashions on the eve of World War I.

The mostly female artists who produced these illustrations were often students of the Applied Arts School and not trained as fashion designers. Active in various aspects of the applied arts industry, they also, at one time or another, worked for the Wiener Werkstätte.

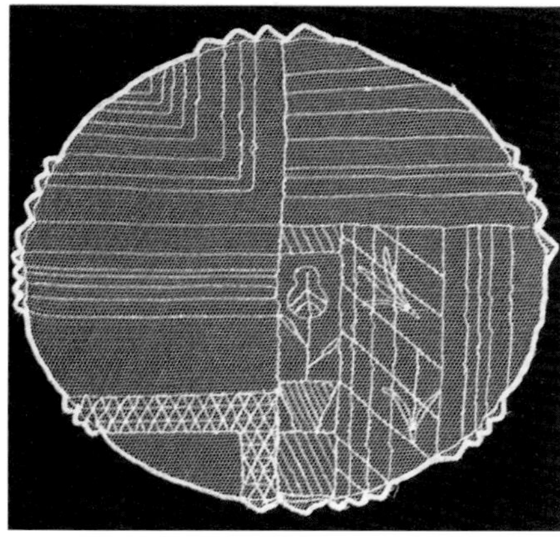

57. Wiener Werkstätte
Embroidered Lacework, ca. 1920s
Fine netting and silk thread, diam. 5 3/4 in. (14.6 cm)
Tag verso: WW/ WIENER/ WERKSTATTE/ no 104/1508/ M 421-25hs/PR
K.97.4

This oval-shaped embroidered lacework is undated, although it probably was made after 1911 when the Wiener Werkstätte textile department began producing lace. The design is dominated by a rectilinear grid structure contrasted by patterns of crosshatching and diagonally running lines. In the lower right quadrant of the oval are a schematically abstracted potted flower and two vegetal motifs. The circular form of the fine-gauge netting complements the slender, consistently ordered lines and geometric patterning, and produces an effect of delicate precision. The oval contour, rectilinear grid structure, delicate lace, and fine, abstract embroidery that fills this piece are similar to Wiener Werkstätte lace designs by Mathilde Flögl that date from 1918.

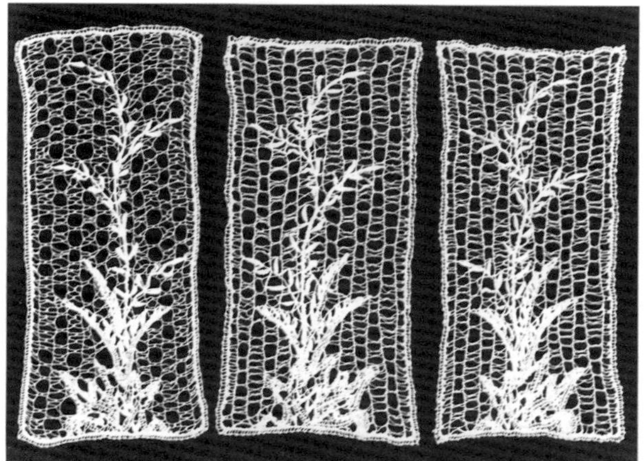

58. Design attributed to Dagobert Peche (Austrian, 1887–1923); Wiener Werkstätte
Three Lace Doilies, ca. 1920
Embroidered heavy lace, approx. 11 1/2 x 5 1/2 in. (29.2 x 14.0 cm) ea. (irreg.)
K.97.3

In contrast to the previous fine and delicate example of Wiener Werkstätte lacework (cat. 57), Dagobert Peche's designs typically use a larger gauge netting and heavier embroidery thread. As in his other decorative works, this group of three rectangular lace pieces incorporates his proclivity for flamboyant, spiky shapes. In this case they are vigorous, arching foliate forms arranged in a triangular composition.

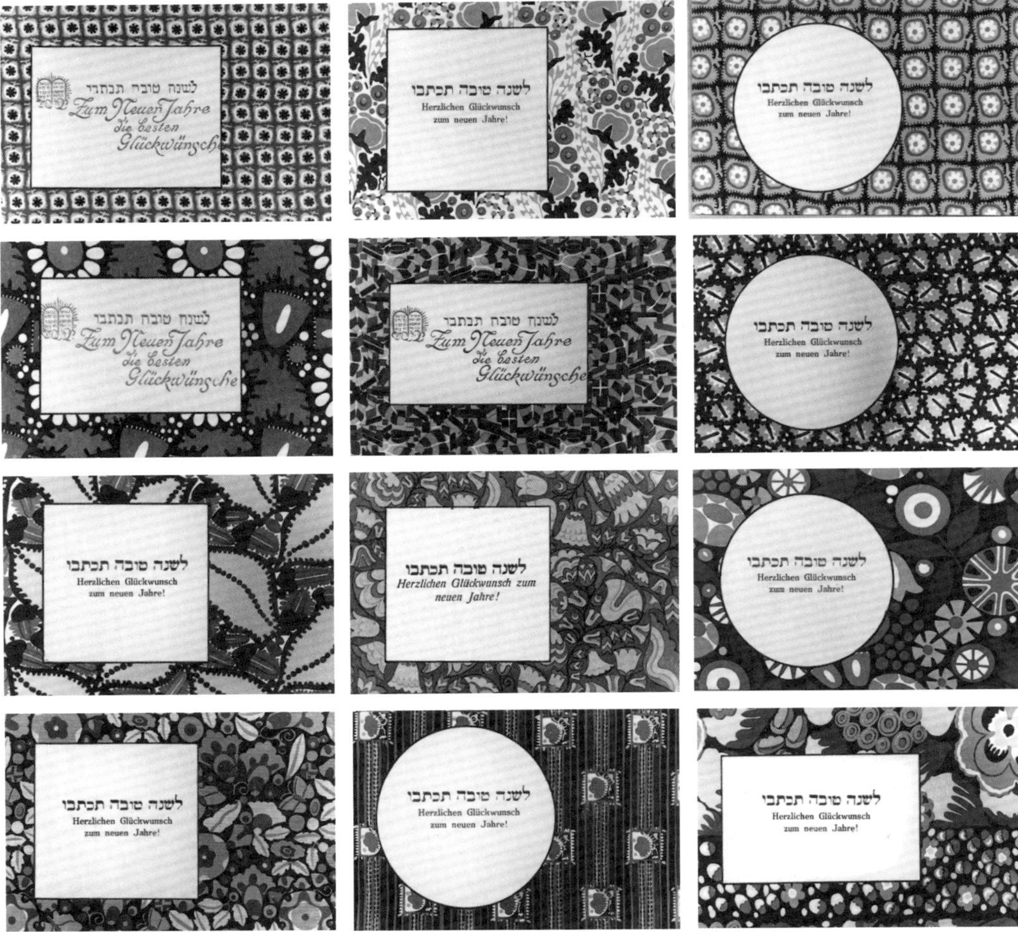

59. Various Wiener Werkstätte Artists
Jewish New Year Post Cards, set of 12, 1910–11
Color-printed cards, ea. 3 1/2 x 5 7/16 in. (8.9 x 13.9 cm)
K.96.15

In this group of works early Wiener Werkstätte textiles were reproduced to make holiday greeting postcards. Each card presents a fabric pattern as a background superimposed with a white rectangle, square, or circle with a Jewish New Year's greeting in Hebrew and German. Among the artists whose designs appear are Carl Otto Czeschka, Wilhelm Jonasch, L. Fochler, Eduard Wimmer-Wisgrill, Karl Riedl, and Martha Alber. The *Lehrlingsheim Zukunft* (Apprentice Home) published the cards through the Brüder Kohn (Kohn Brothers) who were the monarchy's largest postcard printers.[28] It is likely that the Werkstätte put the caché of its textiles and corporate identity at the disposal of the Apprentice Home. The colorful and vibrant designs were highly recognizable and the publishers could have distributed them in large numbers. The source of the fabrics also was indicated clearly on the reverse, which cites the Werkstätte, the name of the fabric designer, and the fabric reproduction. Further underscoring the cultural currency of the Werkstätte's fabrics is Gustav Klimt's 1917–1918 portrait of Johanna Staude in which she wears a dress made of Alber's *Blätter* with its familiar large turquoise leaves and Josef Hoffmann's interior decoration for the Graben Café in Vienna that made ample use of Wilhelm Jonasch's *Krieau* (figure 4).

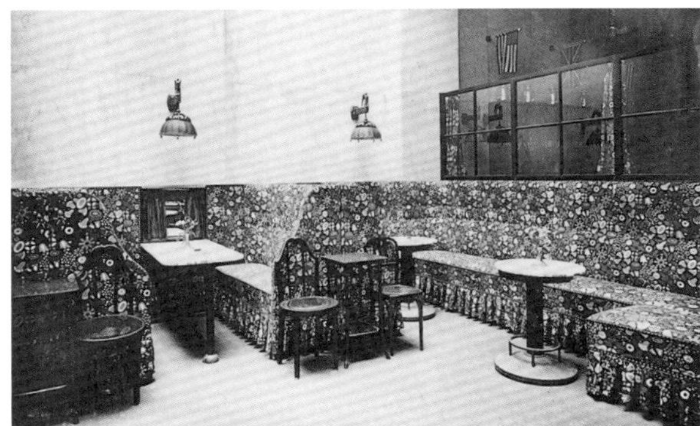

Figure 4. The Graben Café Vienna: interior decoration by Josef Hoffmann, 1912, features upholstery *Krieau*, 1910–1911 by Wilhelm Jonasch. Photograph from Wiener Werkstätte album 105. Photograph courtesy Österreichsches Museum für angewandte Kunst, WWF 105

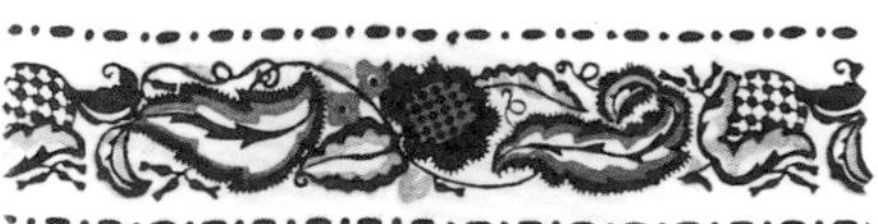

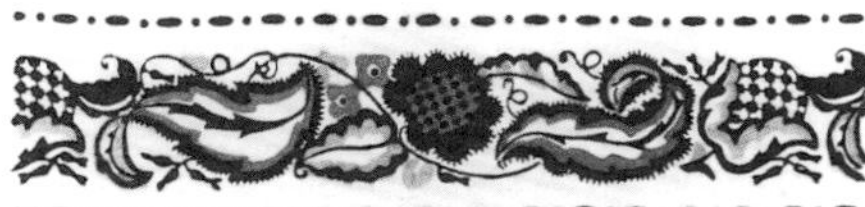

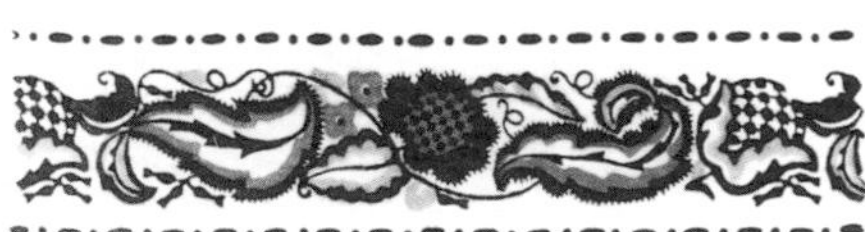

60. Dagobert Peche (Austrian, 1887–1923), designer; Wiener Werkstätte
Freudenau WW #297, 1911–1913
Black, magenta, and blue on white silk, 9 1/4 x 6 5/8 in. (23.5 x 16.8 cm) (irreg.)
WW tag tipped in
K.99.30

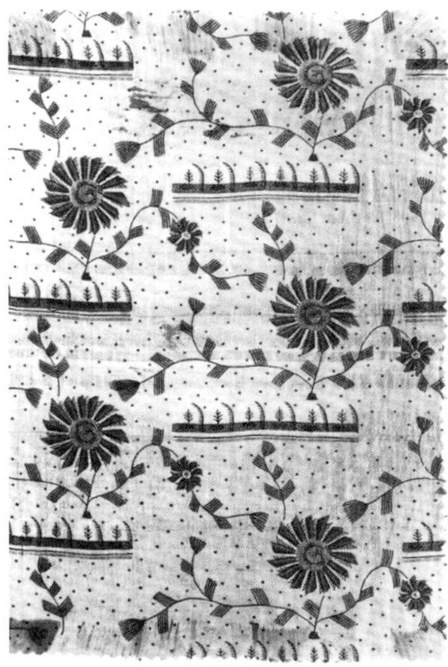

61. Maria Likarz-Strauss (Austrian, 1893–1956), designer; Wiener Werkstätte
Borneo W.W. #805, 1920–1921
Block-printed green silk with orange, pink, and black, 13 5/8 x 9 1/8 in. (34.7 x 23.2 cm) (irreg.)
WW tag tipped inK.99.25

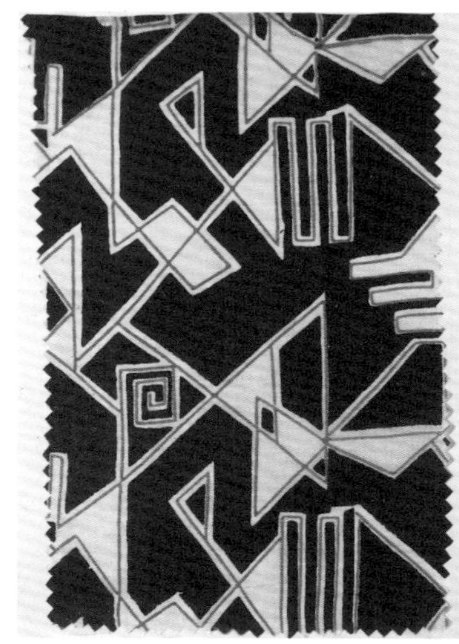

62. Maria Likarz-Strauss (Austrian, 1893–1956), designer; Wiener Werkstätte
Ajax W.W. #911, 1925
Block-printed black and red on white silk, 9 3/4 x 6 3/8 (24.8 x 16.3 cm) (irreg.)
WW tag tipped in
K.99.26; see Color Plate 15

Maria Likarz-Strauss was one of the major textile designers of the Wiener Werkstätte. She trained at the Applied Arts School for Women and Girls from 1908 to 1910 and at the Applied Arts School from 1911 to 1915. She began working for the Wiener Werkstätte in 1912, and in 1922 she and fellow textile and fashion designer Max Snischek ran the fashion division until it closed in 1932.

Likarz-Strauss appears to have contributed textile designs to the Wiener Werkstätte as early as 1912. Her work consistently emphasized abstract, geometric forms, and bright, saturated colors. Whereas many of her colleagues' fabrics of the same period reflect the tendency toward floral and vegetal motifs, Likarz-Strauss's designs clearly stood apart from the outset, anticipating the formal language of the interwar movement that became known as art deco.

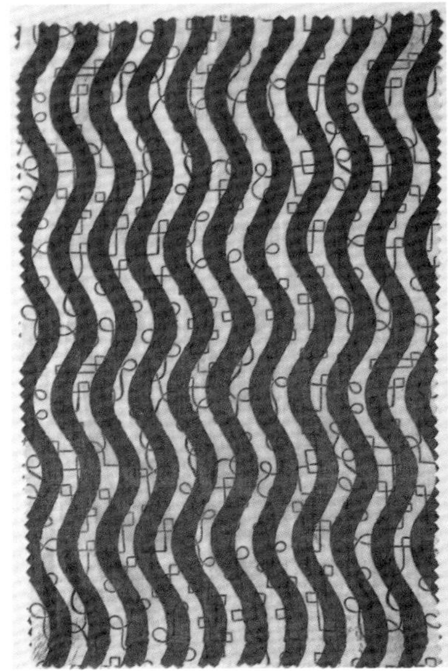

63. Felice Rix-Ueno (Austrian, 1893–1967), designer; Wiener Werkstätte
Biarritz W.W. #883, 6 December 1924
Block-printed blue and black on white silk, 8 1/2 x 5 7/16 in. (21.5 x 13.8 cm) (irreg.)
WW tag tipped in
K.99.31; see Color Plate 16

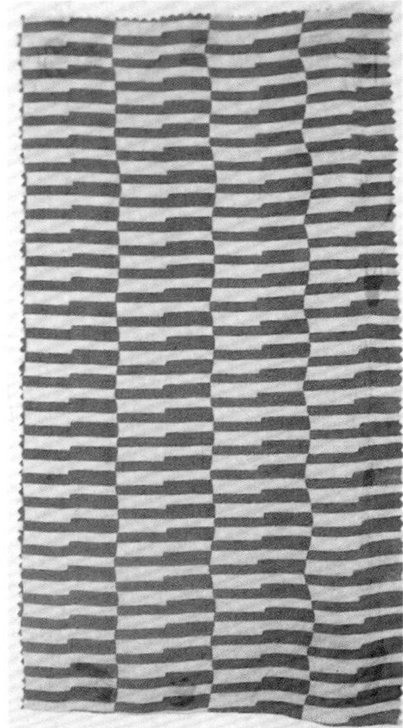

64. Mathilde Flögl (Austrian, 1893–1950), designer; Wiener Werkstätte
Clan W.W. #1007, April 1928
Block-printed red and yellow on crêpe de chine, 14 x 7 5/8 in. (35.5 x 19.3 cm) (irreg.)
WW tag tipped in
K.99.22; see Color Plate 17

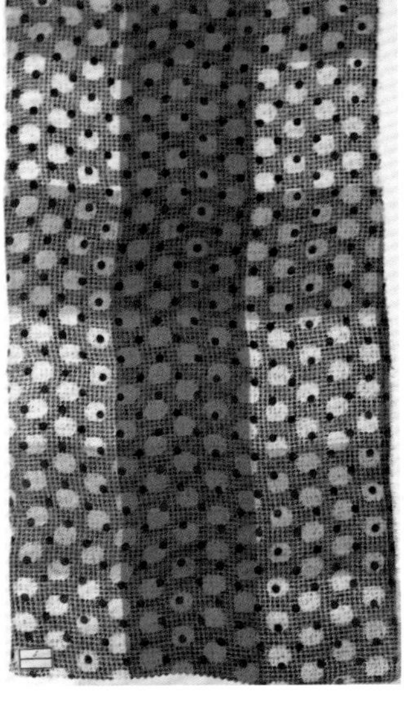

65. Clara Posnansky (Austrian), designer; Wiener Werkstätte
Magnus W.W. #5278, June 1930
Brown, beige, and red on white crêpe de chine, 16 1/8 x 8 5/8 in. (41.1 x 21.9 cm) (irreg.)
WW tag tipped in
K.99.34; see Color Plate 18

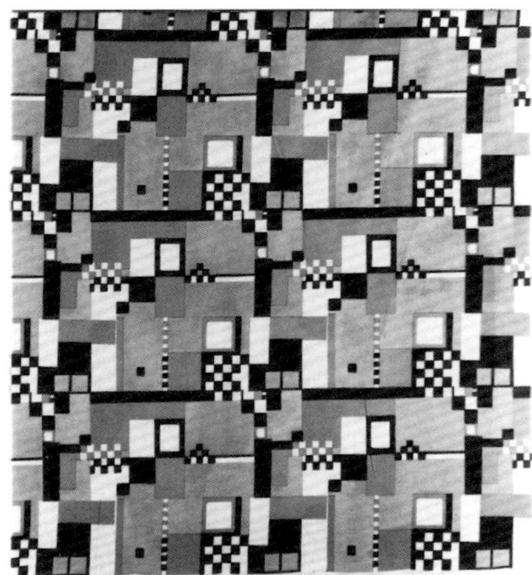

66. Lotte Hahn (Austrian, 1906–?)
Geometric Textile, ca. 1930
Woven cotton, 49 x 77 in. (124.4 x 195.5 cm)
Printed in gray along selvage: WIENER WERKSTÄTTE
K.2000.6

IV. BOOKS, PERIODICALS, PUBLICATIONS

The widely varied published works in this section share two common traits: they were conceived as vehicles to convey written and visual information and designed to be works of art. The Kaerwer collection holds an excellent selection of Viennese publications that range from small ball programs and illustrated children's books to massive histories and lavish collector volumes. These works combine the notion of the *Gesamtkunstwerk* with new printing technologies, theories of graphic design, typography, illustration, a love of book decoration, and a revival of quality bookbinding.

In addition to the improved fin-de-siècle printing technologies that allowed for the combination of image and text on the same page, the element of typography also took on new aesthetic importance. Viennese artists and craftspeople designed their own signature monograms, and ornamental lettering became a carefully integrated element alongside other components of the page such as illustrations and decorative borders. A significant contributor to the art of ornamental lettering was Rudolf von Larisch, professor of typography and heraldry at the Applied Arts School. Larisch published on the subject of typography beginning in 1899 and also developed a theory of graphic composition in which foreground and background were given equal emphasis. He was largely responsible for the development of the Secession's decorative typography and later acted as consultant on matters of lettering for the Wiener Werkstätte. His ideas inspired two generations of Viennese designers, including Koloman Moser and Carl Otto Czeschka.

The Viennese development of the publication as a total work of art had its greatest initial impetus with the Vienna Secession's periodical *Ver Sacrum*. The Wiener Werkstätte further expanded the field, setting up its own letterpress and bookbinding workshop. Their production focused mainly on designing illustrated children's books and limited deluxe editions. The majority of published works presented in this section derives from these two groups and displays a range of purpose, design, and execution. Several other examples demonstrate the production of other contemporary artists and associations active in Vienna.

A. Artist Association Publications

The publications in this section range from periodicals, exhibition catalogues, and histories to a commemorative monograph, produced by or about Viennese art associations and artists during the period from 1900 to 1950. Together, they provide an important overview of the development of Viennese art associations, their aims and activities, and the manner in which they presented themselves to national and international audiences.

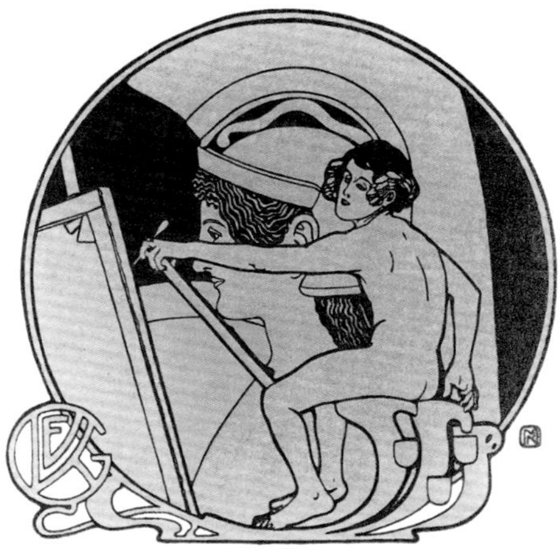

67. Koloman Moser (Austrian, 1868–1918)
Vignette for the *Annual Portfolio of the Society for Reproduction Art (Vignette für die Jahresmappe der Gesellschaft für Vervielfältigende Kunst)*, 1898
Color lithograph, cover for portfolio, 5 5/8 x 5 15/16 in. (14.3 x 15.0 cm)
Lower right, monogram: KM; lower left: GFVK
K.85.12

Moser's 1898 vignette celebrates the graphic reproduction arts as an allegorical hero who thrives under the Society for Reproduction Art's sponsorship. Younger than the traditional arts of architecture, sculpture, and painting, the graphic arts are portrayed as a classical youth who wears a crown of laurel leaves and is protected under the aegis of Pallas Athena, the patron of wisdom and the arts. The young artist appears with burin and metal plate—tools of the graphic arts—and contemplates his reproduction of the painting that stands before him on the left. The image recalls Gustav Klimt's lithograph advertisement for the Secession's first exhibition of the same year. Klimt's Athena is a resolute, even threatening, warrior whose full-length figure appears in the image's foreground, turned in profile to the left. In contrast, Moser depicts Athena as a monumental, bust-length presence that looms behind the figure of the artist like a benign guardian. Moser's stylized monogram of the society (GfVK), which appears in the lower left of the vignette, gives way to tendrils that extend to the right and become a literal support on which the artist sits.

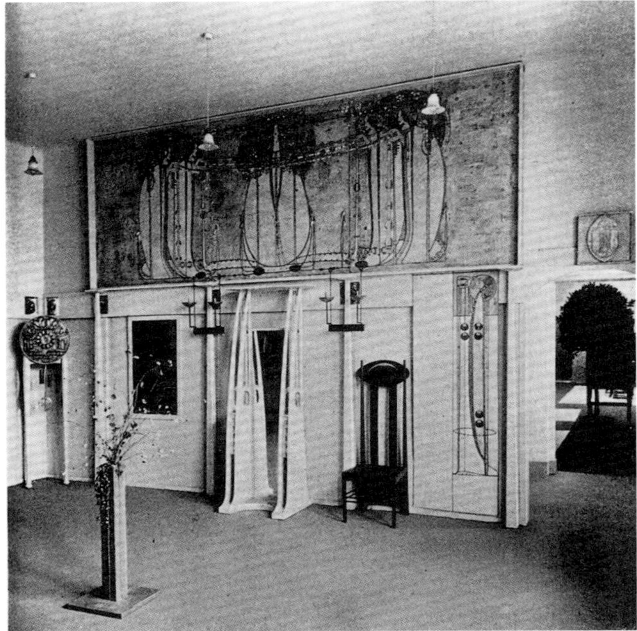

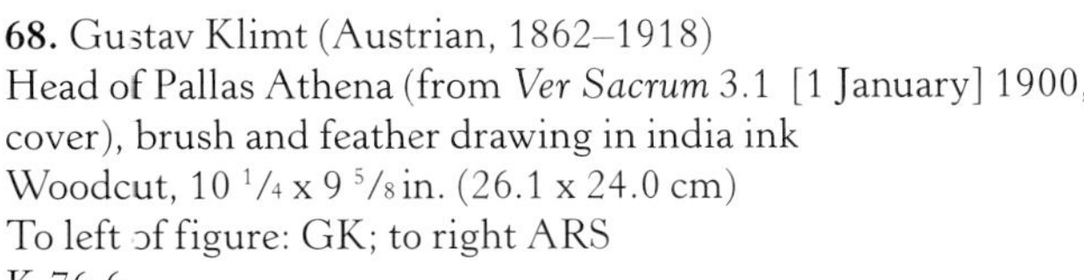

68. Gustav Klimt (Austrian, 1862–1918)
Head of Pallas Athena (from *Ver Sacrum* 3.1 [1 January] 1900, cover), brush and feather drawing in india ink
Woodcut, 10 1/4 x 9 5/8 in. (26.1 x 24.0 cm)
To left of figure: GK; to right ARS
K.76.6

69. Photograph of VIII Vienna Secession Exhibition, Room X showing Charles Rennie Mackintosh and Margaret Macdonald Mackintosh installation (from *Ver Sacrum* 3.24 [15 December 1900]: 385)
Etching, color lithography, woodcuts, 10 1/4 x 9 5/8 in. (26.1 x 24.0 cm) each
K.76.6

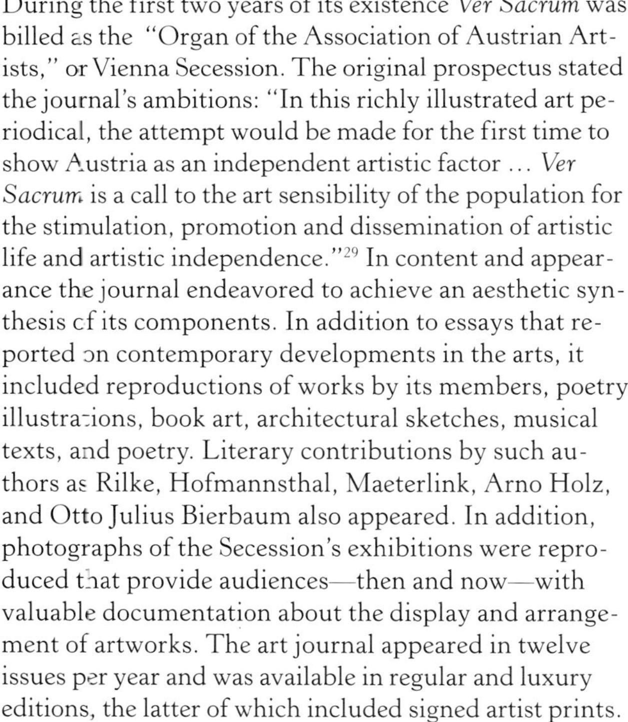

During the first two years of its existence *Ver Sacrum* was billed as the "Organ of the Association of Austrian Artists," or Vienna Secession. The original prospectus stated the journal's ambitions: "In this richly illustrated art periodical, the attempt would be made for the first time to show Austria as an independent artistic factor ... *Ver Sacrum* is a call to the art sensibility of the population for the stimulation, promotion and dissemination of artistic life and artistic independence."[29] In content and appearance the journal endeavored to achieve an aesthetic synthesis of its components. In addition to essays that reported on contemporary developments in the arts, it included reproductions of works by its members, poetry illustrations, book art, architectural sketches, musical texts, and poetry. Literary contributions by such authors as Rilke, Hofmannsthal, Maeterlink, Arno Holz, and Otto Julius Bierbaum also appeared. In addition, photographs of the Secession's exhibitions were reproduced that provide audiences—then and now—with valuable documentation about the display and arrangement of artworks. The art journal appeared in twelve issues per year and was available in regular and luxury editions, the latter of which included signed artist prints.

The year 1900 signaled a change in the periodical's format and, to a certain degree, its aims. Notably, the new title "News of the Association of Austrian Artists" (*Mitteilungen der Vereinigung Bildender Künstler Österreichs*) reflected a different character. An editorial note in the first 1900 issue explained these developments as a response to a desire to make the periodical more frequently available to a greater number of members, to increase its intimate character, and to encourage Secession artists to contribute their views and experiences as frequently as possible.[30] The journal now appeared bimonthly, and its size was reduced from 28.5 x 30 cm to 24 x 26 cm.[31] In place of the previous full-page cover designs often in color, a central vignette was printed on an ivory-colored cover. The cover vignette most often reproduced an image that appeared in the same issue.

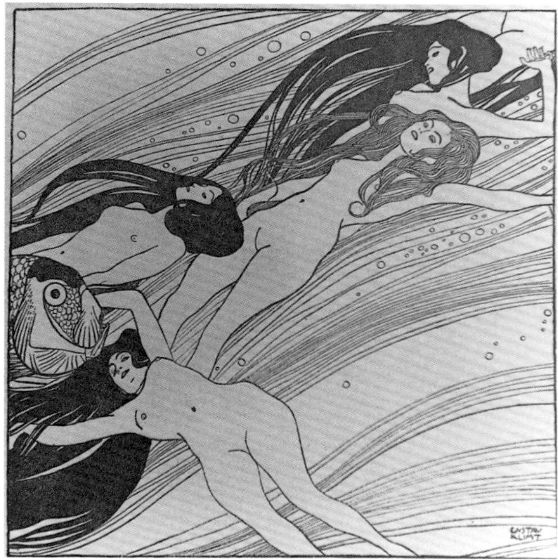

70. Gustav Klimt (Austrian, 1862–1918)
Fish Blood, 1898 (from *Ver Sacrum* 6, special edition [1903]: 53)
Catalogue of the XVIII Vienna Secession Exhibition, November-December, 1903 (Vienna: Druck von Adolf Holzhauser, 1903), 72 pp.
Page, 9 13/16 x 9 5/16 x 5/16 in. (24.9 x 23.7 x 8.0 cm)
K.96.2

Marking Gustav Klimt's status as a leading figure of Viennese modernism and the prominent role he played in the formation of the Vienna Secession, the group mounted a retrospective exhibition of his work in November of 1903. The corresponding issue of *Ver Sacrum* appeared as the exhibition's catalogue. Prior to becoming the Secession's first president in 1897, Klimt had received commissions for decorating public buildings including the Bucharest National Theatre and the Burgtheater and Kunsthistorisches Museum in Vienna. In 1894 he had began work on three allegorical paintings of Philosophy, Medicine, and Jurisprudence for the Aula of the Vienna University. Before these works were displayed together at the 1903 exhibition, they had been celebrated abroad but were the subject of scandal in Vienna for their radically modern style, decidedly pessimistic content, and depiction of nudity.[32]

Along with two of the university paintings, the catalogue also reproduces Klimt's *Pallas Athene, Beethoven Frieze, Judith, Musik,* and *Nuda Veritas.* These works reflect his interest in a variety of artistic sources from Jugendstil and symbolism, to Mycenean, Byzantine, and Styrian art. Often pairing the realistically rendered human form with rich, jewellike surfaces of swirling forms and geometric patterns, Klimt's paintings juxtapose fleshy corporeality with dematerialized symbolic abstraction. In the majority of Klimt's work, which includes portraiture and outstanding drawings, the human—and in particular the female—figure was a favorite subject. He often treated themes of human existence, love, and eroticism. The latter is reflected in *Fish Blood,* an aquatic scene of nude women whose existence, like their bodies and flowing hair, appears to follow the fluid surge of their watery context.

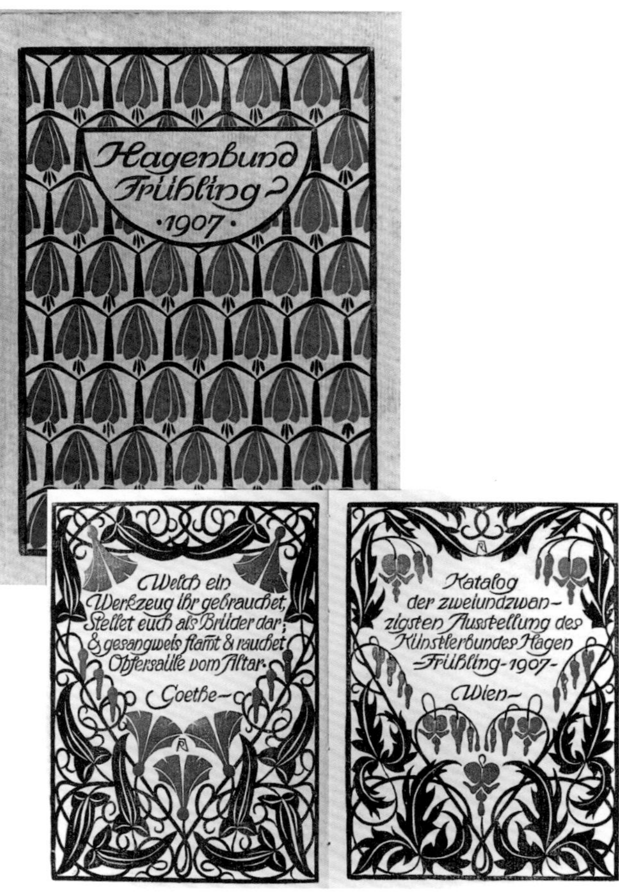

71. Rudolf Junk (Austrian, 1880–1943), book decorator, woodcut designer
Catalogue of the Twenty-second Exhibition of the Hagen Artist Society (*Katalog der Zweiundzwanzigsten Ausstellung des Künstlerbundes Hagen*) (Vienna: Künstlerbundes Hagen, 1907), 96 pp., 11 two-color woodcuts
Book, 7 1/4 x 5 5/8 x 1/4 in. (19.7 x 14.3 x 8 cm)
K.97.9

Rudolf Junk designed this catalogue in black and red woodcut to accompany the twenty-second exhibition of the Hagen Artist Association (*Künstlerbundes Hagen,* or *Hagenbund*). The Hagenbund was officially organized by Heinrich Lefler, Joseph Urban, and other artists on February 3, 1900 and was active until 1938, when the Gestapo forced its closure. The group's artists had met informally since 1876 as the Hagen Society (*Hagengesellschaft)* and convened regularly at restaurants and cafés to discuss various art issues. Their name was taken to honor Josef Hagen, whose "Blaues Freihaus" served as one of the group's later meeting places. Similarly dissatisfied with Vienna's conservative artist organization, the *Künstler-haus,* most of the Hagenbund members withdrew from this institution in 1897 at the same time as the Secessionists.

In addition to the *Künstlerhaus* and the Secession the Hagenbund served as Vienna's third leading contemporary arts organization.

From the outset the Hagenbund endeavored to build an audience from a public that was interested in the developments of modern art such as Jugendstil.[33] The group's leaders, Lefler and Urban, drew inspiration from the socially oriented English Arts and Crafts movement. Many of its artists were also younger and active as illustrators. Given this grounding, the group's designs were less lavish than the decorative arts of the Secession and showed a stronger folk art sensibility. On a stylistic level, their early works embodied a floral Jugendstil; after World War I, expressionism and art deco were more characteristic. Their works were aimed at a consumer base of a more modest income level than those of the Secession and Wiener Werkstätte.

Junk's woodcuts for this publication, with their lively red and black decorative designs printed on heavy paper, reflect the Hagenbund's interest in folk art. The catalogue is organized according to the exhibition's sections that included sculpture, porcelain, stained glass, paintings, drawings, and prints; the Majolica Room (*Majolika-Saal*); black-and-white graphic works (*"Schwarz-Weiss"*), The Four Seasons (*Die vier Jahreszeiten*), Fragments Selected from a Mausoleum (*Fragmente—aus einem Mausoleum*), black-and-white sculpture, drawings, and graphics (*"Schwarz-Weiss"*), portrait room (*Portraet-Saal*), and miscellaneous works (*Varia*).

This 1923 publication for the Vienna Ceramic (Wiener Keramik) provides a brief text and retrospective catalogue of the ceramic firm's works produced during the first seventeen years of its existence. Founded in 1906 by Bertold Löffler and Michael Powolny, the workshop produced ceramics for the Wiener Werkstätte, which took over its distribution in 1907. Later in 1913 the Vienna Ceramic merged with the Gmunder Ceramic to form the United Vienna and Gmunder Ceramic (Vereinigte Wiener und Gmunder Keramik). Perhaps most notably, the workshop contributed decorative tiles to the Palais Stoclet in Brussels and the Cabaret Fledermaus in Vienna.

The ceramics reproduced in the catalogue display the range of the workshop's production from its early, predominantly geometric style utilitarian pieces in a restricted number of colors, to later fanciful designs and polychrome figurines. The frontispiece reproduces a group of ceramic pieces painted in watercolor by Egon Schiele, whom the Werkstätte occasionally employed after he left the Academy in 1909.[34] Schiele's expressionistic rendering of the small, coarsely designed vessels slightly distorts their shapes to emphasize a crude, handmade quality of production. Although his watercolor does not replicate the designs of the Vienna Ceramic itself, it lends a sense of handcrafted authenticity to the workshop's production and suggests its connection to a longer tradition of ceramic making as well as to Schiele's artistic output.

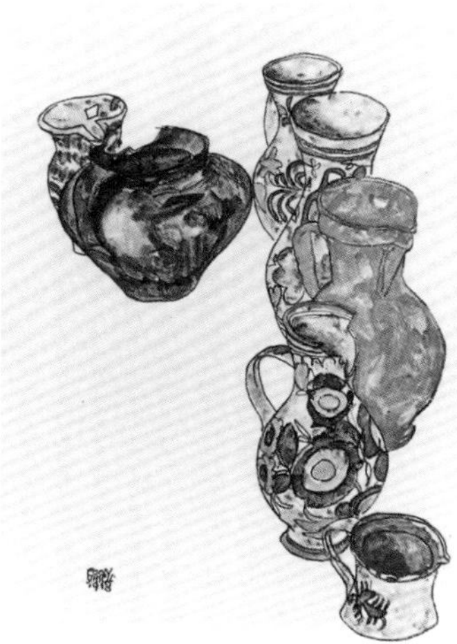

72. Egon Schiele (Austrian, 1890–1918), frontispiece artist
Leopold Wolfgang Rochowanski, *Wiener Keramik* (Leipsiz: Thyrsos, 1923), 183 pp.,145 plates
Printed vellum cover, 1 color reproduction of a Schiele watercolor, hand-bound with cloth spine, 9 1/8 x 6 1/2 x 9/16 in. (23.1 x 16.4 x 1.5 cm)
Signed by author following title page, graphite: L. W. Rochowanski
Edition of 150
K.99.35

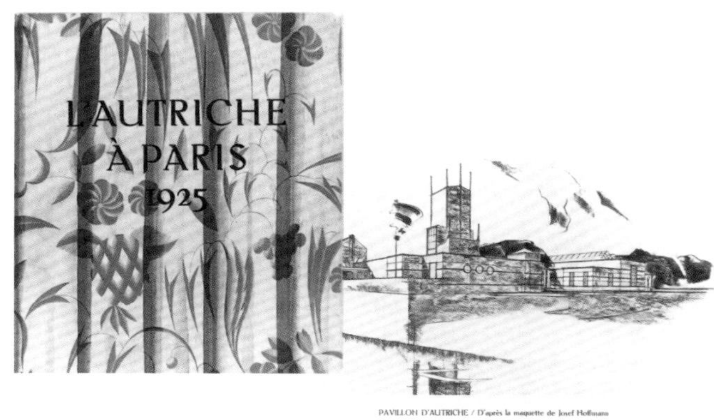

73. Dagobert Peche (Austrian, 1887–1923), cover designer;
Josef Hoffmann (Austrian, 1870–1956), pavilion designer
Hugo Winkler, ed., *Austria in Paris* (*L'Autriche à Paris*) (Vienna: Executive Commission, 1925), 128 pp., 34 single-page plates, 3 fold-out plates
Book, 7 5/16 x 6 11/16 x 5/16 in. (18.6 x 17.0 x .8 cm)
K.99.38

This catalogue for the Austrian pavilion at the 1925 International Exposition of Modern Decorative and Industrial Arts in Paris reproduced a broad range of Wiener Werkstätte applied art works and designs.

Included among them are Josef Hoffmann's architectural renderings for the Austrian pavilion. His designs emphasize low-lying, horizontally based structures with minimal decoration. On a fundamental level, this type of formal vocabulary became associated with the international art deco style, which derived its name from the exposition. In contrast to Hoffmann's reductive, even sober forms, Dagobert Peche's textile pattern for the catalogue's cover depicts fantastically attenuated flowers and leaves in red and pink on a white ground superimposed with translucent dark gray-blue vertical bands. With this choice, Hoffmann paid homage to the recently deceased Peche, whose designs were used generously in the pavilion's case displays of Viennese products.

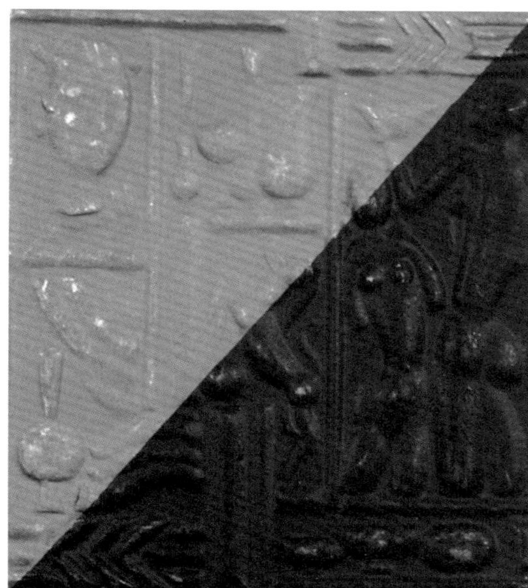

74. Vally Wieselthier (Austrian, 1895–1945), front cover designer; and **Gudrun Baudisch** (Austrian, 1906–1982), back cover designer
Mathilde Flögl, ed., *The Wiener Werkstätte 1903–1928: The Evolution of the Modern Applied Arts* (Vienna: Krystall, 1929), 144 pp.
Bound in orange and black papier mâché, embossed with figures and designs in high relief
Book, 9 1/8 x 8 5/8 x 1 in. (23.1 x 22.0 x 2.5 cm)
K.96.4

Edited by Mathilde Flögl, this twenty-five year history of the Wiener Werkstätte was published in German, French, and English. The art deco style embossed binding, designed by Vally Wieselthier and Gudrun Baudisch and produced in orange and black papier mâché, emulates a molded terracotta relief. This resemblance led to the catalogue's nickname of *Kachelalmanach,* or tile almanac.[35] The text is extensively illustrated and includes short essays on the group's prominent figures such as Gustav Klimt, Josef Hoffman, Koloman Moser, Fritz Waerndorfer, and projects such as the Cabaret Fledermaus. Flögl also provided a compendium of artist's monograms, which are valuable as both graphic design and a tool of identification.

The illustrations that accompany the texts display the group's stylistic and material development of modern applied and fine arts. These range from the early, monumental Palais Stoclet mosaics by Gustav Klimt and his portrait of Mäda Primavesi, to smaller, individual works such as book bindings, metal work, ceramics, textiles, carved boxes, and toys, to interior designs and the pavilion at the 1925 Paris exposition. The designs that span this twenty-five year history of Viennese modern applied arts display a notable shift from its earlier sensibility. Many designs of the 1920s were increasingly expressionistic or folk-art inspired, utilized modest materials, and displayed a marked frivolity. The introductory text acknowledges the challenges that everyone had met over the years. Reflecting on the ideals, successes, and difficulties of the Wiener Werkstätte, Flögl asserts a positive note of perseverance:

> Even now after twenty-five years of hard work and sad disappointments, we are convinced that all creative work must be appreciated and considered rightly, according to the laws of nature, and that the greatness of a nation depends as to whether it is able to realize new ideas quickly enough, and before all others …
> … The choice has been made among those artists who by reason of their great talent and personal note, have proved their value, and have helped to maintain and further that high standard which the W[einer] W[erkstätte] has been out for from its initiation, no matter at what cost and sacrifice; to bar all soulless imitations, leveling mechanism and mercantilism of the so-called art productions of our time. The ever-increasing influence of the WW in the production of the applied arts of the cultured show how just these have become a means of approachment of the Nations. William Morris was fully alive to this fact when in his "Art and beauty of the Earth" he sent forth his message: "All people east of the Atlantic felt this art; from Bokhara to Galway, from Iceland to Madras, all the work glittered with its brightness and quivered with its vigor. It cast down the partitions of race and religion also. Christian and [Muslim] were made joyful by it; Kelt, Teuton, and Latin raised it up together. Persian, Tartar and Arab gave and took its gifts from one another."[36]

As was characteristic for the late Wiener Werkstätte, the book received both favorable responses and harsh criticism. Among the charges was the critique that the book's production was "frivolous" and disregarded typographical progress. Sharper still was the response of Max Ermers, a member of the circle of the prominent modern architect Adolf Loos, who claimed that the publication signaled the "spirit of the very spirit of the WW, culture of the terminal culture proper to the Decline of the West."[37]

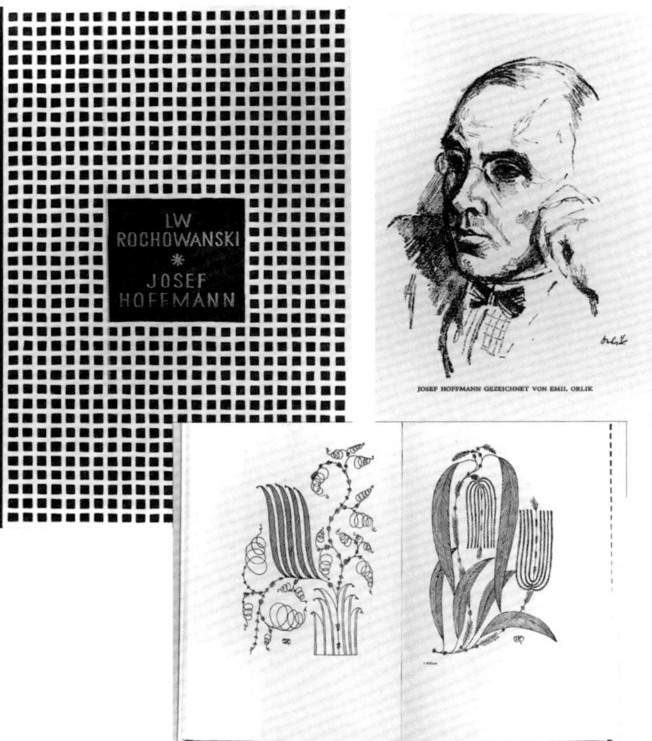

75. **Josef Hoffman** (Austrian, 1870–1956), artist and cover designer
Leopold Wolfgang Rochowanski, *Josef Hoffmann: A Study Written for His Eightieth Birthday* (*Josef Hoffmann: Eine Studie Geschrieben zu seinem 80. Geburtstag*) (Vienna: Österreichischen Staatsdruckerei, 1950), 71 pp., 14 plates
Cover printed with gold-embossed letterpress; cloth spine with gold text, printed *Gitterwerk* endpapers; 1 photolithograph by Orlik, 13 reproductions of Hoffmann's work
Book, 10 15/16 x 7 3/4 x 7/16 in. (27.8 x 19.7 x 1.1 cm)
K.11

This monograph on Josef Hoffmann celebrates his eightieth birthday and commemorates his far-reaching contributions to modern Viennese architecture and applied arts. The brown-and-cream cover presents Hoffmann's *Gitterwerk* (lattice) pattern, the tectonic design motif for which he is perhaps best known. Among the text's illustrations are a portrait drawing of Hoffmann by Emil Orlik and numerous of Hoffmann's own designs, such as floral and foliate motifs and architectural details. Hoffmann's drawings are rendered with a fine, elegant line; a few are sketches for vases, such as the voluptuous type that appeared in the 1920s. In contrast to Hoffmann's early architectonic style, these forms—articulated in clean, thin lines—are more delicate and feminine.

B. State-Sponsored and Commemorative Publications

During the early years following the formation of the Vienna Secession and the Wiener Werkstätte the Austro-Hungarian monarchy commissioned the groups' artists to design and produce artworks and publications. This official support was significant in that it both sanctioned and encouraged high quality avant-garde design.[38] This sponsorship continued until the early twentieth century when government commissions declined and the groups relied more heavily on private patronage from the recently established middle class.[39]

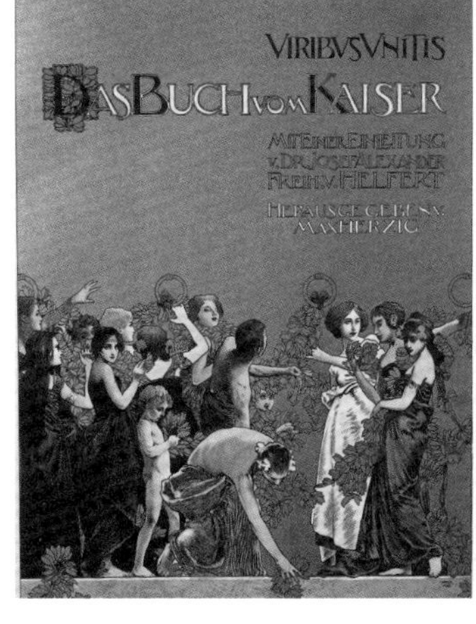

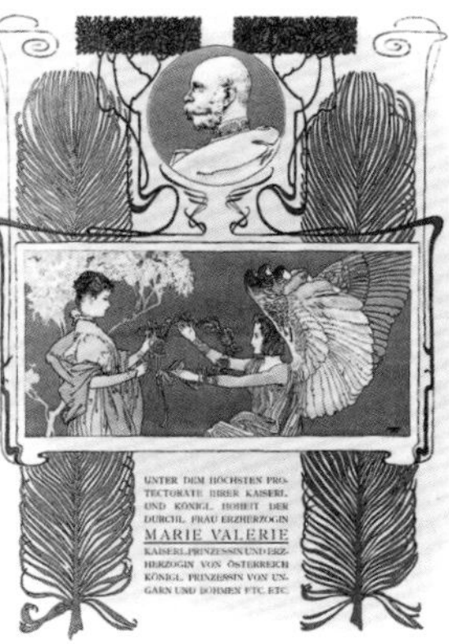

76. **Koloman Moser** (Austrian, 1868–1918), book decorator; **Josef Hoffmann** (Austrian, 1870–1956), book decorator and binding designer
Max Herzig, ed., *Viribus Unitis: Book of the Emperor* (*Viribus Unitis: Das Buch vom Kaiser*), with preface by Josef Alexander von Helfert (Vienna: Herzig, ca.1898), 322 pp., 3 color plates, 82 plates
Leatherette binding, gold-stamped design, book, 18 1/4 x 15 x 2 in. (46.3 x 3.8 x 5.1 cm)
K.96.1; see Color Plate 19

Commissioned by Archduchess Marie Valerie, this lavish volume pays tribute to her father, Franz Josef I in his official role as emperor of the Austro-Hungarian Empire (1848–1916). The title *Viritus Unitis* was the emperor's motto, meaning "with united forces." The volume's editor, Max Herzig, stated that although other histories of the emperor existed, it was his aim with this publication to "describe the life and activities of our emperor in a full and emotionally corresponding manner, a work that in true-to-life representations introduces us to our sovereign in official as well as purely private scenes." Portrayed as the vigorous, beneficent patriarch of an ethnically varied empire, Franz Josef elegantly appears in a range of civic, military, and cultural activities. He receives the populace, hunts, confers with government officials, reviews troops, visits a synagogue, and attends balls and the theater. Included among the book's almost 400 illustrations and ornamental embellishments are Jugendstil pages designed by Hoffmann and Moser and Hoffmann's gold-embossed cover design of the imperial coat of arms framed by a foliate border. Particularly striking are Moser's three decorative pages with idyllic scenes of young men and women set against lavish gold backgrounds. Seen within the framework of Hoffmann and Moser's avant-garde designs, the presentation of Franz Josef and his deeds underscores his identity as a modern leader.

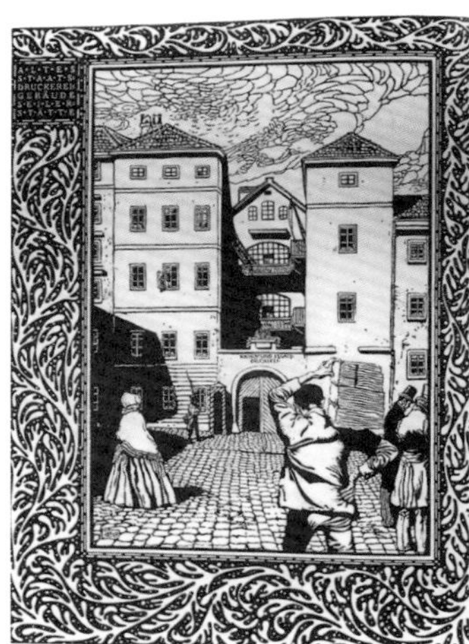

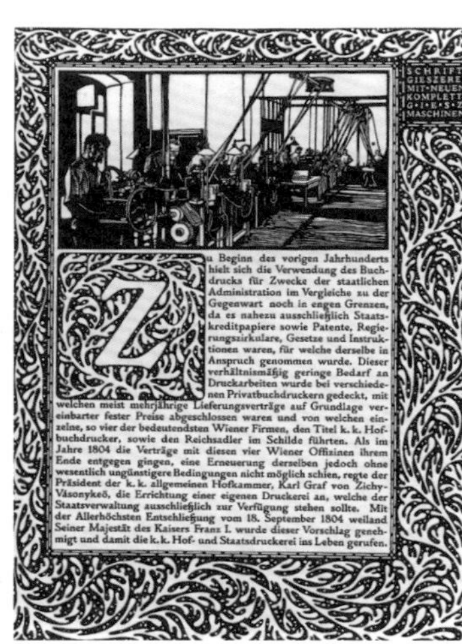

Zu Beginn des vorigen Jahrhunderts hielt sich die Verwendung des Buchdrucks für Zwecke der staatlichen Administration im Vergleiche zu der Gegenwart noch in engen Grenzen, da es nahezu ausschließlich Staatskreditpapiere sowie Patente, Regierungszirkulare, Gesetze und Instruktionen waren, für welche derselbe in Anspruch genommen wurde. Dieser verhältnismäßig geringe Bedarf an Druckarbeiten wurde bei verschiedenen Privatbuchdruckern gedeckt, mit welchen meist mehrjährige Lieferungsverträge auf Grundlage vereinbarter fester Preise abgeschlossen waren und von welchen einzelne, so vier der bedeutendsten Wiener Firmen, den Titel k. k. Hofbuchdrucker, sowie den Reichsadler im Schilde führten. Als im Jahre 1804 die Verträge mit diesen vier Wiener Offizinen ihrem Ende entgegen gingen, eine Erneuerung derselben jedoch ohne wesentlich ungünstigere Bedingungen nicht möglich schien, regte der Präsident der k. k. allgemeinen Hofkammer, Karl Graf von Zichy-Vásonykeö, die Errichtung einer eigenen Druckerei an, welche der Staatsverwaltung ausschließlich zur Verfügung stehen sollte. Mit der Allerhöchsten Entschließung vom 18. September 1804 weiland Seiner Majestät des Kaisers Franz I. wurde dieser Vorschlag genehmigt und damit die k. k. Hof- und Staatsdruckerei ins Leben gerufen.

77. Koloman Moser (Austrian, 1868–1918), designer; **Carl Otto Czeschka** (Austrian, 1878–1960), illustrator; **Rudolf von Larisch** (Austrian, b. Italy, 1856–1943), typographer
A. W. Unger and Joseph Dernjać, *In Celebration of One Hundred Years of the Imperial and Royal Court and State Printing Works (Zur Feier des einhundertjährigen Bestandes der k.k. Hof-und Staatsdruckerei)* (Vienna: k.k. Hof-und Staatsdruckerei, 1904), 112 pp., 21 plates
Paper covers; printed tissues, 7 woodcuts, 14 reproductions of drawings by Czeschka, book, 15 15/16 x 12 3/16 x 15/16 in. (40.8 x 31.0 x 2.4 cm)
K.73.10

This publication of gala bindings for the Imperial and Royal State Press's hundred-year jubilee was the Wiener Werkstätte's first major commission. The project also signaled the beginning of collaboration between the two groups. The edition was limited to 1,700 copies and included a typeface by Applied Arts School professor Rudolf von Larisch, reproductions of woodcuts by Czeschka, and original woodcuts. Moser not only supervised the printing process, but also designed the watermark, initials, decorative borders, title page, plate covers, dust jacket, and bindings.[40] The illustrations present the press's various industrial shops, such as the bookbindery, workshops for electrotyping, zinc etching, lithography, correction, gluing, stamp-cutting, presses for single and double color, stone, quick, and copper printing, and packing area. Foremost among the text's themes is the presentation of the state press as an art institution (*Kunst-Anstalt*).

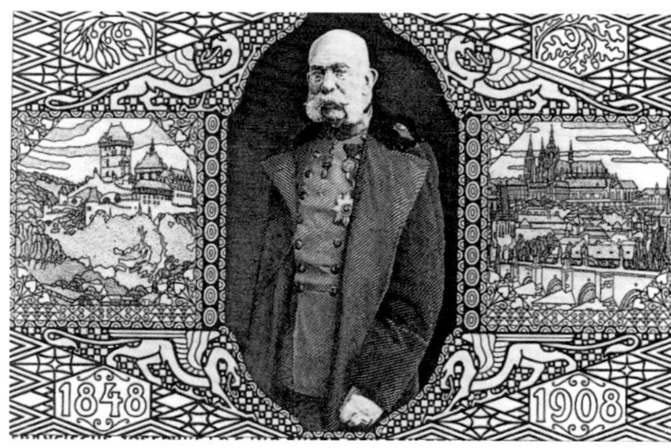

78. Koloman Moser (Austrian, 1868–1918)
Postcard for Emperor Franz Josef's Jubilee [1848–1908] Exhibition, Prague, 1908
Postcard, 3 3/8 x 5 1/4 in. (8.5 x 13.4 cm) (sight)
K.76.1

Moser designed this postcard on the occasion of the sixtieth anniversary of Emperor Franz Josef's accession to the throne on December 2, 1848. He also designed postage stamps related to the event.

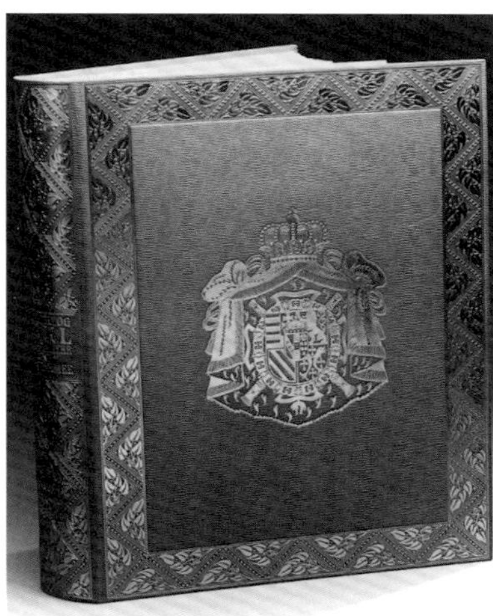

79. Josef Hoffmann (Austrian, 1870–1956), binding designer; bound by Wiener Werkstätte
Wilhelm John, ed., *Archduke and Field Marshal Karl and His Army (Erzherzog Karl der Feldherr und seine armee)* (Vienna: k.k. Hof- und Staatdruckerei, 1913), 444 pp., 65 color plates, 13 B&W illus.
Saffron leather cover, gilt-tooled by Hoffmann, 6 four-color plates by Max Jaffé, 2 etchings by Luigi Kasimir, original book box with coat-of-arms, 16 9/16 x 14 x 3 3/16 in. (42.0 x 35.6 x 8.2 cm); book 15 3/4 x 12 1/2 x 2 3/8 in. (40.0 x 31.8 x 6.0 cm)
52/60 with colored plates and leather binding
K.98.9

Franz Karl, the father of Franz Josef, was the last Holy Roman emperor. As Francis I, he was the emperor of Austria (1804–1835) and as Franz, the king of Hungary (1792–1830) and king of Bohemia (1792–1836). Upon ascending to the throne after the death of his father in 1792 he dealt with ongoing difficulties that resulted from the French Revolution. Between 1792 and 1813 Austria fought several wars against Napoleonic forces. The Holy Roman Empire was dissolved in 1805, and Franz abdicated his title of emperor the following year. As head of the Austrian army Franz at times had taken the field himself. During the battles of 1813–1814 Austria joined the coalition that finally defeated Napoleon, and succeeded in destroying the French emperor's power. Published on the centenary of those victorious battles, the Werkstätte volume is a historical overview of this great period of the Austrian military. It also includes a biographical sketch of Franz Karl, an account of his role as field marshal, and recollections of his contemporaries. Josef Hoffmann designed the gold-embossed leather binding, and other Werkstätte artists produced seventy-nine illustrations.

C. Ball Programs and Card Holders

Music plays an important role in Austrian culture, and royal, civic, and private balls are perhaps the strongest and most enduring reminders of the glittering pomp and ceremony of Ringstrasse Vienna. Organizers often commissioned ball programs and card holders, at times commemorating historic events or persons, which would be given to their guests as favors or souvenirs. The ball programs in the Kaerwer collection display a range of both functionality and craftsmanship, from late nineteenth-century designs that could be used to record dances and partners to more elaborate keepsakes.

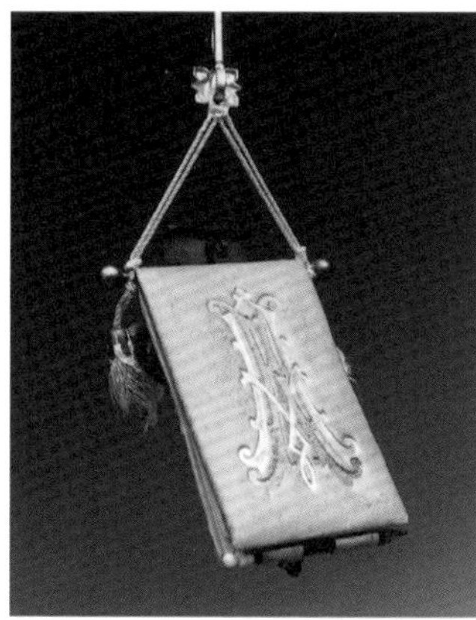

80. Wilhelm Melzer (Austrian, active 1899–1911), designer
Ball Program (*Carnet de Bal*) (Vienna: Melzer, 1889)
Miniature book with black metal folding stand decorated with Habsburg eagle's head and wings. Bound in yellow morocco with AK [*Architekten-Kränzchen*] stamped in gold, 3 x 1 7/8 in. (7.5 x 4.7 cm)
K.99.16

This miniature ball program for the March 11, 1889 Architects' Circle (*Architekten-Kränzchen*) is bound in yellow morocco embossed with the organization's initials, AK. Wilhelm Melzer designed the book with an elaborate gilt black metal-filigree folding stand decorated with an eagle's head and wings. At the bottom, a small ivory-tipped pencil holds the book closed. The gilt hook tied to the book by a silk cord suggests a ball guest could secure the program to her garments during a dance. The text lists the musical program of the ball in two separate sections, "*Vor der Ruhe*" (before intermission) and "*Nach der Ruhe*" (after intermission). Each section lists the names and number of the dances, including waltzes, polonaises, polkas, and quadrilles, along with their composers, such as Johann Strauss, Josef Kaulich, Carl Zeller, and Karel Komzák, among others.

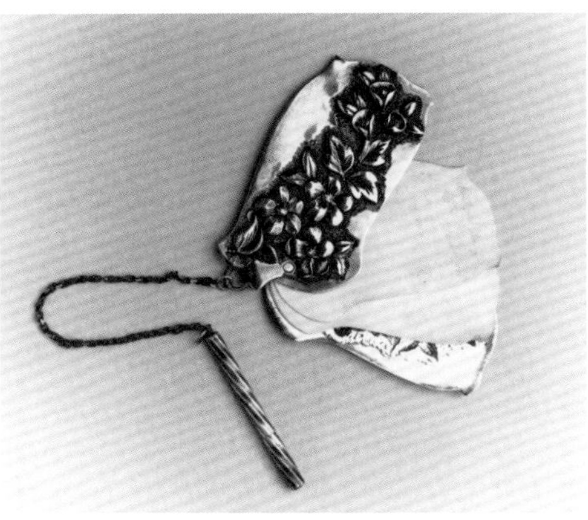

81. Designer unknown, German or Austrian
Dance Card Holder, ca. 1890
Silver repouseé and ivory leaves, 3 1/2 x 1 3/4 in. (8.8 x 4.6 cm)
K.68.8

This lady's dance card holder combines thin leaves of ivory clasped together between silver covers decorated with flowers modeled in low relief. Attached to the cover by a short chain is a small cylindrical writing instrument used to write the names of dance partners. Some writing still appears on the leaves. The asymmetrical design of the cardholder and its floral decoration were both generally in keeping with stylistic tendencies of Jugendstil and also would have been a suitably feminine complement to a woman's formal ball gown.

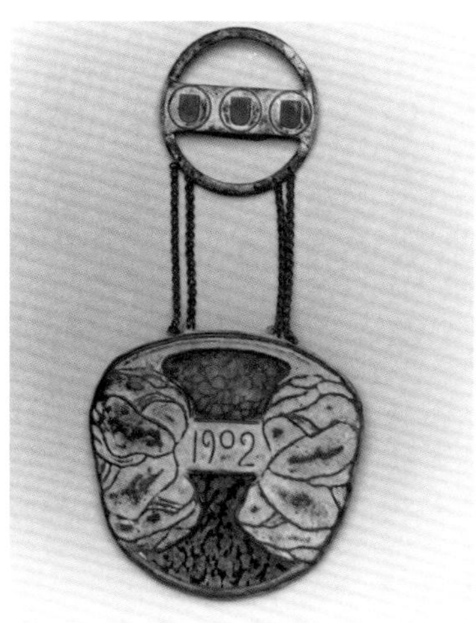

82. **Antoinette Krasnik** (Austrian, 1874–1956); Johann Loetz Witwe
1902 Costum-Fest Ball Card Hanger, 1902
Metal, cobalt papillion glass, folded program insert, 7 7/8 x 3 7/8 in. (19.9 x 9.8 cm)
Recto: 1902; verso: COSTUM-FEST/DER KK KUNSTGEWERBE/SCHULE IN WIEN 31 1 1902/ ANTOINETTE KRASNIK
K.2002.4

The *Ball der Stadt*, or Municipal Ball, was instituted in 1890 as a civic counterpart to the royal court ball that took place at the Hofburg. This annual event was held at the recently built town hall. For the 1909 *Ball der Stadt*, the ball committee commissioned Remigius Geyling and Wilhelm Melzer to design a program as a ladies' souvenir.[41] The book celebrated two particularly significant matters of civic pride: the life of composer Josef Haydn, who died in 1809, and the centenary of the Austro-Hungarian victory over Napoleonic forces.

In the manner of a *Gesamtkunstwerk*, each of the book's components—text, illustrations, patterned borders, decorative endpapers, and binding—is synthesized with the others to produce an organic unity. Geyling's brightly colored, near square-format lithographs present commemorative scenes of 1809 and reflect the neoclassical style of that period. He rendered such memorable images as Master Haydn's last day at the spinet, the uniformed members of the Viennese Citizen Grenadier Division, and the nocturnal bombardment of Vienna by the French on May 11 and 12. The series ends with Archduke Karl's victorious entry into Aspern on May 23, 1809, and portraits of Vienna's mayors bracketing the period, Stephan Edl von Wohlleben (1809) and Karl Lueger (1909).

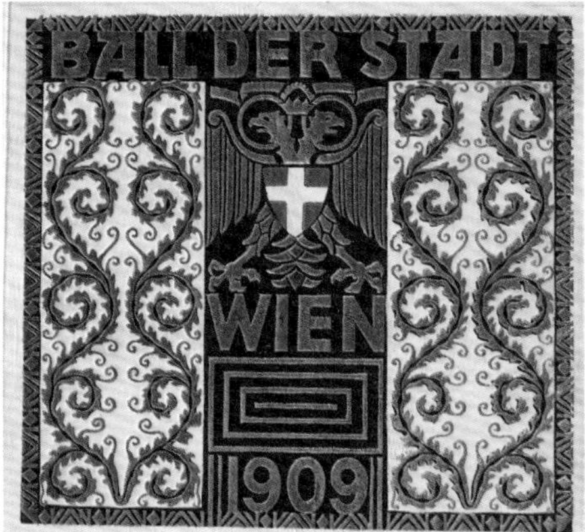

83. **Remigius Geyling** (Austrian, 1878–1974), illustrator; **Wilhelm Melzer** (Austrian, active 1889–1911), binder
City Ball 1909 (*Ball der Stadt* 1909) (Vienna: Berger, 1909), 12 color plates
Color-printed book box with ribbon handles; leather-bound and tooled with gold; color printed endpapers, color lithographs; book cover: Jugendstil gold tooling brackets Vienna's heraldic banner. Below is Melzer's logo designed by Koloman Moser. Original book box, 6 3/8 x 7 7/16 x 1 1/4 in. (16.2 x 18.9 x 3.2 cm); book, 5 3/4 x 6 11/16 x 5/8 in. (14.7 x 17.0 x 1.6 cm)
K.98.10; see Color Plates 20, 21

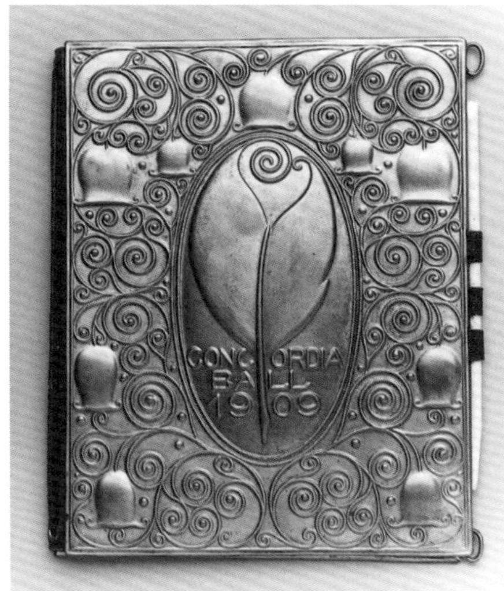

84. **Josef Hoffmann** (Austrian, 1870–1956), designer; Wiener Werkstätte
Concordia Ball Program Cover, 1909
Gilt brass, marbled endpapers, paper, leather, ivory, book, 5 9/16 x 4 3/4 in. (14.2 x 12.1 cm); case: 8 x 6 x 1 in. (20.4 x 15.2 x 2.6 cm)
Stamped inside bottom edges of cover: WIENER WERK-STÄTTE
K.2002.5

Josef Hoffmann designed this well-known ball program cover for the 1909 Winter Ball of the Concordia Journalists and Writers' Association.

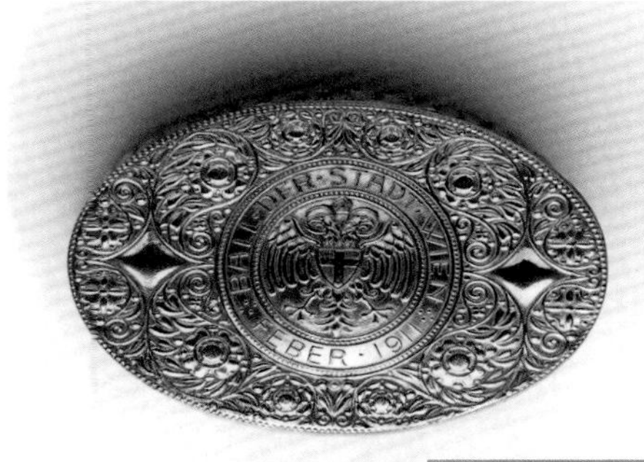

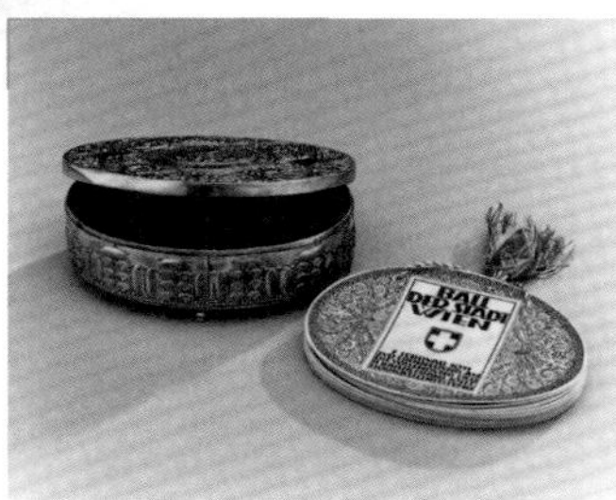

85. Remigius Geyling (Austrian, 1878–1974), designer;
Wilhelm Melzer (Austrian, active 1889–1911), silversmith
City Ball of Vienna, 7 February 1911 (*Ball der Stadt Wien, 7. Februar 1911*) (Vienna: Gerlach & Wiedling, 1911), 36 plates
Silver plate box, lid lined with green moiré, pages caught together by a tasseled cord, 3 x 4 1/4 x 1 in.
(7.6 x 10.9 x 2.6 cm) oval
K.90.8
Engraved bottom of box: Wilhelm Melzer, Wien. VII

This oval-shaped ball program, accompanied by a silver box, was commissioned as a favor for a Viennese gala in honor of Emperor Franz Josef. Thirty-six black-and-white plates list the sequence of musical arrangements performed at the ball and depict Austrian notables and landscapes, each identified on the reverse. Picturesque landscapes with images of aqueducts, bridges, and reservoirs celebrate and commemorate imperial modernization achievements. The final image includes the caption: "The inauguration of the second Emperor Franz Josef High-Source Pipeline (*Hochquellenleitung*) through his Majesty the Emperor on the 2nd Dec. 1910."[42]

D. Fine Bindings

Reflecting the larger international fin-de-siècle revival of bookbinding, the notion of the book as a work of art was of central importance to the Wiener Werkstätte. In addition to the establishment of a bookbinding workshop on their Neustiftgasse premises, the group's 1905 working program articulated their strongly held convictions on the subject:

> The good binding has become completely extinct. The hollow back, tacking with string, the unpleasant cut, the badly stitched leaves, and poor leather are ineradicable. The so-called individual volume, that is, the factory-produced cover printed full of advertisements, is all that we have. The machine works busily and fills our bookcases with deficiently printed volumes; the result is cheapness. Every civilized person should nevertheless be ashamed of this material abundance, the easy production of which on the one hand brings a diminished responsibility, while on the other hand the abundance leads to superficiality. How many books do we really make our own? And should one not own these bound in the best manner, in the best jackets, on the best paper, in marvelous leather? Should we have forgotten that the love with which a book is printed, outfitted, and bound brings us into another relationship with it, that the interaction with beautiful things embellishes ourselves as well? A book should be a whole work of art and its value must be measured as such.[43]

Despite their alarmist tone regarding carelessly mass-produced books, the Viennese bookbinding tradition that originated in the fourteenth century had not completely died out. In fact, the Wiener Werkstätte discovered local craftsmen skilled in traditional techniques that included leather intarsia, braiding, and manual gilding.[44] Not surprisingly, this combination of excellent craftsmanship and high-quality materials led to the production of exquisite volumes that could only be sustained on a small scale. As such, the group most often took on private commissions for single bindings or printed small editions through special publishers.[45] The books in this section, which include art books, commemorative publications, novels, and a fairytale, have been selected primarily for the high quality and aesthetically interesting design and execution of their bindings.

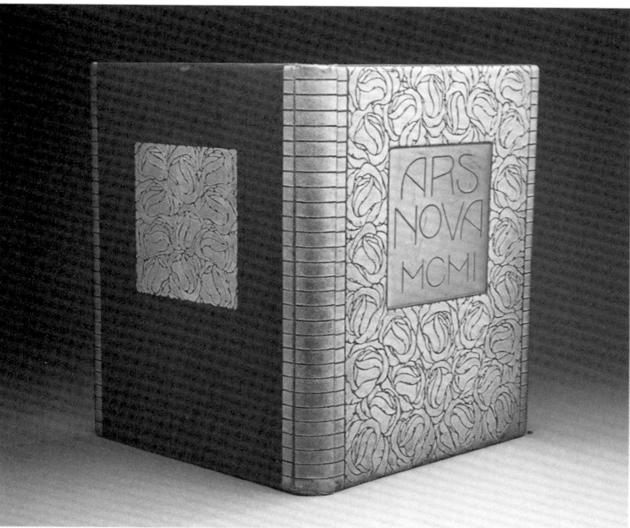

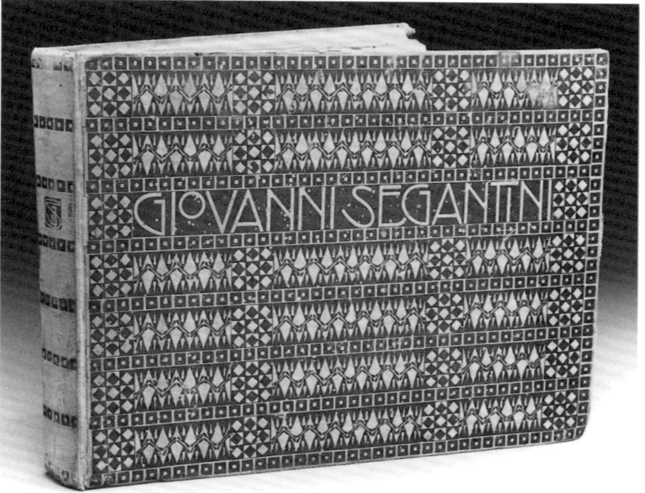

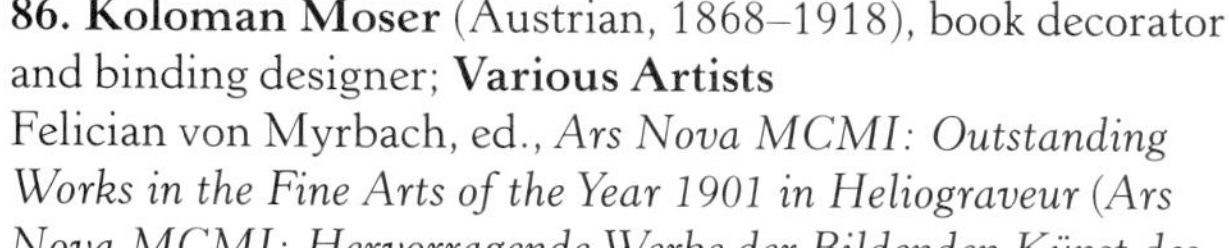
86. Koloman Moser (Austrian, 1868–1918), book decorator and binding designer; **Various Artists**
Felician von Myrbach, ed., *Ars Nova MCMI: Outstanding Works in the Fine Arts of the Year 1901 in Heliograveur* (*Ars Nova MCMI: Hervorragende Werke der Bildenden Künst des Jahres 1901 in Heliogravure*) vol. 1 (Vienna: Herzig, 1901), 114 pages, 45 plates
Silver-tooled clothboard, heliograveur, 18 1/16 x 13 15/16 x 1 5/8 in.
(46.2 x 38.0 x 4.2 cm)
K.97.13.1; see Color Plates 22, 23, 24

This first of two volumes entitled *Ars Nova* (New Art) exemplifies the Secession's interest in contemporary avant-garde art by a range of international artists. A compendium of outstanding production in the fine arts exhibited during 1901, the tome includes works by such celebrated European artists as Cuno Amiet, Hans Baluschek, Eugène Carrière, August Gaul, Max Klinger, Gustav Klimt, Walter Leistikow, Max Liebermann, Elias Repin, Auguste Rodin, Fritz von Uhde, and Ignacio Zuloaga. The volume pays tribute to the latest in excellent artistic achievement. With its exquisite bindings, endpapers, and decorative borders by Koloman Moser, it is also a significant example of Jugendstil book design itself. The cover's silver-tooled rose motif is repeated in the gold-colored text borders. This motif, which likely derived from a similar design by Charles Rennie Mackintosh, was a favorite emblem of Moser and anticipates the geometric Rosemark stamp developed for the Wiener Werkstätte's trademark logo.

87. Koloman Moser (Austrian, 1868–1918), binding designer
Franz Theodor Hubert Servaes, *Giovanni Segantini: His Life and His Work* (*Giovanni Segantini: Sein Leben und sein Werk*) (Vienna: Gerlach, 1902), 134 pp., 63 plates
Gilt-embossed cover; letterpress, 63 plates after oil paintings, pastels, tempera, book, 11 3/8 x 15 7/16 x 2 in.
(28.8 x 39.2 x 5.1 cm)
K.73.9; see Color Plate 25

The Italian symbolist Giovanni Segantini was an exponent of the late nineteenth-century painting technique known as divisionism. Raised in the Italian Alps and later resident in the Engadin region of the Swiss Alps, Segantini is best known for his landscapes and allegories. Through his development of divisionism, a post-impressionist technique that breaks down light through the juxtaposition of shades of pure color, Segantini's works achieved a remarkable luminosity and clarity of atmosphere. Championed in both Germany and Austria, Segantini was among the artists included in the Secession's first exhibition in 1898. In 1900 the *Ver Sacrum* dedicated an entire issue to the artist's work. Their ninth exhibition (13 January to 28 February 1901) was a memorial show of Segantini's works, marking the artist's death in 1899. Inspired by this monumental display of the artist's work, the Imperial and Royal Ministry of Culture and Education organized a committee in March 1901 for the production of a Segantini monograph. This 1902 luxury edition, designed by Koloman Moser, reproduces the artist's oil and tempera paintings and pastels and has a gold-embossed cloth cover dominated by Moser's characteristic checkerboard pattern of alternating squares and diamonds.

Among Segantini's works exhibited by the Secession was his *Wicked Mothers* of 1894. This work reflects the artist's interest in the theme of motherhood beginning around 1890. His resulting works present both positive and negative allegories of motherhood that combine the natural and spiritual as well as Christian and non-Christian symbolism. Set in an eerie, near-empty landscape, the *Wicked Mothers* depicts the punishment and redemption of women who had rejected the duties of motherhood.

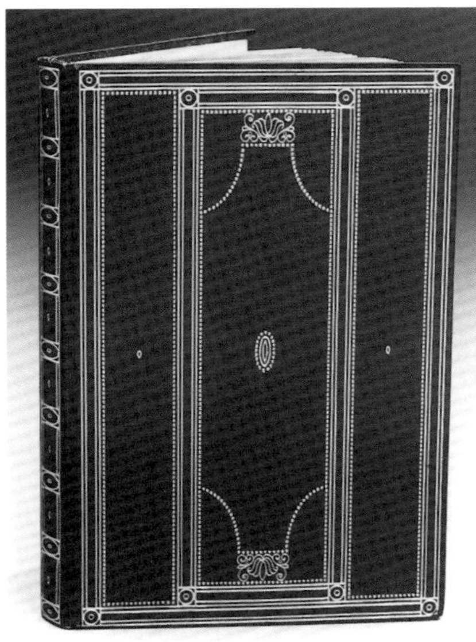

88. Josef Hoffmann (Austrian, 1870–1956), binding designer; **Ferdinand Schmutzer** (Austrian, 1870–1928), illustrator
Arthur Schnitzler, *The Shepherd's Pipe* (*Die Hirtenflöte*)
(Vienna: Deutsch-Österreichischer, 1912), 104 pp., 9 etchings
Leather bound with gold tooling, book, 6 9/16 x 4 1/2 x 1/2 in.
(16.7 x 11.4 x 1.2 cm)
Limited edition, 315/ 400
K.90.7; see Color Plate 25

Hoffmann's green leather binding with simple and elegant gold embossing gives this modest-sized volume of *The Sheperd's Pipe* a refined look. The Austrian playwright and novelist Arthur Schnitzler had practiced medicine for much of his life with a primary interest in psychiatry. Among Vienna's most distinguished early twentieth-century writers, Schnitzler first gained recognition with *Anatol* (1893). His later works were probing explorations of human psychology, complexities of the erotic life, and a fear of death, often evoking the atmosphere of fin-de-siècle Habsburg decadence. He also produced plays, novels, collections of stories, and medical tracts.

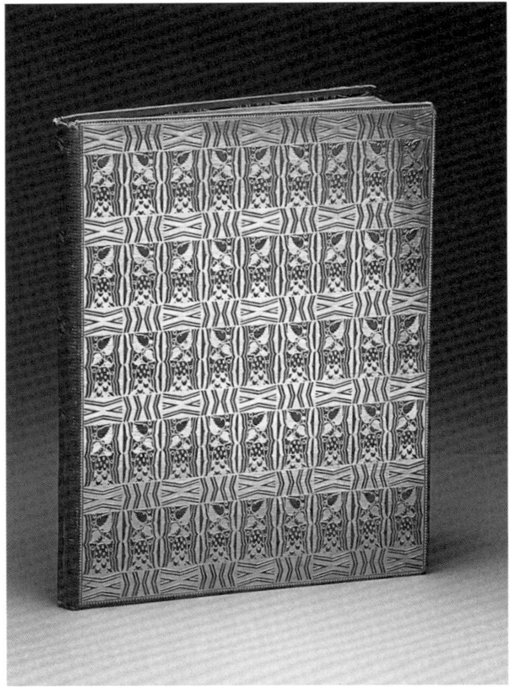

89. Josef Hoffmann (Austrian, 1870–1956), binding designer, bound by the Wiener Werk-stätte
Franz Grillparzer, *The Poor Fiddler* (*Der Arme Spielmann*)
(Vienna: k.k. Hof-und Staatsdruckerei, 1915), 82 pp.
Golden leather cover with gilt tooled design; typeset with border and endpapers by Hoffman, book, 10 3/8 x 8 1/8 x 15/16 in.
(26.3 x 20.7 x 2.4 cm)
1/50 deluxe copies in edition of 500
K.94.13; see Color Plate 26

This deluxe edition of *The Poor Fiddler* is one of fifty examples bound in golden leather by the Wiener Werkstätte. Josef Hoffmann's lavish gilt binding, with a pattern of bell-shaped flowers and leaves, repeats the same motif produced in black and white on the book's endpapers, title page, frontispiece, and text pages. Originally published in Hungary in 1847, *The Poor Fiddler,* by Austrian poet and dramatist Grillparzer, is set in Catholic Vienna and relates the story of a poor musician. A socially marginal character, he is goodhearted but a failure in practical life and cheerfully accepts life's disappointments. That Grillparzer's text enjoyed popularity into the twentieth century is due to a certain Austrian conservatism and taste for tradition.[46] Its narrative evokes a way of life linked to an Austrian affection for the country's landscape, capital, and society. *The Poor Fiddler* belongs to an Austrian literary tradition characterized by a tension between meditation and action, and the transition from a disillusionment with idealism to a compromise with reality.

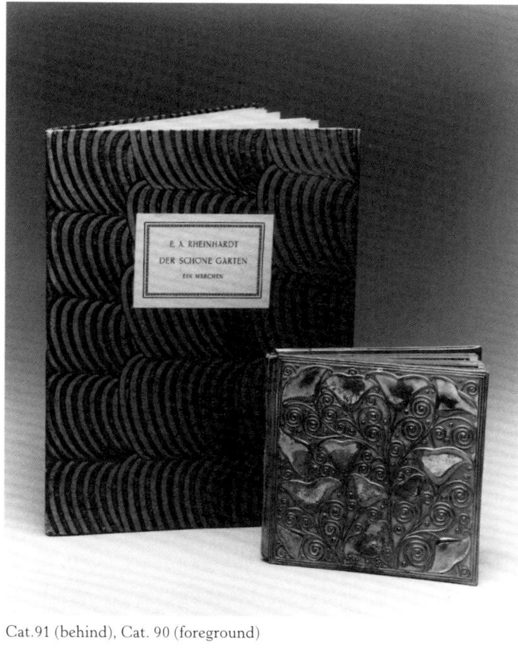

Cat.91 (behind), Cat. 90 (foreground)

90. Josef Hoffmann (Austrian, 1870–1956), designer and editor; **Carl Otto Czeschka** (Austrian, 1878–1960), cover designer; and various WW artists
Pictures from Karlsbad (*Bilder aus Karlsbad*) (Wiener Werkstätte, ca. 1911), 25 pp., 25 color plates
Repousée gilt brass cover designed by Czeschka, with color prints, book, 4 3/4 x 5 x 1/2 in. (12.0 x 12.7 x 1.2 cm)
Stamped bottom edge brass cover: WIENER WERKSTÄTTE
K.ca.75/12; see Color Plate 27

The small, near square-format *Pictures from Karlsbad* was published on the occasion of the opening of the Wiener Werkstätte's branch in the Austrian resort town. Carl Otto Czeschka's repousée brass cover is decorated with a lively, folk-art inspired pattern of flowers and scrolling foliage, an abstracted organic motif that recalls the work of Gustav Klimt. The book's lithographic illustrations celebrate Karlsbad with simplified, colorful depictions of the fashionable resort's historical sites and buildings. These include the Stag's Leap (Hirschensprung), Small Versailles Café and Restaurant, Castle Fountain (Schlossbrunn), New Theater House (Neue Schauspielhaus), Theresien Fountain (Theresienbrunnen), Café Helenehof, city tower (Stadtturm), Schiller's house, the Ring, market square, and the city park health spa (Kursalon im Stadtpark).

91. Bohuslav Kokoschka (Austrian, 1892–1976), illustrator
Emil Alphons Rheinhardt, *The Lovely Garden: A Fairytale* (*Der schöne Garten: Ein Märchen*) (Vienna: Strache, 1920), 43 pp., 4 plates
Lithographic plates; pages uncut; cover color-printed reproduction with B&W appliqued sheet, book, 9 7/16 x 7 1/4 x 5/16 in. (24.0 x 18.4 x .8 cm)
367/ 500
K.75.1; see Color Plate 27

Emil Rheinhardt's *The Lovely Garden: A Fairytale*, with expressionistic illustrations by Bohuslav Kokoschka (younger brother of Oskar Kokoschka) is one of an edition of 500 printed on japan-type velum. The cover's repeating pattern of curving green and turquoise stripes suggests densely packed leaves or foliage evocative of a lush garden. The fairytale is written in the form of a drama and begins with brief sketch that describes the initial setting and characters: "The foreigner lies in the beautiful garden, dazed from much journeying, sleeping under a blooming pomegranate tree. Gazelles, silvery pheasants, peacocks, and a panther come close and rest around the figure."[47]

E. Book Illustration

The majority of works in this section reflects a dominant reform trend among fin-de-siècle book illustration that aimed to produce affordable books meant for more a democratic distribution. This movement countered the decadent literary tendency derived from romanticism that was characterized by outsider themes, pessimism, and a taste for the unusual. In contrast, its subjects were oriented toward the general interest of its readership.[48] Late nineteenth-century efforts to reform pedagogy also led to a new interest in aesthetically driven forms of childrearing that found expression in children's and youth literature. Viennese art and applied art schools played a vital role in these developments as students produced illustrations for children's books. Vienna's Applied Arts School, Art School for Women and Girls (est. 1897), and the Graphic Text and Research Institute (est. 1888) all incorporated a consciousness of the new pedagogy into their training. This not only led to the production of high artistic quality and commercially driven children's books, but also to the production of school murals, schoolbook illustration, and toys. Stylistically spanning from Jugendstil to postwar realism, the illustration examples in this section reflect a pleasure in formal and technical experimentation, a taste for tectonic picture construction, and a splendid use of color and decorative surface patterns.

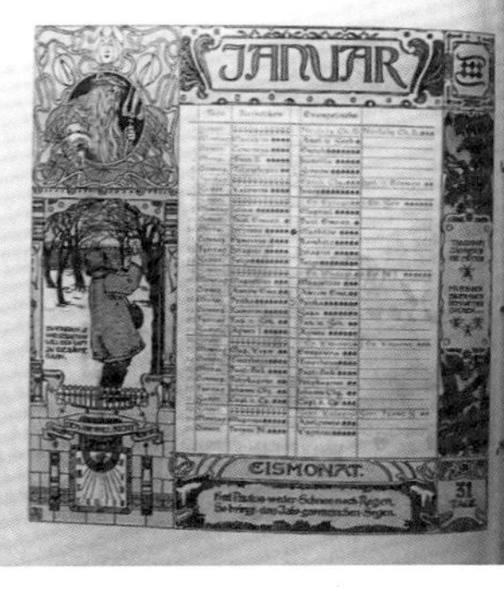

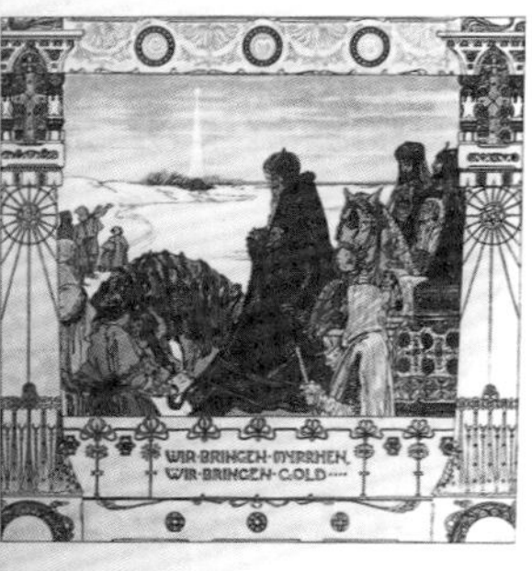

92. Heinrich Lefler (Austrian, 1863–1919) and **Joseph Urban** (Austrian, 1872–1933), illustrators
1899 Austrian Calendar Month-Pictures (1899 *Österreichischer Kalender Monatsbilder*) (Vienna: Artaria, 1899), 25 pp., 25 color plates
Color-printed paper and bindings, bound with silk ribbon, book, 12 5/8 x 11 1/8 x 5/16 in. (32.0 x 28.4 x .8 cm)
K.95.2; see Color Plates 28, 29

Heinrich Lefler and Josef Urban designed this finely illustrated calendar for the year 1899. In February of the following year, the artists founded the Hagen Artist Association (see cat. 71). Composed in book format, each month is divided over an intricately decorated two-page layout such that each month's calendar has a corresponding image on the opposite page. A somber landscape scene of the three journeying Magi, for instance, accompanies January's calendar. An ornamental border in the form of architectural structure frames the image. The initials representative of the three kings, Caspar, Melchior, and Balthasar appear in the circular vignettes along the top lintel-like border.

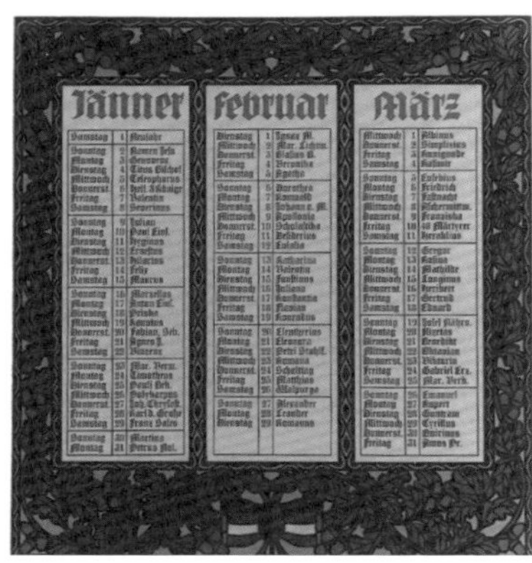

93. Wiener Werkstätte, possibly by Dina (Bernhardine) Kuhn (Austrian, 1891– ca. 1956), designer
1916 Calender (Vienna: k.k. Graphische Lehr- und Versuchsanstalt, 1916)
Color cover and printed ornamental borders around 12-month calendar, folio of 2 folded sheets, page 10 1/2 x 9 7/16 in. (26.6 x 24.0 cm)
In graphite on upper right edge of sheet: D. Kuhn
K.96.5

In contrast to the 1899 calender by Lefler and Urban (cat. 92), this 1916 Wiener Werkstätte calendar, possibly designed by Dina Kuhn, is a total work of art in more abbreviated form. The year is divided into four parts with three months, listed vertically with day, date, and corresponding saint's name, combined on one page. A broad, ornamental border with dark green oak leaves and golden acorns frames the first three months and repeats the colors used for the text, thus unifying the whole.

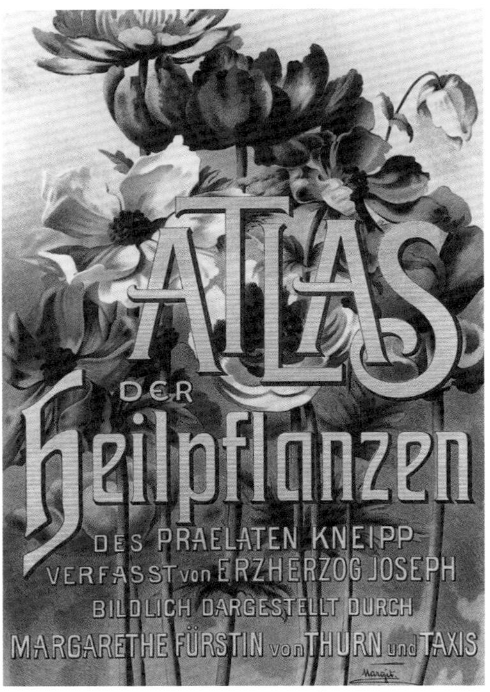

94. Margarethe, Princess of Thurn and Taxis (German, b. Hungary, 1870–1955), illustrator
Josef, Archduke of Austria, *Atlas of Father Kneipp's Medicinal Plants* (*Atlas der Heilpflanzen des Praelaten Kneipp*) (Regensburg: Wunderling's Hofbuchhandlung, ca. 1903), 214 pp., 210 color lithographs
Bound in cloth with color-illustrated cover, Jugendstil gilt-printed endpapers, 12 1/8 x 9 1/16 x 2 3/8 in. (30.8 x 23.0 x 6.0 cm)
K.99.37; see Color Plate 30

Josef, the archduke of Austria, dedicated this medicinal atlas to Sebastian Kneipp (1821–1897), a Bavarian priest whose herbal remedies provided a cure for the illnesses the archduke suffered in the last decades of the nineteenth century.[49] The sumptuous, organic forms of the book's Jugendstil cover, endpapers, and decorative vignettes complement the naturalistic illustrations of Kneipp medicinal plants produced by the archduke's daughter, the painter and sculptor Princess Margarethe of Thurn and Taxis. Each medicinal plant image includes text that identifies its Latin and German names, the geographical region in which it grows, and which plant part is used. The treatments Kneipp developed in the late nineteenth century applied multifarious herbal and water therapies for the "cure of diseases and preservation of health."<50> He advocated a natural, rational mode of life and system of cure that he considered the prerequisite to maintaining good health. Popularized through such publications as *My Water Cure* (1886) and *How You Should Live* (1889) that were translated into several languages, Kneipp's remedies also significantly influenced modern physical therapy and balneology (medical therapy with mineral baths).

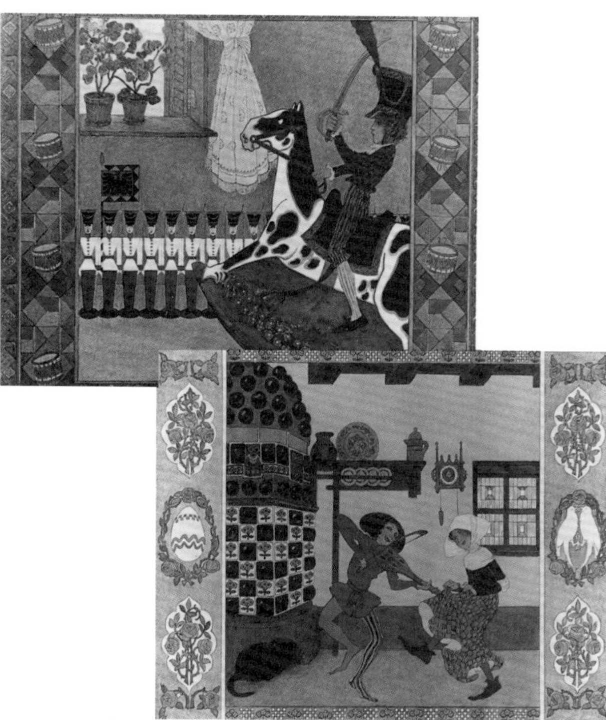

95. Heinrich Lefler (Austrian, 1863–1919) and **Joseph Urban** (Austrian, 1872–1933), illustrators
W. Labler, ed., *Kling-Klang Gloria: German Folk and Children's Songs* (*Kling-Klang Gloria: Deutsche Volks- und Kinderlieder*) (Vienna: Tempsky and Freytag, 1907), 66 pp., 16 color plates
Song book: color paperboard cover, black-and-white ornamentation around music scores
Book, 10 1/8 x 12 11/16 x 7/16 in. (25.6 x 32.3 x 1.0 cm)
K.90.9

The selection of German folksongs, *Kling-Klang Gloria,* is among the best-known German language songbooks for children. The songs' scores and texts are paired with colorful narrative illustrations by Lefler and Urban. Their vivid and often playful compositions combine a central image, derived from the song's theme, flanked laterally with decorative borders or narrative vignettes. Lefler's work as a stage designer no doubt influenced the theatrical arrangement of the characters and scenes. As in the illustration for *Little Hansel, Little Gretel* [*Hanselein (Gretelein)*], the use of bright complementary colors and a multitude of patterns juxtaposed with flat, open surfaces, projects the liveliness of the dancing boy and girl across the entire scene.

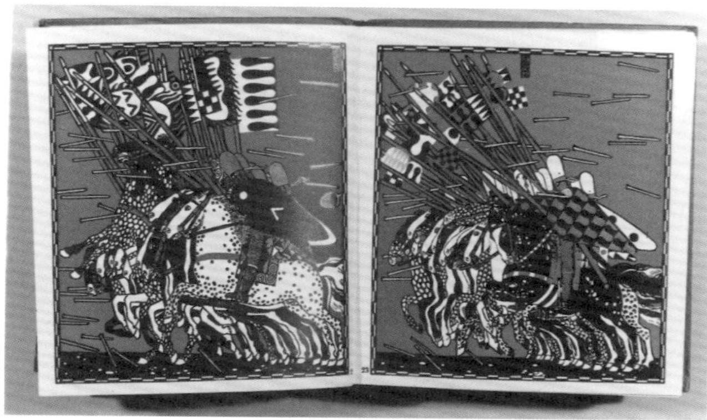

96. Carl Otto Czeschka (Austrian, 1878–1960), book designer
Franz Keim, *The Nibelungs Retold to the German Nation* (*Die Nibelungen dem Deutschen Volke wiedererzählt von Franz Keim*) 2nd ed. (Vienna: Gerlach & Wiedling, 1924), 68 pp., 16 plates
Letterpress, book, 6 x 5 5/8 x 7/16 in. (15.2 x 14.3 x 1.1 cm)
K.76.5; see Color Plate 31

Both Franz Keim's text and Carl Otto Czeschka's illustrations for this version of the Nibelungs make this book a particularly significant document of its time. The schoolteacher Keim (1840–1918) became an independent writer after retirement and composed dramas, epics, and lyric works. His adaptation of the twelfth-century epic reduced the original's 2400 stanzas to thirty pages. It also evokes the psychology of his characters, an especially modern quality that would have appealed to a broad middle class audience. The design of the publication exemplifies the Viennese notion of the *Gesamtkunstwerk.* The graphic artist Czeschka trained at the Vienna Academy from 1894 to 1899 and taught at the Applied Arts School from 1902 to 1907 before he took a teaching post in Hamburg. He joined the Wiener Werkstätte in 1905 and remained a member after he moved to Hamburg. For the *Nibelungs,* Czeschka not only produced the innovative two-page illustrations but also the frontispiece, decorative borders that frame each page, and small, square-format vignettes. His typographical selection of the Jugendstil Eckmann font also reflects the overall modern interpretation of the epic's medieval character.[51]

Czeschka's images articulate his fondness for medieval subject matter and combine a strong architectonic composition, a limited range of colors (blue, red, gold), and a brilliant juxtaposition of flat, open planes and decorative patterns. The resulting scenes, which extend horizontally over two pages, are either statically arrested or energetically animated, although they consistently achieve a sense of monumentality that belies their small scale. The book's publisher, Martin Gerlach, printed it as part of his Jugendbücherei (young people's library) series intended to improve the quality of children's books. The series produced thirty-four moderately priced editions of the Keim/Czeschka *Nibelungs*.[52]

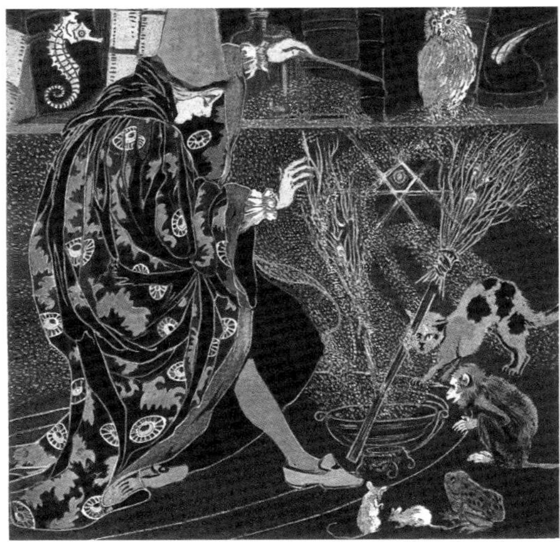

97. Ilona Wittrisch (Austrian, 1879–1946), illustrator
Josef Bindtner, *The Spiders: A German Fairytale* (*Die Spinnen: Ein deutsches Märchen*) (Vienna: k.k. Graphische Lehr- und Versuchsanstalt, 1914), 34 pp., 5 color plates
Book, 10 3/4 x 9 3/8 in. (27.2 x 23.5 x 14 cm)
K.2000.8; see Color Plate 32

A magician, witch, lovely blond princess, and host of animals all play a role in Josef Bindtner's fairytale of adventures narrated by a spider. Illona Wittrich's narrative style of illustration recalls nineteenth-century romanticism in which a scene appears fantastically alive. Balancing realism and caricature, dynamic composition and delicate rendering, she animates all the elements of her images such that humans and animals as well as atmosphere and inanimate objects become remarkably expressive.

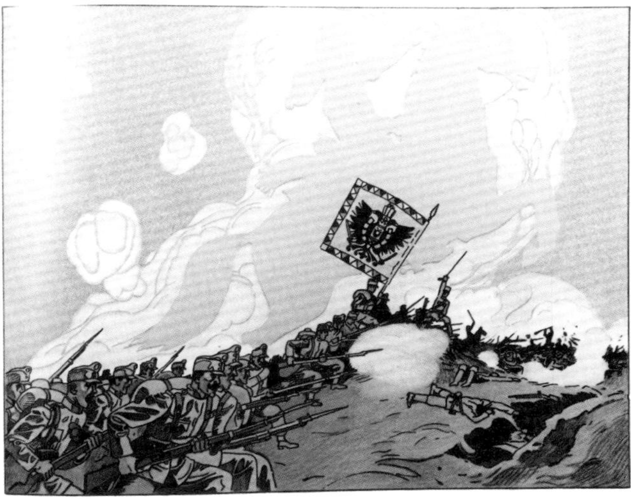

98. Franz Wacik (Austrian, 1883–1938), illustrator
Hugo von Hofmannsthal, *Prince Eugene the Noble Knight: His Life in Pictures* (*Prinz Eugen der edle Ritter: Sein Leben in Bildern. Erzählt von Hugo von Hofmannsthal*) (Vienna: L. W. Seidel & Sohn, 1915), 46 pp., 12 original lithographs
Decorative text border of oak leaves and acorns and pictorial endpapers. Bound in cloth-backed pictorial boards, 10 1/4 x 12 7/8 x 7/16 in. (26.1 x 32.7 x 1.1 cm)
K.94.5

Prince Eugene of Savoy's (1663–1736) reputation as a great military leader in the service of the Holy Roman Emperor made him a legend within Austro-Hungarian history. Born into the Carignan line of the house of Savoy, he later distinguished himself by fighting against the Turks in central Europe and the Balkans and against France in the War of the Grand Alliance and the War of the Spanish Succession. An imperial field marshal by the age of twenty-nine, his battles were known for their bloodiness as well as their daring and success. After the Turkish siege of Vienna and their defeat in 1638, Prince Eugene became known as the "terror of the Turks and commander in chief of all Austrian armies" and was later even referred to as the "secret emperor."[53] The title of the text, *Prince Eugene the Noble Knight*, derives from a traditional hymn of the Habsburg armies.

The text by Hugo von Hofmannsthal, one of Vienna's most distinguished fin-de-siècle writers, gives the life of Eugene of Savoy the character of a legend-in-the-making. He recounts the battles with the French and Turks, as well as Eugene's civic accomplishments. These include the building of the Vienna City Palace (*Stadtpalais*) and Belvedere and advising the emperor to make Trieste into a powerful harbor city. Hofmannsthal writes of Eugene, "Under the contemporary Austrians, he alone was capable of the thought that not only Spain and Venice, not only England and the Netherlands, but also Austria should signify something on the sea."

The book's twelve lithographic illustrations produced by Secession member and art teacher Franz Wacik combine theatrical composition, vivid color, and dramatic lighting to underscore the legendary quality of Eugene's life and reputation. In the book's final battle scene, for instance, Wacik presents a landscape of charging Austrian World War I soldiers. The image follows the song text, "Prince Eugene's spirit is always there, where our soldiers fight and triumph." Figures, weapons, and the imperial flag dynamically incline toward the right of the composition and convey the unified thrust of the attack. Looming above the troops is the pale gray silhouette of Eugene seated on a rearing horse, framed by a voluminous yellow cloud. Presented in hierarchic proportion, Eugene appears as a fantastic, charismatic force leading the charge, his spirit illuminating the troops below.

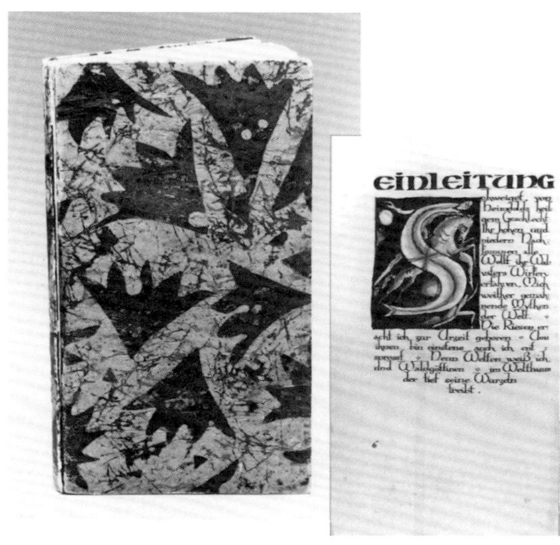

99. Julius Zimpel (Austrian, 1896–1925)
The Prophecy of the Sibyl of the Voluspa (Die Kunde der Wala Völuspá), 1916, 59 pp. 16 watercolors, 2 vignettes
Ink, watercolor, graphite, 8 3/16 x 4 3/4 x 1/2 in.
(20.9 x 12.2 x 1.6 cm)
K.2002.3

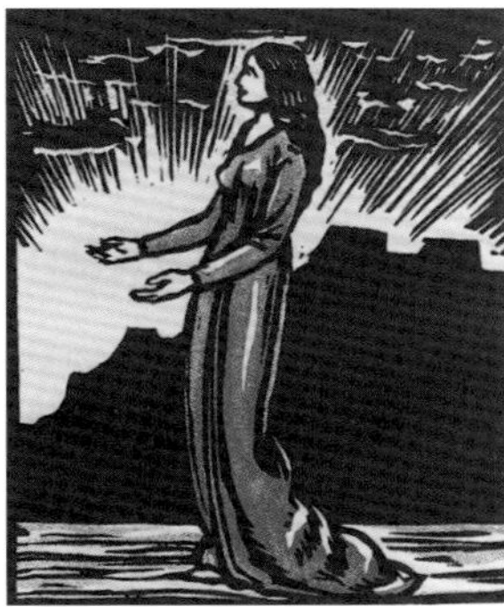

100. Erwin Lang (Austrian,1886–1962), illustrator; Jutta Schulhof, typographer
Arthur Koessler, ed., *German Minnesong (Deutscher Minnesang: Ausgewählt und Übertragen von Arthur Koessler)* (Vienna: Konegan, 1921), 41 pp., 6 color woodcuts
Book, 4 1/2 x 4 1/16 x 1/4 in. (11.4 x 10.0 x .6 cm)
K.94.14

This small, modest book is a collection of German lyric poetry known as Minnesong. Developed by poet musicians in the twelfth and thirteenth centuries, this type of medieval song originally dealt with themes of courtly love, although the term has since been applied more broadly to a variety of verse. Many poems in this selection are by anonymous authors. They pay tribute to a host of courtly themes dealing with love, hope, longing, secret desire, sorrow, and parting. Erwin Lang's six crisply colored woodcuts display elements of expressionism. By focusing on a single subject presented in the composition's foreground, his small but surprisingly monumental images capture the somber and melancholic tone of the poems.

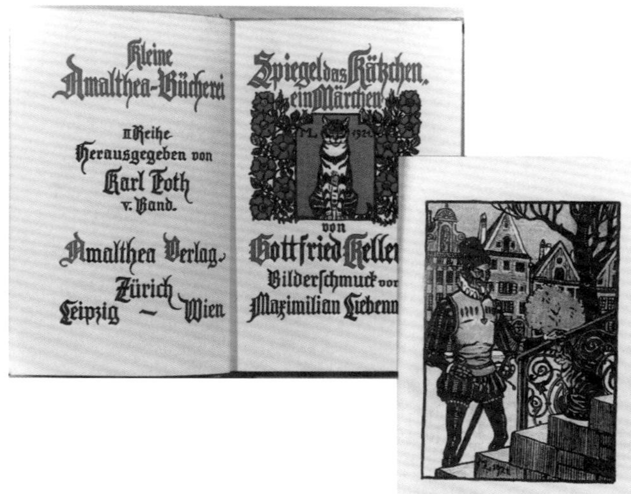

101. Maximilian Liebenwein (Austrian, d. Munich, Germany, 1869–1926), illustrator
Gottfried Keller, *Spiegel, the Kitten: A Fairytale (Spiegel, das Kätzchen: Ein Märchen)* (Zurich: Amalthea, 1922), 117 pp., 8 B&W illus.
Book, 6 x 4 1/4 x 1/2 in. (15.2 x 10.8 x 1.2 cm)
K.97.10

Spiegel, the Kitten, written by the major late nineteenth-century realist writer Gottfried Keller, was first published in 1865. The fairytale is a humorous critique of the people of Seldwyla, a fictive town often interpreted as a Keller's native Zurich. Based on the proverb "the cat is in the bag," the fairytale follows Spiegel's amusing encounters with the town wizard, Herr Pineiss. In the course of the story, the narrative reveals the Seldwylers' character flaws, gullibility, and restrained but positive feelings toward others. In what can be called a cat-lover's delight, Maximilian Liebenwein's illustrations celebrate the tale's protagonist, Spiegel the cat. The book's boldly designed cover and frontispiece, and playfully composed endpapers, black and white vignettes, and color illustrations—all rendered in a clear, realist style—depict the feline subject as an intelligent and lively character.

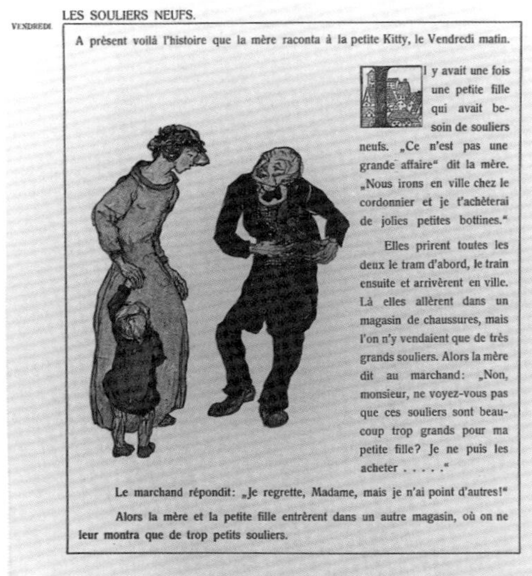

VENDREDI

LES SOULIERS NEUFS.

A prèsent voilà l'histoire que la mère raconta à la petite Kitty, le Vendredi matin.

Il y avait une fois une petite fille qui avait besoin de souliers neufs. „Ce n'est pas une grande affaire" dit la mère. „Nous irons en ville chez le cordonnier et je t'achèterai de jolies petites bottines."

Elles prirent toutes les deux le tram d'abord, le train ensuite et arrivèrent en ville. Là elles allèrent dans un magasin de chaussures, mais l'on n'y vendaient que de très grands souliers. Alors la mère dit au marchand: „Non, monsieur, ne voyez-vous pas que ces souliers sont beaucoup trop grands pour ma petite fille? Je ne puis les acheter . . . . ."

Le marchand répondit: „Je regrette, Madame, mais je n'ai point d'autres!"

Alors la mère et la petite fille entrèrent dans un autre magasin, où on ne leur montra que de trop petits souliers.

102. Herta Zuckermann (Austrian, active 1923), illustrator
C. de Leeuw-Schönberg, *Mother's Tales for Little Kitty: Seven Tales Translated from the Dutch* (*Les Contes de maman à la petit kitty: Sept contes de Madame C. de Leeuw-Schönberg traduits du Hollandais*) (Amsterdam: Metz & Co's Magazijnen, 1923), 14 pp., 13 color plates; 3 B&W illus.
Book, 9 1/4 x 8 1/8 in. (23.6 x 20.7 cm)
K.99.13

The design of *Mother's Tales for Little Kitty* adheres fundamentally to the Viennese tradition of the total work of art, although Herta Zuckermann's articulation of that ideal presents a striking stylistic contrast to the majority of books in this section. As a young student, Zuckermann had participated in Professor Franz Cizek's classes at the Applied Arts School for students of ages six to fifteen.[54] Cizek's reformist pedagogy was intended to foster the creativity inherent in young children. In order to develop expressive abilities, children were provided a broad range of media and encouraged to experiment freely and positively critique each other's work. Rhythmic movement was also introduced into Cizek's methodology, and music was played as children worked on their projects. Reflecting a fin-de-siècle interest in music, rhythm, and dance as means to mental and physical liberation, Cizek believed that "[music] stimulates work, spirit and body take on the impetus of the sounds, the rhythmic production increases."[55] Such elements appear to have inspired Zuckermann's proclivity toward a fluid and rhythmic handling of line. Unlike many other illustrations in this section, Zuckermann's technique is sketchy, fluid, and even nervous. Although her rendering recalls somewhat the meandering, curvilinear forms of Jugendstil, it is less stylized and even whimsical.

F. Pattern Books

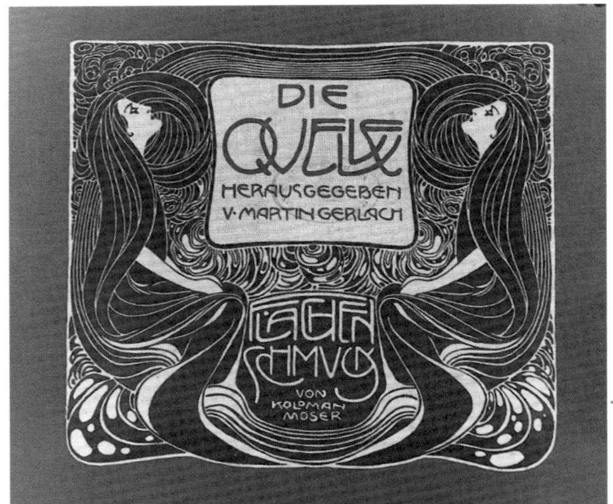

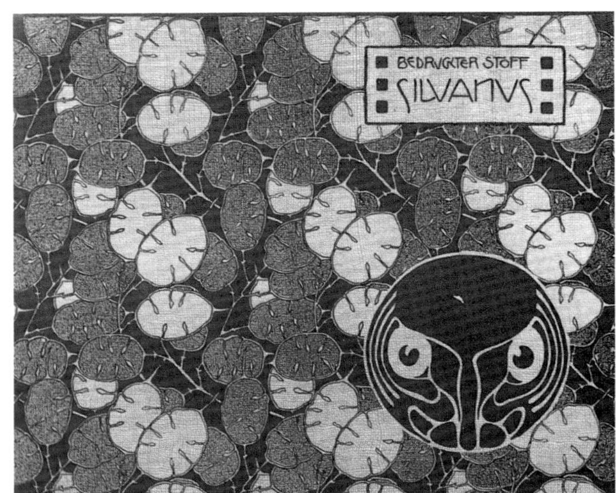

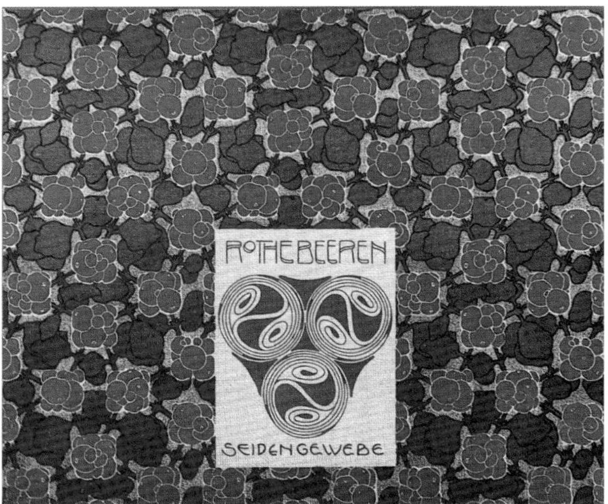

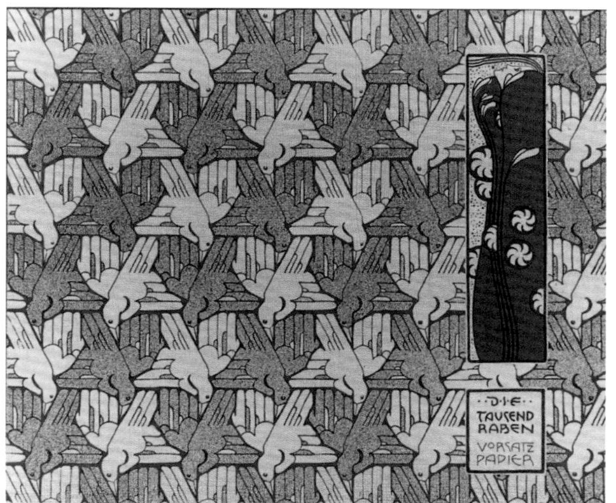

103. Koloman Moser (Austrian, 1868–1918), designer
The Source: Surface Ornament (Die Quelle: Flachen Schmuck)
(Vienna: Gerlach, 1901), 30 plates
Original linen cover; sheet, ea. 9 7/8 x 11 3/4 in. (25.0 x 29.9 cm)
K.78.1

This variation on the total work of art concept is a splendid collection of pattern designs by Koloman Moser. Many of the colorful patterns combine interlocking abstracted forms of figures, animals, or foliage. Reflecting his interest in the graphic theories of Rudolf von Larisch, Moser plays with fore- and background space through the juxtaposition of form, color, and pattern. The result is spatial tension that verges on optical illusion. Inspired by Japanese prints, Moser also superimposed square or rectangular insets on the patterns that identify the name of the design and its suggested use. The recommended applications include fabrics, wallpaper, tapestries, wrapping paper, weaving, wall decorations, floor coverings, block-printed silk, and upholstery.

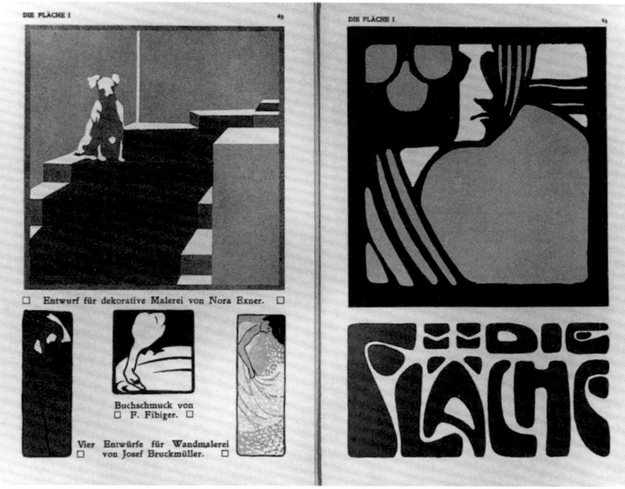

104. Various artists
Felician von Myrbach et al., eds., *The Surface I (Die Fläche I)*
(Vienna: Schroll, 1903–1904), 30 pp.
Color designs (algraphs) for paintings, posters, books, and prints; some pages from I.7 and some from I.8; sheet (each): 12 5/16 x 8 1/8 in. (31.3 x 20.6 cm)
K.90.13

Edited by members of the Wiener Werkstätte, this pattern book is a portfolio of brightly colored Jugendstil surface decorations. The designs were intended for practical aesthetic applications such as decorative painting, monograms, posters, book decorations, tapestries, weaving, woodcuts, business cards, silk fabric, and embroidery. Reflecting contemporary efforts to develop a distinctive Viennese style in a broad range of media, Josef August Lux's introductory statement asserted that "people, who for decades usually fetched their models from Paris, already demand the 'Viennese style' today. *The Surface* manifests this style in its most austere and purified form."[56]

Notes

1. See the notes from the fourteenth exhibition, *Vereinigung bildender Künstler Österreichs* (Vienna: Vereinigung bildender Künstler Österreichs, 1902, quoted in Peter Vergo, *Art in Vienna 1898–1918: Klimt, Kokoschka, Schiele and Their Contemporaries* (Ithaca: Cornell University Press, 1975), 70.

2. Quoted in Sharon L. Hirsch, *Hodler's Symbolist Themes* (Ann Arbor: UMI Research Press, 1983), 3.

3. Sharon L. Hirsch, *Ferdinand Hodler* (New York: Braziller, 1982), 112.

4. See Tag Gronberg, "The Inner Man: Interiors and Masculinity in Early Twentieth-Century Vienna," *Oxford Art Journal* 24, 1 (2001): 73.

5. Michael Pabst, "Diktatur des Quadrats," in *Wiener Grafik um 1900*, ed. Michael Pabst (Munich: Silde Schreiber, 1984), 191–227; see especially pages 204–7. See also Carl G. Jung, *Psychology and Religion* (New Haven: Yale University Press, 1938), 115.

6. For a fuller account of this psycho-geographical split in Kalvach's history, see Hanna Egger, *Expressive und Dekorative Graphik in Wien Zwischen 1905 und 1925: Rudolf Kalvach und Hedwig Mailler* (Vienna: Österreichisches Museum für angewandt Kunst, 1979), 11–15.

7. For an early article on Orlik, see Richard Muther, "Emil Orlik," *The Studio* 20, 89 (August 1900): 159–64.

8. Tsuneo Takeda, *Kanō Eitoku* (New York: Kodansha International & Shibundo, 1977), 43.

9. Bernhard Denscher, "Literatur um Jung-Wien," in *Wien 1870–1930: Traum und Wirklichkeit*, ed. Robert Waissenberger (exh. cat.) (Salzburg: Residenz, 1984), 46.

10. *Die Bilderwelt im Kinderbuch: Kinder- und Jugendbücher aus fünf Jahrhunderten* (exh. cat.) (Cologne: Greven & Bechtold, 1988), 357.

11. Cf. the listing in Robert Waissenberger, *Ver Sacrum: Die Zeitschrift der Wiener Secession, 1898–1903* (exh. cat.) (Vienna: Museen der Stadt Wien, 1982), 112. The color woodcuts by Exner, Uchatius, and Fiebiger were indeed meant for an animal alphabet book, although they never appeared on the book market. *Die Bilderwelt im Kinderbuch,* 357.

12. Jennifer Hawkins Opie, "The New Glass: A Synthesis of Technology and Dreams," in *Art Nouveau 1890–1914*, ed. Paul Greenhalgh (exh. cat.) (New York: Abrams, 2000), 215.

13. Victor Arwas, *Glass: Art Nouveau to Art Deco* (New York: Rizzoli, 1977), 8.

14. Waltraud Neuwirth, *Das Glas des Jugendstils: Sammlung des Österreichischen Museums für angewandte Kunst, Wien* (Munich: Prestel, 1973).

15. Victor Arwas and Helga Hilschenz both mention that in 1902 Loetz produced designs by Moser and his students in an arrangement coordinated by Bakalowits. Helga Hilschenz, *Das Glas des Jugendstils: Katalog der Sammlung Hentrich im Kunstmuseum Düsseldorf* (Munich: Prestel, 1973), 390; Arwas, *Glass,* 119, 144. See also Neuwirth, *Das Glas des Jugendstils.*

16. Opie gives the dates for Kirschner's collaboration with the Loetz firm as 1899 to 1914. See Opie, "The New Glass: A Synthesis of Technology and Dreams," 216.

17. Josef Hoffmann, Working Program, Wiener Werkstätte, published 1904–05 in the *Wiener allgemeine Zeitung* 26, 16 (March 1905): 2. Quoted in Werner J. Schweiger, *Wiener Werkstätte: Kunst und Handwerk, 1903–1932* (Vienna: Branstätter, 1982), 42–43. Translation mine.

18. *Deutsche Kunst und Dekoration* 17, 3 (1905–06): 192.

19. Ludwig Hevesi, *Altkunst-Neukunst: Wien, 1904–1908* (Vienna: Konegen, 1909), 228, 230. Quoted in Schweiger, *Wiener Werkstätte: Kunst und Handwerk, 1903–1932*, 60.

20. Carl E. Schorske, *Fin-de-Siècle Vienna: Politics and Culture* (New York: Knopf, 1980), 237.

21. The covered box was formerly attributed to Kitty Rix, although evidence that it is the work of her sister Felice is more conclusive. Whereas Kitty's first documented Wiener Werstätte ceramic work dates from 1924, Felice was active in the ceramic workshops from 1917 to 1923, a period within which the date of the box falls. Moreover, the artist's stamp on the bottom of the box bears the initials, F. R. and an unbroken rectilinear outline found in other examples of Felice's monogram. See also Bärbel Hamacher, ed., *Expressive Keramik der Wiener Werkstätte, 1917–1930* (Munich: Bayerische Vereinsbank, 1992), 132.

22. From Jesser-Schmidt's resume, personnel archives, Hochschule für angewandte Kunst in Vienna. Quoted in Hamacher, *Expressive Keramik*, 14.

23. Werner J. Schweiger, *Wiener Werkstätte: Design in Vienna, 1903–1932*, trans. Alexander Lieven (New York: Abbeville Press, 1984), 220.

24. Elisabeth Rücker, *Wiener Charme: Mode 1914/15: Graphiken und Accessories* (Nuremberg: Germanisches Nationalmuseum, 1984), 31.

25. Angela Völker in collaboration with Ruperta Pichler, *Textiles of the Wiener Werkstätte 1910–1932* (New York: Rizzoli, 1994).

26. Jane Kallir, *Viennese Design and the Wiener Werkstätte* (exh. cat.) (New York: Galerie St. Etienne and Braziller, 1986), 29–30.

27. Corresponding criticism refers to a growing provincialism with the increasing expressionist styles and looking toward primitive, folkish, childlike forms. The Werkstätte was seen as regressive rather than really in step with the times, despite the fact that much of the prewar abstraction—especially in the area of textile design—anticipated international developments during the interwar period. See Völker, *Textiles of the Wiener Werkstätte,* 111, 119.

28. Völker, *Textiles of the Wiener Werkstätte*, 153.

29. Waissenberger, *Ver Sacrum*, 43. Translation mine.

30. Editorial note published in the first 1900 issue, reproduced in Waissenberger, *Ver Sacrum*, 75.

31. Waissenberger, *Ver Sacrum*, 73.

32. Vergo, *Art in Vienna 1898–1918*, 50–60.

33. Robert Waissenberger, ed., *Vienna: 1890–1920* (New York: Rizzoli, 1984), 148–49.

34. Kallir, *Viennese Design and the Wiener Werkstätte*, 135.

35. Kallir, *Viennese Design and the Wiener Werkstätte*, 124.

36. Mathilde Flögl, *The Wiener Werkstätte 1903–1928: The Evolution of the Modern Applied Arts* (Vienna: Krystall, 1929), introduction.

37. Schweiger, *Wiener Werkstätte: Design in Vienna, 1903–1932,* 123–24.

38. Kallir, *Viennese Design and the Wiener Werkstätte*, 22–25.

39. Kallir, *Viennese Design and the Wiener Werkstätte*, 22–25, 33.

40. Schweiger, *Wiener Werkstätte: Kunst und Handwerk, 1903–1932*, 40.

41. The text's frontispiece reads, "*Gedenktage aus dem Jahre 1809/ Eine Erinnerung/den Damens Wien Gewidmet/Vom Ballkomitte/der Stadt Wein.*"

42. The German text reads, "*Die Eröffnung der zweite Kaiser-Franz-Josef-Hochquellenleitung durch se. Majestät den Kaiser am 2. Dez. 1910.*"

43. Josef Hoffmann, Working Program, Wiener Werkstätte, 1905. Quoted in Schweiger, *Wiener Werkstätte: Kunst und Handwerk, 1903–1932*, 42–43. Translation mine.

44. Hoffmann, Working Program, Wiener Werkstätte, 1905. Quoted in Schweiger, *Wiener Werkstätte: Kunst und Handwerk, 1903–1932*, 42.

45. Schweiger, *Wiener Werkstätte: Design in Vienna, 1903–1932*, 183.

46. Franz Grillparzer, *The Poor Fiddler*, trans. Alexander and Elizabeth Henderson (New York: Ungar, 1967), 13–15.

47. The German text reads, "*Der Fremde liegt im schönen Garten, vertaubt von vieler Wanderschaft, schlafend unter einem blühenden Granatbaum. Gazellen, silberne Fasane, Pfaue und ein Panther kommen nahe und lagern um die Erscheinung.*"

48. See Joseph Lammers, "Bild und Werk. Zu Themen illustrierter Bücher," *Vom Jugendstil zum Bauhaus: Deutsche Buchkunst 1985–1930* (exh. cat.) (Munster: Westfälisches Landesmuseum für Kunst und Kulturgeschichte, 1981), 55–65.

49. Josef, archduke of Austria, "Vorwort," *Atlas der Heilpflanzen*.

50. Sebastian Kneipp, *The Kneipp Cure* (New York: Nature Cure, 1949), frontispiece.

51. *Die Nibelungen. In der Wiedergabe von Franz Keim*. Fore- and afterword by Helmut Brackert, illustrations by Carl Otto Czeschka (Frankfurt am Main: Insel, 1972), 9.

52. *Bilderwelt im Kinderbuch*, 357.

53. Paul Hofmann, *The Viennese: Splendour, Twilight, and Exile* (New York: Anchor Press, 1988), 63.

54. Franz Cizek, "Introduction," in C. de Leeuw-Schönberg, *Les Contes de maman à la petit kitty* (Amsterdam: Metz & Co's Magazijnen, 1923).

55. "*... die Musik die Arbeit fördert, Geist und Körper nehmen das Schwingen der Töne auf, das rhythmische Schaffen steigert sich.*" L. W. Rochowanski, *Die Weiner Jugendkunst: Franz Cizek und seine Pflegestätte* (Vienna: W. Frick, 1946), 45. Quoted in Wanda A. Bubriski, "Franz Cizek—Ein Pionier der Kunsterziehung," in *Wien 1870–1930: Traum und Wirklichkeit*, ed. Robert Waissenberger (Salzburg: Residenz, 1984), 164.

56. Josef August Lux, "Die Fläche," in *Die Fläche I*, ed. Felician von Myrbach et al. (Vienna: Schroll, 1903–04), n.p.

Selected Bibliography

Ankwicz, Hans von. "Wacik, Franz." In *Allgemeines Lexikon der bildenden Künstler* 35. Edited by Ulrich Thieme und Felix Becker. Zwickau: Ullmann, 1964–1966.

Arwas, Victor. *Glass: Art Nouveau to Art Deco.* New York: Rizzoli, 1977.

Aynsley, Jeremy. *Graphic Design in Germany: 1890–1945.* Berkeley: University of California Press, 2000.

Bahr, Hermann. *Briefwechsel mit seinem Vater: Ausgewählt von Adalbert Schmidt.* Vienna: Bauer, 1971.

Bahr, Hermann. *Secession.* Vienna: Wiener, 1900.

Bailey, Colin B., ed. *Gustav Klimt: Modernism in the Making.* Exh. cat. New York: Abrams; Ottawa: National Gallery of Canada, 2001.

Baroni, Daniele, and Antonio D'Auria. *Kolo Moser: Graphic Artist and Designer.* New York: Rizzoli, 1986.

Die Bilderwelt im Kinderbuch: Kinder- und Jugendbücher aus fünf Jahrhunderten. Exh. cat. Cologne: Greven & Bechtold, 1988.

Bisanz-Prakken, Marian. *Gustav Klimt: Der Beethovenfries: Geschichte, Funktion und Bedeutung.* Salzburg: Residenz, 1977.

Bubriski, Wanda A. "Franz Cizek—Ein Pionier der Kunsterziehung." In *Wien 1870–1930: Traum und Wirklichkeit,* edited by Robert Waissenberger. Exh. cat. Salzburg: Residenz, 1984, 161–67.

Campbell, Joan. *The German Werkbund.* Princeton: Princeton University Press, 1978.

Carey, Frances, and Antony Griffiths. *The Print in Germany, 1880–1933.* Exh. cat. London: The British Museum, 1984. Reprint. New York: Dover, 1993.

Carter, Sebastian. *Twentieth Century Type Designers.* London: Trefoil, 1987.

Comini, Alessandra. *Egon Schiele's Portraits.* Berkeley: University of California Press, 1974.

Comini, Alessandra. *Gustav Klimt.* New York: Braziller, 1975.

De La Grange, Henry-Louis. *Gustav Mahler. Vienna: The Years of Challenge.* Oxford: Oxford University Press, 1995.

Denscher, Bernhard. "Literatur um Jung-Wien." In *Wien 1870–1930: Traum und Wirklichkeit,* edited by Robert Waissenberger. Exh. cat. Salzburg: Residenz, 1984, 45–57.

Egger, Hanna. *Expressive und Dekorative Graphik in Wien Zwischen 1905 und 1925: Rudolf Kalvach und Hedwig Mailler.* Vienna: Österreichisches Museum für angewandt Kunst, 1979.

Fahr-Becker, Gabriele. *Wiener Werkstätte: 1903–1932.* Translated by Karen Williams and High Warden. Cologne: Taschen, 1994.

Fanelli, Giovanni. *La Linea Viennese: Grafica Art Nouveau.* Florence: Cantini, 1989.

Fenz, Werner. *Koloman Moser: Graphik, Kunstgewerbe, Malerei.* Salzburg: Residenz, 1984.

Flögl, Mathilde. *The Wiener Werkstätte 1903–1928: The Evolution of the Modern Applied Arts.* Vienna: Krystall, 1929.

Gluck, Frans, and Fritz Novotny. *Wien um 1900.* Exh. cat. Vienna: Historical Museum of the City of Vienna, Künstlerhaus, Secession, 1964.

Goldwater, Robert. *Symbolism.* New York: Harper & Row, 1979.

Greenhalgh, Paul, ed. *Art Nouveau 1890–1914.* New York: Abrams, 2000.

Gronberg, Tag. "The Inner Man: Interiors and Masculinity in Early Twentieth-Century Vienna," *Oxford Art Journal* 24, 1 (2001): 67–88.

Der Hagenbund. Exh. cat. Vienna: Museen der Stadt Wien, 1975.

Hamacher, Bärbel, ed. *Expressive Keramik der Wiener Werkstätte, 1917–1930.* Munich: Bayerische Vereinsbank, 1992.

Hanisch, Ernst. *1890–1990. Der lange Schatten des Staates. Österreichische Gesellschaftsgeschichte.* Vienna: Ueberreuter, 1994.

Hansen, Traude. *Wiener Werkstätte: Mode, Stoffe, Schmuck, Accessories.* Vienna: Brandstätter, 1984.

Heller, Friedrich C. "Gerlachs Jugendbücherei," *Die Schiefertafel* 4, 3 (December 1981): 138–62.

Hevesi, Ludwig. *Acht Jahre Sezession.* Vienna: Konegen, 1906. Reprint. Klagenfurth: Ritter, 1984.

Hevesi, Ludwig. *Altkunst—Neukunst: Wien, 1904–1908.* Vienna: Konegen, 1909.

Hilschenz, Helga. *Das Glas des Jugendstils: Katalog der Sammlung Hentrich im Kunstmuseum Düsseldorf.* Munich: Prestel, 1973.

Hirsch, Sharon L. *Ferdinand Hodler.* New York: Braziller, 1982.

Hirsch, Sharon L. *Hodler's Symbolist Themes.* Ann Arbor: UMI Research Press, 1983.

Hofmann, Paul. *The Viennese: Splendour, Twilight, and Exile.* New York: Anchor Press, 1988.

Howard, Jeremy. *Art Nouveau: International and National Styles in Europe.* Manchester, U.K.: Manchester University Press, 1996.

Hummel, Julius. *Koloman Moser: 1868–1918.* Exh. cat. Vienna: Hochschüle für angewandte Kunst in Wien & Österreichisches Museum für angewandte Kunst, 1979.

Johnston, William M. *The Austrian Mind.* Berkeley: University of California Press, 1972.

Jung, Carl G. *Psychology and Religion.* New Haven: Yale University Press, 1938.

Kallir, Jane. *Egon Schiele: The Complete Works.* New York: Abrams, 1990.

Kallir, Jane. *Viennese Design and the Wiener Werkstätte.* Exh. cat. New York: Galerie St. Etienne and Braziller, 1986.

Kneipp, Sebastian. *The Kneipp Cure.* New York: Nature Cure, 1949.

Kunsthandwerk: Jugendstil, Werkbund, Art Déco. Catalogue by Karl H. Bröhan, 2 vols. Berlin: Sammlung Bröhan, 1977.

Lammers, Joseph. "Bild und Werk: Zu Themen illustrierter Bücher." In *Vom Jugendstil zum Bauhaus: Deutsche Buchkunst 1985–1930.* Exh. cat. Munster: Westfälisches Landesmuseum für Kunst und Kulturgeschichte, 1981.

Lux, Josef August. "Die Fläche." In *Die Fläche I,* edited by Felician von Myrbach et al. Vienna: Schroll, 1903–04, n.p

Morton, Frederic. *A Nervous Splendor: Vienna, 1888–1889.* London: Weidenfeld and Nicolson, 1979.

Müller, Guido. *Deutsch-französische Gesellschaftsbeziehungen und europäische Gespräche nach dem Ersten Weltkrieg. Das Deutsch-Französische Studienkomitee und der Europäische Kulturbund 1923/24–1932/33.* Munich: Oldenbourg, 2002.

Muther, Richard. "Emil Orlik," *The Studio* 20, 89 (August 1900): 159–64.

Nebehay, Christian M. *Gustav Klimt: Dokumentation.* Vienna: Galerie Christian Nebehay, 1969.

Nebehay, Christian M. *Wien speziell. Architetktur und Malerei um 1900.* Vienna: Brandstätter, 2000.

Neuwirth, Waltraud. *Glas 1905–1925: Vom Jugendstil zum Art Deco*, vol. 2. Vienna: Selbstverlag Dr. Waltraud Neuwirth, 1987.

Neuwirth, Waltraud. *Das Glas des Jugendstils. Sammlung des Österreichischen Museums für angewandte Kunst, Wien.* Munich: Prestel, 1973.

Neuwirth, Waltraud. *Die Wiener Werkstätte: Avantgarde, Art Deco, Industrial Design.* Vienna: Neuwirth, 1984.

Die Nibelungen. In der Wiedergabe von Franz Keim. Fore- and afterword by Helmut Brackert. Illustrations by Carl Otto Czeschka. Frankfurt am Main: Insel, 1972.

Noever, Peter, ed. *Dagobert Peche and the Wiener Werkstätte.* Vienna: Österreichisches Museum für angewandte Kunst, 2002.

Nostitz, Oswalt von. "Hofmannsthal, Hugo von." In Caspar v. Schrenck-Notzing, *Lexikon des Konservativismus.* Graz: Stocker, 1996.

Novotny, Fritz and Hubert Adolph. *Max Kurzweil: Ein Maler der Wiener Sezession.* Munich: Jugend & Volk, 1969.

Opie, Jennifer Hawkins. "The New Glass: A Synthesis of Technology and Dreams." In *Art Nouveau 1890–1914*, edited by Paul Greenhalgh. Exh. cat. New York: Abrams, 2000.

Otto Prutscher: 1880–1949. Vienna: Hochschule für angewandte Kunst, 1997.

Pabst, Michael. "Diktatur des Quadrats." In *Wiener Grafik um 1900*, edited by Michael Pabst. Munich: Silde Schreiber, 1984.

Pabst, Michael. *Wien um 1900: Grafik und Buchkunst 1895–1914.* Munich: Villa Stuck, 1982.

Phillips, Lisa. *Frederick Kiesler.* Exh. cat. New York: Whitney Museum of Art and Norton, 1989.

Reifenberg, Benno. "West-Kunst-Gewerbe. Zur internationalen Ausstellung in Paris," *Frankfurter Zeitung*, 5 August 1925.

Rennhofer, Maria. *Koloman Moser.* Vienna: Brandstätter, 2002.

Rochowanski, L.W., ed. *Ein Führer durch das Österreichische Kunstgewerbe.* Leipzig: Heinz, 1930.

Rochowanski, L. W. *Die Weiner Jugendkunst: Franz Cizek und seine Pflegestätte.* Vienna: Frick, 1946.

Rücker, Elisabeth. *Wiener Charme: Mode 1914/15: Graphiken und Accessories.* Nuremberg: Germanisches Nationalmuseum, 1984.

Schmuttermeier, Elisabeth. "Die Wiener Werkstätte." In *Wien 1870–1930: Traum und Wirklichkeit*, edited by Robert Waissenberger. Salzburg: Residenz, 1984, 145–50.

Schmuttermeier, Elisabeth. *Schmuck von 1900–1925.* Exh cat. Vienna: MAK-Austrian Museum of Applied Arts, 1986.

Schorske, Carl E. *Fin-de-Siècle Vienna: Politics and Culture.* New York: Knopf, 1980.

Schütte, Margret. *Emil Orlik.* Berlin: Mann, 1983.

Schweiger, Werner J. *Wiener Werkstätte: Design in Vienna, 1903–1932.* Translated by Alexander Lieven. New York: Abbeville Press, 1984.

Schweiger, Werner J. *Wiener Werkstätte: Kunst und Handwerk, 1903–1932.* Vienna: Branstätter, 1982.

Sekler, Eduard F. *Josef Hoffmann: Das architektonische Werk: Monografie und Werkverzeichnis.* Vienna: Residenz, 1982.

Sekler, Eduard F. *Josef Hoffmann: The Architectural Work. Monograph and Catalogue of Works.* Princeton: Princeton University Press, 1985.

Silver, Kenneth. *Esprit de Corps.* Princeton: Princeton University Press, 1989.

Silverman, Debora L. *Art Nouveau in Fin-de-Siècle France: Politics, Psychology, and Style.* Berkeley: University of California Press, 1989.

Steinberg, Michael P. *The Meaning of the Salzburg Festival.* Ithaca: Cornell University Press, 1990.

Takeda, Tsuneo. *Kanō Eitoku.* New York: Kodansha International & Shibundo, 1977.

Troy, Nancy J. *Modernism and the Decorative Arts in France: Art Nouveau to Le Corbusier.* New Haven: Yale University Press, 1991.

Varnedoe, Kirk. *Vienna 1900: Art, Architecture and Design.* New York: Museum of Modern Art, 1986.

Vergo, Peter. *Art in Vienna 1898–1918: Klimt, Kokoschka, Schiele and their Contemporaries.* Ithaca, NY: Cornell University Press, 1975.

Vienna Moderne, 1898–1918: An Early Encounter between Taste and Utility. Exh. cat. Houston: Sarah Campbell Blaffer Gallery, University of Houston, 1979.

Vienna: Turn of the Century Art and Design. Exh. cat. London: Fischer Fine Art, 1979.

Völker, Angela, with the collaboration of Ruperta Pichler. *Textiles of the Wiener Werkstätte, 1910–1932.* New York: Rizzoli, 1994.

Vom Jugendstil zum Bauhaus: Deutsche Buchkunst, 1895–1930. Exh. cat. Munster: Westfälisches Landesmuseum für Kunst und Kulturgeschichte, 1981.

Waissenberger, Robert, ed. *Traum und Wirklichkeit: Wien 1870–1930.* Exh. cat. Vienna: Museum der Stadt Wien, 1985.

Waissenberger, Robert. *Ver Sacrum: Die Zeitschrift der Wiener Secession, 1898–1903.* Exh. cat. Vienna: Museen der Stadt Wien, 1982.

Waissenberger, Robert, ed. *Vienna: 1890–1920.* New York: Rizzoli, 1984.

Weiss, Walter. "Salzburger Mythos? Hofmannsthals und Reinhardts Welttheater," *Zeitgeschichte* 2, 5 (February 1975): 109–19.

Wien 1870–1930: Traum und Wirklichkeit. Edited by Robert Waissenberger. Salzburg: Residenz, 1984.

Wien um 1900: Kunst und Kultur. Vienna: Brandstätter, 1985.

Die Wiener Werkstätte: Modernes Kunsthandwerk von 1903–1932. Exh. cat. Vienna: MAK-Austrian Museum of Applied Arts, 1967.

Index

Designed by David Alcorn
Alcorn Publication Design
Graeagle, California

Edited by Patricia Powell
Elvehjem Museum of Art

The cover, section display, and drop caps are set in Blue Island from Adobe.
The body text is set in Horley Old Style in its normal, semibold, bold, and italic forms.

The cover stock is #100 Centura Silk and the interior text stock is #100 Centura Silk Book.